The Quare Women's Journals:

May Stone & Katherine Pettit's Summers in the Kentucky Mountains and the Founding of the Hindman Settlement School

To Dave & Phyllis
who have been w. Me
on all of my important
Journies during the
last thirty years

With love

Jess

August 22, 1997

A picture taken during one of the first county fairs held at Hindman, sponsored by the Hindman Settlement School.

The Quare Women's Journals:

May Stone & Katherine Pettit's Summers in the Kentucky Mountains and the Founding of the Hindman Settlement School

Edited by
Jess Stoddart

The Jesse Stuart Foundation
Ashland, KY
1997

The Quare Women's Journals:
May Stone & Katherine Pettit's Summers in the
Kentucky Mountains and the Founding of the
Hindman Settlement School

Copyright © by The Jesse Stuart Foundation

FIRST EDITION

Library of Congress Cataloging-in-Publication Data

Stone, May.
    The quare women's journals : May Stone & Katherine Pettit's summers in the Kentucky mountains and the founding of the Hindman Settlement School / edited by Jess Stoddart. [OBN]
        p.   cm.
    Includes bibliographical references (p.).
    ISBN 0-945084-67-6
    1. Stone, May--Diaries. 2. Pettit, Katherine--Diaries. 3. Teachers--Kentucky--Diaries. 4. Hindman Settlement School--History. 5. Education, Rural--Kentucky--History. I. Pettit, Katherine. II. Stoddart, Jess, 1937- . III. Title.
LA2317.S86A3 1997
371.1'0092'2--dc21   97-25374
                                                          CIP

Published By:
The Jesse Stuart Foundation
P.O. Box 391 Ashland, KY 41114
(606) 329-5232
1997

For my mother, Marie Stewart Stoddart
her sisters and brothers
Nancy, Maude, Albert, and Sidney
children of the Hindman Settlement School

Where the raincrow mourns his hoarse prayer at night
And minnows drowse in crystal gardens of the dark,
Where shafted sunlight spans green oaten meadows
And jarflies sizzle their July mowing machine songs,
You walk familiar hills seeding a land of memory.

You know the place where the humming bird nests,
The moist coves where bees make wild lin honey
And the haunts of mountain tea and partridge berry.
The master oak plummets an acorn in your path
And by Edenic waters mint beds lift lavender cones.

The ceremonial seasons revolve/recycle around you:
The delicate watercolor Persephone spring, the lush
Thrush and whippoorwill summer, the grieving
Sacrificial autumn, the on-hold Redbird winter.

This is your land, Mountain Child.
Live on in this quiet country of the mind,
Unharmed and harmless here,
Charmed in time and child famous.

Mountain Child
by Albert Stewart

Camp Industrial at Hindman, Knott
County Kentucky from June 12 to August 31, 19__

On June 12, a party of six, Miss Katherine
R. Pettit, Miss Curry Breckinridge and Miss
Katherine Christian of Lexington, Miss Laura
Campbell of Philadelphia, Miss Eva W. Bruner
and Miss May Stone of Louisville, started to
Hindman, Knott Co. Kentucky to establish a
Social Settlement there, under the auspices
of the Kentucky Federation of Women's Clubs.
All the winter before, two of us had been busy
planning for the work, getting the necessary
helpers as well as materials for the different
classes.

The journey from Louisville to Hindman
occupied three days and was full of incident
and interest. The first day we went nearly 200
miles on the Railroad to Jackson and the other
two days were spent going 45 miles over a very
rough, mountain road. We had quite a caravan
three large wagons, heavily loaded with supplies.

Acknowledgments

I am fortunate to have worked on two projects in my career that became labors of love. The first, more than a decade ago, was a book celebrating the centenary of Eleanor Roosevelt, a woman I came to see as a true American heroine. In a different way, this current project was, from its inception, also a labor of love. My involvement with it came about because many members of my family, including my mother, were graduates of the Hindman Settlement School. I had grown up hearing stories about the school. And after becoming an historian I wondered about its name and if it had any relationship to the Settlement House Movement of the Progressive Era. The opportunity to edit this manuscript has been not only a journey into America's past but my mother's also and, through her, into my own as well. In the course of this journey I came to appreciate the significance of the school and social settlement to generations of mountaineers.

Katherine Pettit and May Stone deserve a place alongside reform leaders such as Eleanor Roosevelt even though their contributions are far less known. Indeed, one of the first connections I saw between these three women was that at the very moment when Pettit and Stone began their settlement house work, deciding to establish a school and social settlement at Hindman, Eleanor Roosevelt began volunteer work at the Rivington Street Settlement House in New York

City. For each, the fulfillment of her social conscience led to a remarkable life achievement. I consider myself fortunate to have a part in telling the stories of each of these women.

No work of this type is published without the assistance of many people other than the editor. I would like to thank Mike Mullins, Executive Director of the Hindman Settlement School for giving me the opportunity to undertake this project, for valuable personal attention to it, and for providing me the resources of the Hindman Settlement School staff and archives during my research visits. I especially want to thank Cassie Mullins, Mike's daughter, for her help during my first trip to the archives and Jana Everage, administrative assistant at the Hindman Settlement School, for her enthusiastic aid and interest in the project. My uncle, Albert Stewart, has been a fund of knowledge on many issues and I also wish to thank David Smith of the Knott County Historical Society for his assistance with a number of questions. Thanks also go to my aunts, Nancy Boatright and Maude Stacy, to my mother's classmates, Alma Pigman and Gertrude Maggard, to Sophie Holiday and to Ruby Boleyn Allen for supplying me with valuable personal reminiscences of their experiences at the Hindman Settlement School. Robert C. Young of Hindman kindly supplied me with help on the weaving terminology found in the Sassafras diary.

I would like to express my gratitude to Margaret Dennis, a graduate student at San Diego State University, for her careful assistance in the preparation of the manuscript and for her many insightful comments during that process. Finally, I express my continuing appreciation to Philip Flemion who has been a shadow editor for me for three decades and who provided both expert advice on content and style and many critical rescues for an historian who remains an inveterate computerphobe.

Jess Stoddart
May, 1997
San Diego, California

Contents

Foreword

The turn of the twentieth century was accompanied by a great zeal on the part of privileged folk to do missionary work among those to whom life had dealt a poor hand, and not even China and Africa got more attention than the Southern Mountains. The major church denominations sent thousands of workers into the upland region that stretched from West Virginia to Alabama to win people from what was perceived as an odious fundamentalism to a more optimistic faith. But earlier explorers for the denominations had also seen the need for temporal help as well. They found only one-room schools in most places, with a few private academies in the county seats, few doctors working in primitive conditions, and houses and agriculture that met only the barest needs. Three movements were converging as the century began: Progressivism, The Social Gospel, and Settlement Houses. All were responsive to social and economic inequality. The Social Gospelers, such as Walter Rauschenbusch, Shailer Mathews, and Washington Gladden, wanted to apply religious principles to temporal inequality. To them, winning souls was not enough; Christianity must make life better for God's children here and now. Those in the Progressive Movement were not necessarily connected to religious institutions.

Progressive ideas appealed to many privileged women, and as more of women's work moved from the home to the factory, in the production of food, clothing, and utensils, women had more time for other things. More went to school at all levels. Some went to work.

With more time on their hands, and with their new-found ideas, women began to create new institutions, such as the General Federation of Women's Clubs and the Women's Christian Temperance Union. They also studied the progressive ideas of John Dewey and Jane Addams who had created Hull House in Chicago to help new immigrants. Addams was forerunner of a small army of women bent on making the world a better place through an institution imported from England, the Settlement Institution. They operated from the three Rs: Research, Residence (among those to be served), and Reform. They were indeed social reformers, intent on changing people's personal habits and also the practices of institutions that created problems.

Katherine Pettit, May Stone, and the others who accompanied them to Eastern Kentucky during the summers of 1899, 1900, and 1901, were from well-to-do homes. They were well-educated, some at elite women's colleges in the East. There was not a great deal of opportunity for employment of women in that age despite their intelligence, education, and ability, and thus most of their energies went into volunteer service. The authors of these dairies came to Eastern Kentucky under the sponsorship of the Kentucky Federation of Women's Clubs and later the Women's Christian Temperance Union, but the ideas that inspired them was the Settlement movement.

Much has been written about the good work that missionaries, such as Pettit and Stone did among mountain people, because many of them wrote at length about their work. Not so much was heard about the downside of do-goodism until Henry Shapiro published his *Appalachia on Our Minds*, and David Whisnant his *All That is Native and Fine*. These books show how the mountaineers were stereotyped and often maligned by well-meaning do-gooders, who were often appalled at finding people so different from themselves and who set to work to make the people like themselves. As Professor Stoddart has said, these dairies are important in showing the cultural conflicts inherent in such work.

The Settlement workers, however, were different in many ways from the church workers. They were social reformers. Their approach, as Walter Trattner (*From Poor Law to Welfare State: A History of Social Welfare in America*), put it, was fraternal rather than paternal. They wished to share the lives of those they served; they wanted to accept and to be accepted. Yet, they were foremost reformers and, therefore, could be just as intolerant of unkept houses and poor cooking habits as the religious missionaries could be of religious fundamentalism. Since Pettit and Stone were also religious people they promoted hymns (from their backgrounds), as well as Sunday Schools, and they were appalled that the Old Regular Baptists were opposed to Sunday Schools and sang a strange (to them) lined-out monophonic hymnody. Although they admired the old British ballads and were gratified that they were much alive among the people, there are no words of appreciation for the local renditions, only the comment that the tunes are "equally as unusual as the words."

The local people dubbed them "The Quare Women," because of their strange ways, and they, in turn, judged the local people to be strange in baffling ways. All of this shows how hard it is for people reared in one culture to readily accept those of another. Even well-educated Americans of the time had meager experience for the idea of multi-culturalism. The conventional wisdom of the Settlement workers was that, while they must show an interest in the lives of those they wished to help, the main agenda was Americanization–of new immigrants, or old ones who had been isolated from the mainstream–to change their ways so that they could become like those in the mainstream. One activity, for example, was teaching patriotic songs.

No doubt, living conditions in Knott, Perry, and Letcher counties at the turn of the century were often inadequate, to say the least. Yet, the shock of the contrast between their lives and those of the residents led the women to say rather extreme and judgmental things, and one sometimes has to question whether or not their observations were accurate, for example, that "most mountain men do little or no work….The women and children do all the work. They plow the fields or hoe them. . .put in the crops and tend them, build and repair the fences, make the garden, keep the house, cook, wash, milk, sew and everything else done at all." They also averred that all of the Old Regular Baptist hymns were sung to the same tune. Yet, there were qualities among Eastern Kentuckians that they admired, such as "their lack of self-consciousness," and they came to admire the coverlets and blankets that the women carded, spun, dyed, and wove from wool and flax, and they ended up collecting them, although sometimes dictating the colors, and also ordering linsey dresses for themselves. They even learned to weave. They also collected ballads and baskets.

They grew fond of the people, taught them everything from Bible stories to sewing and cooking, cajoled them, preached the evils of drink and tobacco, and arranged for several to go elsewhere to school, often on scholarship.

These "quare" women were hardy souls, living or teaching in tents, walking ten or twelve miles in a day to visit homes and teach classes, or riding mules through streams and over precarious trails to help teachers with new pedagogical methods. They attended church and funerals in far-flung locations, and visited homes where families had medical or other problems. Once, John, their bony and usually reliable, borrowed mule, in fright or orneriness, threw them both down a bank into a creek, with Stone landing on a rock and Pettit landing on top of her. Even though both had broken ribs and Pettit a sprained wrist, they rushed down the stream to recover their hairpins, fixed their hair, and went on to a Sunday School they had arranged. Stone spent the next day in bed, but Pettit set off as usual by muleback on her rounds, even though Montgomery and Carr Creeks were in high tide from heavy rains, and ended up wading Yellow Creek to get to her destination. After the floods receded, both were back to their usual tiring schedules with few complaints about their broken ribs.

When they left after their last summer to catch the train in Jackson, they elected to float down the North Fork of the Kentucky, rather than go by wagon, in deference to their knitting ribs. Their conveyance was "a very, dirty boat" which had to be hastily caulked with tar and rags. Poled by a boy in front and paddled by another in the rear, the boat sometimes had to be pulled over the shoals while the women walked or waded. The trip to Jackson was a hundred circuitous miles.

Pettit and Stone were to show the same uncompromising and adventurous spirit when they founded Hindman Settlement School in 1902, and Pettit was even more determined when she went off to the Harlan County wilderness to found Pine Mountain Settlement School in 1913. Over a hundred young women followed Pettit and Stone to Eastern Kentucky, most of them graduates of such colleges as Smith, Bryn Mawr, Mt. Holyoke, Wellesley, and Vassar. One, Elizabeth Watts, came to stay a year and stayed a lifetime, becoming director of the Hindman Settlement School, Watts perhaps having the most positive attitude toward the mountaineers. If she harbored negative thoughts about the ways of the people, she mostly kept them to herself, or couched them in kind and positive words. These women were extraordinary in their intellect and their ability to cope and to work. Not always valued at home, they sought other avenues for their passion for social reform and their wish to serve humankind. And here is the irony, Stone, Pettit and those who accompanied or succeeded them, came to a decidedly patriarchal culture. Yet the men of the mountains accepted, appreciated, and assisted them because of what they did for them and their families. An apocryphal story told at Hindman illustrates the success of these pioneering women in establishing themselves as people of consequence. After the "women" had established the school, a male teacher was eventually hired to teach shop classes. Walking down the road one day, he met an old patriarch, who inquired, "Be you one of the women down at the settlement?"

Loyal Jones
Berea, Kentucky

"I never seed any quare wimmen like you all before"

May Stone

Katherine Pettit

"We mostly choose the things that suit us best."
From the poem, "Books" by Ann Cobb

Introduction

THE JOURNALS OF THE QUARE WOMEN

The Hindman Settlement School, founded by Katherine Pettit and May Stone in Hindman, Kentucky in 1902, is one of the first rural social settlement institutions in America. It became a model for many others which followed. Prior to the school's founding, Pettit and Stone spent portions of the three preceding summers holding social settlement camps at various locations in the mountains of Eastern Kentucky before settling permanently in Hindman. Pettit kept records of these summers and the three manuscripts were put into typescript as early as 1901. They have been used by scholars and also served as the source for four novels by Lucy Furman as well as poems by Ann Cobb (both long time faculty members of the school). The manuscripts have intrigued everyone who has come into contact with them. For example, Elizabeth Watts, who succeeded May Stone and Katherine Pettit as director of the Hindman Settlement School, wrote her mother a weekly letter about events at the settlement. They provide one of the richest sources of information on the formative years of the school. Early in 1912 she wrote:

> I said the fair was the best fun of the week, didn't I? Well, I lied. Sunday afternoon was the very best, when all the Hillside family collected before a jolly big open fire and Miss Stone read us the diary that she and Miss Pettit kept the summer before they came

to Hindman when they were over to Carr…and it was perfectly
<u>fascinating</u>. Parts of it ought to be published but of course they
never can be.[1]

Seventy five years later, Elizabeth Watt's wish will come true as
the Sassafras diary, along with the journals of the Cedar Grove camp
and Camp Industrial at Hindman are now made accessible to a general audience. The diaries of the three social settlements are, themselves, quite different in length and structure. The first two, for the
six week Cedar Grove camp in 1899 and the ten week Camp Industrial in 1900, are basically reports, briefly summarized versions of
events and activities. The first is only eight pages and was probably
prepared to be read at the annual meeting of the camp's sponsor, The
Kentucky Federation of Women's Clubs. The second is thirty pages,
although doubled in length by separate reports on the sewing, cooking and kindergarten classes and other addenda. These contrast
sharply with the record of the third summer at Sassafras in 1901
which is a daily diary one hundred fifty pages long.

Our information about the "quare women's" experiences proceeds
from the very general to the very specific. The Cedar Grove narrative focused on what the women brought with them and how they
organized the camp. Cooking, sewing and kindergarten classes formed
the main activities in keeping with the request which had brought
them to the area.

Pettit and Stone with two other women went to Cedar Grove at
the invitation of the Reverend Mitchell of Hazard, specifically to
train girls and women in modern methods of domestic science and
housekeeping. They directed their program almost entirely to females. There are only a couple of references to boys joining in Sunday reading groups and one mention of the tutoring of a local male
school teacher in shorthand.

Even this brief report revealed the structure of their social settlement work. A basic schedule was provided setting days and times

for the main classes. Yet the women were very flexible and allowed the needs of those served to determine or change routine. Many times at Cedar Grove and the later camps, someone would arrive to seek assistance or training–to "larn" something–and they would receive individual attention. Normally the lessons consisted simply of how to sew a necktie or make beaten biscuits. The camp became a source of great curiosity and people traveled considerable distances to see "the quare women" or "fotched-on women" as they were often called by the mountaineers. The photographs they preserved help us understand the fascination with these women and their camp festooned with bright banners and pictures.

The Cedar Grove narrative contains brief observations on the local living conditions, mainly negative comments on the dirt and squalor of many cabin dwellings, the mountaineer's poor food and health, the widespread use of tobacco, and the hard life of the women. Both Pettit and Stone found some of the patriarchal assumptions of mountain society amusing including the notion that, as single women over twenty, they were "culls." Offers to remedy this with a "widder man" needing someone to milk his cows and take care of his dozen children were duly recorded. In summarizing their first experience with a social settlement, they were clearly moved by the response they received and Pettit ended the account by relating how the local citizens told them on their final day, "the good you have done will live with us."

Immediately after the camp closed, Pettit and Stone began plans for another the next summer, again with the sponsorship of the State Federation. At Camp Industrial (a name which replicates the name given by the Women's Christian Temperance Union to its all-day educational programs) the teachers included four other women; Katherine Christian and Eva Bruner of Lexington, Laura Campbell of Philadelphia and Curry Breckingridge of Louisville. Curry was a member of one of Kentucky's most prominent families. The local people gave special names to each of the women with Katherine

Pettit the "up-and-comingest," May the "ladyest," Katherine Christian the "goodest-cooking," and Curry Breckingridge the "commonest" (friendliest).[2] *The Lexington Herald* which Curry's brother, Desha, edited ran an extensive account of the Cedar Grove camp shortly before the Hindman venture began with the intent of drumming up support and money for the later venture.

Camp Industrial, sited at Hindman, the county seat of Knott County, represented a much more ambitious undertaking than Cedar Grove. A large quantity of special supplies and teaching materials went along with them, enough to fill three large wagons. They laid the camp out on five terraces on the hillside across from the town, the same site as the later, permanent school. All of the participants brought special teaching skills. Breckingridge and Bruner were experienced kindergarten teachers, Campbell and Stone took charge of sewing, and Christian, trained in "hygienic cooking" at Battle Creek, Michigan, taught cooking and music classes.

In their second summer, the women did considerably more traveling into the countryside. What is especially notable was their work with local teachers. They participated in the annual Teacher's Institute held at Hindman. The journal includes a detailed description of the clothing of one of the teachers who attended the Institute and who could only be called a turn-of-the-century "clothes-horse" right down to the "ashes of roses" satin ribbon necktie which adorned her. They held a picnic for outlying schools and their teachers and, at every opportunity, they distributed flags, pictures, and teaching materials to liven the one-room school houses in which most of these teachers labored. They taught the teachers games to play with their children reflecting contemporary theories of early education. The new kindergarten movement which they advocated, stressed the importance of the development of younger children through games and other activities. Pettit described all of this explicitly as "social settlement" work. Indeed, in the conclusion to the report, Pettit wrote, "we feel after three months work at Hindman that the settlement plan is the best way of reaching and helping these people."

Excellent photographs of the brightly festooned tent city survive to illustrate the fascination it had for the local people. They found Hindman an excellent site for their work. While Camp Cedar Grove had been only a short distance from Hazard, the county seat of Perry County, Camp Industrial was in a well populated town with two hundred ninety children in the school district. Both children and adults had easy access to the camp and the location guaranteed a prosperous group of citizens who appreciated and supported their work. While they were there, Mrs. Cora Smith, who had been sent by the Board of the Reformed Church to locate a site for a permanent missionary school, spent a month with them. A public meeting was held to try to persuade her to establish the school at Hindman but Pettit noted that Mrs. Smith eventually chose a site in Jackson County nearer to the railroad. That evening was probably not an entire failure for the townfolks since only a year later May and Katherine decided to establish their own social settlement school in Hindman.

Mary Stacy and Rhoda, her helper, spent a great deal of their "spare" time at the farm preparing wool for spinning. The farm was the headquarters of Katherine and May during the Sassafras summer. Here we see Rhoda picking wool shorn from their sheep.

Another event that summer which, in hindsight, takes on a pro-phetic quality was a horseback trip they all made to Pine Mountain, the place where Pettit would found a second school in 1913. She was clearly taken with the beauty of the area and wrote, "the view from that point was superb...the moon shone over the Big Black Mountain, flooding the dark valley of the Cumberland with its sil-very light, while the sun was shining on the ridges in the Kentucky valley."

The success of the Hindman camp led the State Federation to authorize a third summer settlement at Sassafras, also in Knott County. A sum of two hundred sixty-two dollars was given by the various chapters and individuals to further the work. A daily diary from June 25 to October 4 provides a detailed account of these weeks. The Sassafras summer, however, might as easily be renamed the summer of tribulations although the two women endured their problems with remarkably good humor.

It began with a two day trip from the railhead in Jackson to Hind-man and was filled with mishaps. One of the horses rolled down a bank, the wagons ended up in quicksand, and they had to be con-stantly "prized" over logs and rocks which caused Pettit to write, "we were out of the wagon more than we were in it." The four day river trip back to Jackson in October was equally beset by difficul-ties. The camp's location explains part of the problems. The Stacy farm, their headquarters, was located at the mouth of Montgomery Creek at Carr's Fork, near the North Fork of the Kentucky River. It was about a mile and a half from Sassafras. But Sassafras was noth-ing more than a post office location. The previous summer they had accepted an invitation from Mary Stacy to bring their social settle-ment to her community the following summer. The attraction of the location was that, situated as it was near the borders of three counties and only fifteen miles from the three towns of Hazard, Hindman and Whitesburg, the social settlement was expected to have a wide im-pact. The opposite seems to have been the case.

Choosing what Pettit described as "the most remote spot in all the southern mountains," a place "no end of miles from anything else but wilderness and thick forest," made their work difficult. It was hard for people to reach the camp and their own visiting of the remote cabins required very strenuous, daily excursions. Nonetheless, visiting the remote cabins became the most significant part of their activity.

The weather also conspired against them. The summer seems to have been unusually rainy. On a number of occasions rain and "tides" threatened their tents which were pitched near the river rather than high on a hillside as in earlier summers. Pettit recorded one rainy morning waking to water standing on her bed cover and dripping on her head. Sometimes rain cut them off entirely and made travel impossible.

These circumstances affected camp routine. Normally visitors did not begin to arrive until after dinner, around noon, for the sewing, cooking, singing, and kindergarten classes scheduled for the afternoon. At first they attracted few students. The early sewing lessons had only three persons including Jasper, the young man hired by them as a general helper for the summer. The sewing class at Camp Industrial had enrolled more than one hundred. Gradually the novelty of their presence, the usefulness of their lessons, and their generous dispersal of Bibles, pictures, and books guaranteed good sized classes and much "dropping in" on them. Learning to make "risen" bread and beaten biscuits as well as having a look at the "quare wimmen" became a favorite local pastime.

The group staffing the camp was smaller at Sassafras than at Hindman. Katherine and May were assisted by Mary McCartney and Rae McNab, both of whom left before the summer's end. McNab, who taught the kindergarten, became a special favorite with the local people. Each morning the women traveled, usually separately, up the branches of the creeks to the remote cabins. Pettit's love of the outdoors comes through strongly in her descriptions of these trips and the beauty of the countryside. It often contrasted with the terrible housing and bleak isolation found at the end of these journeys. Here is her description of a trip up Montgomery branch for afternoon Sunday School on the first Sunday of the camp:

> More than half of the way the path is in the bed of the creek and we had to jump from one large rock to another. Soon we came to a old mill which is almost hidden from sight by the trees, vines and rocks. On one side of it is a waterfall. Looking up the creek there is a curve and the shadows of the trees and rocks falling on the water make it a scene of beauty indeed. On one side of this fall the path leads up a very steep and rocky hill to a level stretch where there are fallen trees to rest on in the shade. Then down again right into the creek to scramble over more rocks and here was perhaps the most beautiful spot of all. There were cascades running swiftly down on either side over ledges of rock, which in some places were covered with mosses, vines and ferns. We next passed a grove of beech trees where the sunlight, touching the top branches, lighted the whole grove, changing the color of the leaves to pale shimmering green.

Concern with poor housing, lack of sanitation, primitive health conditions, and bad food figure prominently in the record as do their steadfast attempts to discourage the use of tobacco and alcohol. The decision to record each day's events, however, provides much greater description, especially of the people who were important to their work that summer. Mrs. Stacy and her "titan haired" helper, Rhoda; Jasper, their always willing and indispensable jack-of-all-trades; Uncle Ira Combs, the area's most noted preacher; Dr. Roark, the local doctor and one of the few persons Pettit pokes fun at in her entries are only some of the figures which the diary brings to life.

The area also had a few African-American families living along one branch whom Pettit and Stone came to know. Initial contact took place when several of the local black women arrived at the camp to wash and iron for them. At first nameless, the washerwomen gradually took on both names and personalities. Pettit made at least one visit to their branch and noted five cases of the flux and homes which she described as "wretched."

In the middle of the summer they broke off their activities for a week's visit to Hindman to attend the Teacher's Institute. During the visit another public meeting of citizens was organized by Professor Clarke, head of the local school, to discuss support for establishing another school. Not long after their return to Sassafras, Pettit wrote that she and May had begun plans for the founding of the Hindman Settlement School. Lucy Furman, in a later article, described the moment:

> when at last the decision must be made, the two sat long one night on a high hill shoulder in the moonlight, considering deeply, prayerfully....From that high hill shoulder the two stepped out at midnight upon faith alone.[3]

But the trials of that summer were not over yet. About two weeks before their camp was to close, the women were thrown down a bank from the mule, John. Both suffered broken ribs. Even this additional disaster only slowed them down a little. Katherine had been the principal recorder of the summer camps but May took on the diary on August 8 when Katherine sprained her wrist in another fall. After the second mishap, May wrote that her chest hurt so much the following morning that she could not get up. Since it was Sunday, Katherine tried to carry on anyway. She set off to keep their regular Sunday School appointment at the Sassafras school. A typical Sunday included both a morning and an afternoon Sunday School with walks of ten to twelve miles. This day was another rainy one and Pettit reached the school to find it locked and empty. She went on to the post office to try to get a key but it was locked also so she finally gave up and walked home. By then the rain had swollen the river to such an extent that she would have been marooned if Uncle Jim Stacy had not appeared with John, the offending mule, to carry her across while there was still time. Eight days later, on September 21, May noted anxiously in the diary that she had feared that Katherine was coming down with pneumonia the night before and had put her to bed with a mustard plaster. But, she recounted, they had been told on the day of their accident that, within eight days they would know if any ribs had been broken. Her entry on September 22 reported that, rather than pneumonia we "were relieved to know it is only two broken ribs knitting together."

From their earliest visits to the mountains both Katherine and May had been fascinated by the handicrafts, especially the woven blankets and "coverlids" made by many women. They ordered hand-woven linsey dresses from Mrs. Enoch Combs who had the closest thing to a general store in the area. They also sought hand-woven blankets. At first it appeared that they were not going to be success-ful since those offered were either used or not in the bright colors they desired. However, during the final days as the camp was break-ing up, people came to say good-bye and leave gifts. Mrs. Combs brought their newly finished dresses and five blankets described as very beautiful.

Katherine and May not only got their blankets, they fulfilled an-other long standing desire. That summer gave them the opportunity to learn to weave, something they had wanted to do for three years. Mrs. Stacy had a loom and early in the diary there is the description of redheaded Rhoda washing dyed wool in a basket in the stream. But the all-consuming duties of the summer precluded time for weav-ing lessons. Only as the summer was nearly gone, with just a week until their departure, did the two get down to learning to weave. On September 23, they began preparation of the loom. Mrs. Stacy was dubious that they could even prepare the loom in the time left much less weave anything. But juggling their schedules and showing the same kind of tenacity that had overcome all other obstacles, they set about to weave something before they left. Jasper was called in, as so many times before, for assistance; in this case to help in the tedious process of getting the loom ready. In a few days it was done. May noted on September 26, "weaving has not stopped as today, first one and then the other at the loom and Mrs. Stacy thinks it a marvel that we have woven a whole yard." On their final day at camp, May noted triumphally, "the piece was finished early this morning and is out of the loom in less time than Mrs. Stacy said it would take to put it in."

All in all, the diary leaves the impression of a summer exceptionally plagued by weather and other misfortunes but full of social settlement work over a large territory. Even the final river trip to Jackson followed the pattern of unexpected difficulties. It lasted four days and was filled with loading and unloading of the boat, constant bailing to keep from sinking, and problems in finding places to stop at night. Their faithful Jasper was along on the trip, supplemented by two other local men with a third one hired on the way to ease the trip.

This final adventure reveals as much about the character of these two women as anything else to be found in the journals. It highlights a quiet courage and unflappability in the face of hardship along with a generous sense of humor. May described the party as it began the journey as "a unique boat load it was, starting 100 miles down the North fork of the Kentucky River, a blind girl, a lame boy...all in the charge of two girls with broken ribs and a sprained wrist."

After traveling four days, when they were only a mile from Jackson, it became clear that logs in the river would make it impossible to go further by boat so, as the diary recounts the end of their journey and their Sassafras summer;

we stepped from floating log to log until we reached the land and then climbed a steep bank...and with the lame boy, blind girl and all the luggage, waded through the mud a mile to Jackson. Here we had as great a sensation when we saw the newly fitted up hotel, with the dressed up ladies and gentlemen walking around on brussels carpets as they must have had when this muddy, wet forlorn looking crowd from 100 miles up the river appeared in the hall and asked for rooms.

As this was being written, we know that the die had already been cast for the young "quare women" from the "level-land." They had made a decision to found a rural social settlement and school. No lives of brussels carpets for them but rather ones devoted to an ideal: to bring "the strong, wealthy, and learned Kentuckians into healthful touch with the poorest, most ignorant, and humblest mountaineer and at the same time make the one appreciate the vitalizing, strengthening influence of the other." This belief, that each could contribute to the other was the underlying premise of the Hindman Settlement School. For them and for many others who would leave lives of comfort for work in the mountains, at times Pettit and Stone must have mused at what fate had chosen for them. A stanza of one of Ann Cobb's poems catches this feeling–and, perhaps, helps explain their decision as well:

> I'm working for the fotched-on women now;
> Sweeping out weeds and rocks from posy-beds,
> Running out hawgs off'n the tater-patch,
> Puttering here and there about the place.
> Quare the high hopes a body sets out with,
> And ends with weeding women's garden-truck!
> Not that I aim to quarrel at my life,
> We mostly choose the things that suit us best.[4]

Katherine Pettit and May Stone chose a life of service. It not only suited them; it left a remarkable legacy for generations of mountain people. Can we take ourselves back nearly a century to understand the sense of mission that inspired them?

PRACTICAL IDEALISTS

The founding of the Hindman Settlement School by Katherine Pettit and May Stone in 1902 is part of a larger story of change and reform in America at the opening of the twentieth century. These two were remarkable women but not unique for their age. In fact, they lived in a time of many exceptional women. A few of these reformers, such as Jane Addams, became national heroines. Most of them, Pettit and Stone included, achieved much but have been lost to the history books. Pettit and Stone deserve to have their work better known and to be given a more prominent place among the leaders of Progressivism in Kentucky. The publication of this record of the three summer camps provides a good understanding of their personalities, motivations and the ideals which underlay their work in the mountains of Eastern Kentucky.

Pettit's and Stone's efforts flowed from a belief that, through education and social settlement activities, people in the Kentucky mountains could be better prepared to adapt to the changes occurring within their economy and culture and better control their own destiny. These two young women, not yet out of their twenties, found themselves leaders in an educational and social revolution transforming Kentucky and the entire South.

Progressivism is the name given to a loose association of individuals and organizations which arose in the late nineteenth century and dominated American politics through World War I. Called forth by urbanization and industrialization and deeply influenced by a similar social movement in England, these reformers have been called "practical idealists." Sharing a set of moral values more than a platform or program, their "aroused Christian conscience" was a critical part of the spirit of reform found everywhere in the nation at the end of the nineteenth century.[5]

Southern Progressivism shared many of the same broad concerns and values as its northern counterpart. However, its leading historian, Dewey Grantham, believes that it was the dramatic enlargement of the role of the middle and professional classes in public policy which explains the movement for reform which swept the region. While it included conservative attitudes which emphasized the need to expand government to achieve social control (in the South this manifested itself particularly in the area of race relations), Progressivism also rested on a strong commitment to a new form of social justice, sometimes called "scientific charity." It focused on helping the poor to help themselves rather than on simple charity. These ideals underlay many programs which the middle class supported as newly recognized social needs of their communities.[6]

Katherine Pettit and May Stone fit very well into the definition of Southern Progressives, especially into the great educational awakening in the South which became a focal point of the social justice movement. For more than a half century, arguments for compulsory public schooling in the rest of the nation had made an inextricable link between education and national progress. This view was now embraced by the middle classes in the South.

Outside of the larger cities of the South, there was really no system of public education worthy of the name. The Census of 1910 gave the figure of 18.2% illiteracy (defined as inability to write) among Kentucky mountain whites over the age of ten. Someone familiar with rural schools described them as "a little house on a little ground with a little equipment, where a little teacher at a little salary, for a little while, teaches little children, little things."[7] Schools were generally ungraded with terms that depended on weather and crops. They were not always taught through consecutive months nor by the same teacher. School was not compulsory and many parents doubted the need for formal education, especially for females.

Progressives like Pettit and Stone brought to their work a strong belief that education would contribute directly to individual well-being, to wider economic development and to the more literate citizenry required by a democratic society. At the moment when Pettit and Stone were laying the groundwork for the Hindman Settlement School, across the South states were creating universal public education systems for the first time. They doubled their per capita expenditures on education, raised teacher's salaries and requirements, lengthened school terms, introduced compulsory attendance, and otherwise brought Southern schools up to the level of those created a half century earlier in the North. In a number of ways, the Hindman Settlement School served as a model for the public schools of Kentucky in matters of curriculum.

Pettit's and Stone's work on the cutting edge of an educational revolution which helped transform Kentucky should have guaranteed them an important place in the history of their state. But the Hindman Settlement School was far more than an educational institution for mountain children. Pettit and Stone introduced some of the most advanced ideas associated with Progressive reform, those of the social settlement movement, into the mountains. They did so at a time of momentous change for the people and culture of Eastern Kentucky. While they could not, alone, stem the inevitable, negative consequences which were a part of industrial capitalism, they sought to mitigate them. Their efforts aided many mountaineers to bridge the gap between their subsistence agricultural economy and the new world of twentieth-century America rapidly advancing into their hills and hollows.

Considerably more is known about Katherine Pettit's life and views than May Stone's. Katherine came from a pioneer family of Central Kentucky. Born February 3, 1868, she was raised on a farm near Lexington, educated at the Sayre Female Institute there, and by her mid-twenties had become an energetic "club woman" involved with many schemes for social, moral and civic improvement.

Her interest in the mountain region is said to have been piqued first by the stories of the feuds in the area which were prominently reported in the Bluegrass area newspapers and other sources in the 1880s. Her interest may have been further activated by a family friend, the Reverend E. O. Guerrant whose Presbyterian mission work in the mountains received considerable publicity in these years. She made her first sight-seeing trip to the region in 1895 staying for several weeks at Hazard. She returned twice again before the Cedar Grove camp. The second trip, in 1896, included the head of the Kentucky Women's Christian Temperance Union, Francis Beauchamp, and led the organization to the establishment of a traveling library system with Katherine as its director.[8] The WCTU would also provide the primary support for the Hindman Settlement School during its first decade.

The final trip, in 1899, just a month before the opening of the Cedar Grove camp, illustrates the way in which the expansion of reform activity at this time depended significantly upon a network of like-minded women. Katherine was accompanied on this trip by Madeline McDowell Breckingridge, a member of Kentucky's premier family of Progressive reformers and herself destined to become the most prominent female Progressive leader in Kentucky. Breckingridge was already helping to found an Industrial School in the mountains and would later lend critical support to the establishment of the Hindman Settlement School.[9]

Indeed, both Katherine and May were well connected to the network of women and religious and civic institutions that drove reform in the state. Both had links to the Breckinridge family. In May's case, she was a classmate at Wellesley of Sophinisba Breckinridge, the elder daughter of the family and sister-in-law of Madeline. Sophinisba Breckinridge had a truly remarkable career even among the many female reformers of her day. The first woman to be admitted to the bar in Kentucky, she also earned a doctorate and taught social work at the University of Chicago which was then the wellspring of much Progressive social and educational thought, especially

Below. This is the home of one of their neighbors during the Sassafras summer, Jordan Smith who lived up the Montgomery Branch.

Above. One of several school houses where Katherine and May held Sunday School during the Sassafras summer. This was up George's Branch.

that associated with the Settlement House Movement. Equally important, Sophinisba was one the closest friends of Jane Addams, the founder of the social settlement movement in America.[10] This connection was of enormous importance both for the formulation of the ideas which guided the social settlement at Hindman and also for the financial support and volunteers provided by this contact. Katherine and May visited Addams at Hull House to seek her advice just months before they launched their school in 1902.[11] And the latest ideas about social settlement work were certainly exchanged between Sophonisba and her sister, Curry, who was one of the six teachers at Camp Industrial. Although the Hindman Settlement School was not the first rural social settlement in America, it was certainly one of the earliest and a revolutionary experiment for its day. Its programs reflect many of Addams' most strongly held ideas about the goals and activities needed in settlement work.

Katherine, May and their work would be connected to the

Breckingridges in still another way. Madeline McDowell Breckingridge was the wife of Desha Breckingridge, the influential editor of the *Lexington Herald* newspaper. The paper gave valuable publicity to the summer camps and to the fund-raising appeal put out in 1902 to establish the school. Articles, often written by Madeline, kept the school before a large, sympathetic, state-wide audience and undoubtedly aided its long term success.

Both Katherine and May were club women and they first met in May, 1899, in Frankfort at a statewide meeting of the Kentucky Federation of Women's Clubs. Kentucky had established the first state chapter of this national organization in the South five years earlier. Katherine was a member of the Lexington branch and May of the Louisville one. May also served as secretary of the state organization. Their partnership came about when Katherine gave a report on the Federation's traveling library project to the mountains. During the same meeting a letter was read from the Reverend T. J. Mitchell, a Presbyterian minister in Hazard, which asked the Federation to send someone to provide classes for women and girls in basic homemaking. He wanted "a gentle, womanly woman, a dear old-fashioned woman."[12] The membership approved of the request and asked Katherine to head up the project. May Stone described the initial encounter, writing;

> This was the first time I had ever seen Katherine Pettit. She stood and told of her recent visit to Harlan County. She thought the settlement work would be a good beginning of help. Club members raised about $180 by subscription and the president asked Katherine if she could take charge of it and get someone else to go with her. After the meeting, Miss Hamilton (the president) and I said when she got things started we would go up and have a part in it. This was the beginning of our work together.[13]

This partnership led to the founding of two important institutions in the mountains; the Hindman Settlement School in 1902 and the Pine Mountain Settlement School in 1913. For Pettit it seems to have been the next logical step in a progression that had begun at least five years earlier. May Stone later wrote that Katherine had urged the WCTU to establish a social settlement as early as 1896. For May Stone it was certainly an unexpected turning point in her life. Indeed there is even some reason to believe that her participation in the Cedar Grove camp may have been accidental. In the Settlement School archives is a typescript report of the Traveling Library Committee which also contains Reverend Mitchell's request. At its bottom is a handwritten notation that Miss McCartney was supposed to go with Pettit but she could not so May Stone went instead. The Reverend Mitchell had his entreaty answered but he did not get any "dear old-fashioned" ladies.

As active club women, Pettit and Stone were part of a phenomena critical to the success of Progressive reform. A wave of organizations had been created by and for women, epitomized by groups such as the Federation and the Women's Christian Temperance Movement. They brought together women who previously had known few public outlets for their energies and ideals beyond church and charity work. The social settlement movement, in particular, acquired much of its enthusiasm and human resources from the graduates of the new women's colleges in the Northeast which had been created to provide women with educations similar to the best available to men. As women like Katherine and May received the new education (May was class of 1888 at Wellesley) they began to seek ways to use their talents and training. They focused on the many problems of contemporary life generated by the Industrial Revolution. Included was everything from education and social settlement work–the heart of the activities of Katherine and May–to concerns with child labor, "fallen women," industrial conditions, and moral and political reform. As one author writing about the phenomena noted, "the power of association had its own inner dynamic which carried many women to points they had not, in the beginning, been able to envision."[14] This would prove true for both Katherine and May.

Indeed, part of the transformation that American society was undergoing was a revolution in basic notions about women's role in American culture. The languid, sheltered, submissive, genteel "Victorian" lady who was often held up for emulation in mid-century America gave way to a new ideal of women as vigorous, capable, participants in public life. Leaders such as Addams often justified women's new activism as "social housekeeping" and the widespread entrance into the ranks of Progressive reform by young, well educated females cemented this cultural transformation.

If Katherine came from a solid middle class background, May's was even more privileged. She was born in Owingsville, Kentucky, the only child of an affluent family. The family moved to Louisville in 1885, the year after May started at Wellesley. Her father served as city attorney and later as chief counsel for the Louisville and Nashville Railroad. He also spent four terms in the Kentucky legislature. Although May left before her senior year, the Wellesley connection was invaluable. Armies of volunteers from there and other women's colleges later worked at Hindman and other settlements. Ann Cobb, for instance, was a Wellesley graduate who became one of the longest-serving and most revered teachers at the school as well as a well known regional poet. This network guaranteed a steady stream of educated teachers and financial support over the years. After leaving Wellesley and before embarking on her adventures with Katherine, May had focused her energies on work with the Louisville chapters of the Daughters of the American Revolution and the Federation of Women's Clubs.[15]

The personalities of these two women were quite different but complimentary. John Campbell, who undertook an extensive social survey of Appalachia for the Russell Sage Foundation and who was a leader in Progressive mountain work, knew them both well. He believed that they provided an excellent balance for each other since

Katherine was clearly an impressive figure with strong opinions and a vigorous, outgoing personality while May was quiet, serene and unflappable with, what one person called "radiant charm."

Katherine was the dominant one, described as friendly, forceful, extroverted, energetic, outspoken and "vivid." A former student, remembering how her mother's generation had viewed Katherine, said that she was thought to be "more of a mixing person." Elizabeth Watts wrote that her principal personality trait was "indomitable courage." Watts noted that she had more energy than anyone she had ever known and was also very frank and didn't hesitate to find fault or tell you how to correct things. Some appreciated this directness such as the former pupil who wrote, "I liked the way you always hit straight from the shoulder." Such frankness didn't sit well with everyone, however, and at least one worker at Pine Mountain described her as "brutally frank."[16] Certainly she was a perfectionist and admitted to being hard to get along with and brusque. These qualities may have been the reason why the young Elizabeth Watts, who arrived at the school in 1909 at the age of nineteen, exhibited considerable anxiety over an impending first visit of Pettit to her family in Rhode Island. She wrote to her mother, "I'm a little scared for fear you won't like Miss Pettit because you have to sort of get used to her but you just must anyway."[17]

Despite her extroverted nature, Pettit was uncomfortable as a public speaker and almost pathological in her dislike of personal publicity according to her school chum, Lucy Furman, who joined the staff in 1907 and spent more than twenty years as a housemother here. Furman became widely known for the four popular novels which she wrote with the school and its work as their settings. They did much to publicize it to the outside world.[18] Katherine also had an aversion to having her picture taken and only a few survive from the early years at Hindman. One was taken surreptitiously and sent by Elizabeth Watts to her mother with the warning, "don't for pity's sake let…Miss Pettit see it for Miss Pettit doesn't like her picture taken and doesn't know that this was."[19]

May Stone's much more subdued temperament fitted better what would have been thought of as a "typical" or ideal Southern gentle-woman of her day. The qualities of her personality are best captured by the title, "the ladyest" of the fotched-on women which she was given by her mountain neighbors. While everyone who knew her emphasized her serenity and exquisite manners, Lucy Furman noted that both May and Katherine were adventurous and allowed no ob-stacle to daunt them. The journals are ample proof of that. May's response to the trials encountered in the summer camps and in keep-ing the school operating may have been more low keyed. But to leave the comforts of her background for the hardships of mountain life could not have been easy. Patience and reserve were personal strengths which she brought to the partnership along with consider-able administrative and financial skills. Elizabeth Watts suggested that her work issued from an "exceptionally deep faith."[20]

Both women showed fascination with the local crafts from the beginning of their acquaintance with mountain culture. Stone often purchased quilts, furniture and antiques from her neighbors. A teacher recalled that she was also very interested in genealogy and knew more about it than any person she had ever met. The daughter of one of the students at the original Camp Industrial recalled that her mother remembered Stone as a slender young woman of medium height, fair skinned, blonde-haired, blue-eyed and dressed in white or pastels. By the time this daughter was herself a student in the 1920s, Stone had become stout, her hair had turned snow white, and she favored pince-nez glasses which hung from a gold chain.[21]

When Katherine set up the Pine Mountain School in 1913, finan-cial problems increased at Hindman and May must have felt over-whelmed. She wrote in the 1914 newsletter that, "when Miss Pettit drove away amid the snow and holly a year ago last Christmas Day, to establish the Pine Mountain School, it seemed as if however fast we ran, we could never quite keep up with the pace that 'workingest woman' had set."[22] These trials led her to offer to turn the school over to any interested party who would agree to keep it going. No one came forward, so she soldiered on, continuing as its titular director but increasingly turning over the day-to-day administration to Elizabeth Watts. After this Stone spent considerable time away from the school, eventually the entire winter. She would return for graduation ceremonies in May and stay until Fall, allowing Watts to take a vacation. She remained titular head of the school until her death in 1946 and, on a number of occasions during the Depression, used her personal income to keep the school running.

Publicity materials regularly went out from the Settlement School for fundraising purposes, A founding myth, which featured an eighty year old mountain patriarch, Uncle Solomon Everidge, became especially important. It recounted how he walked barefoot twenty-two miles to entreat them to start a school at Hindman. The story, constantly reiterated, could easily make one believe that no schooling was available at Hindman when Katherine and May arrived. But theirs was not the first educational institution in Hindman. George Clarke had established one fifteen years earlier. So why they chose Hindman and why George Clarke sold his school remains something of a mystery.

Clarke had established a school in 1887 and provided five months of common or primary school (paid for by county taxes) and five months of subscription school (privately paid-for instruction) each year. Pettit and Stone took over the common school work along with the three room building formerly belonging to Clarke's Buckner Academy. According to Rhonda England who has written an excellent doctoral dissertation on the Hindman Settlement School and its first three directors, "Voices From the History of Teaching: Katherine Pettit, May Stone and Elizabeth Watts at Hindman Settlement School," Clarke's approach to teaching represented the older "common school" method while Pettit and Stone introduced ideas associated with Progressive educational theory as well as the concept of industrial or vocational education.[23]

Clarke was originally asked by the citizens to found a school and was given a site by the town. Through his success he soon controlled the public school funds available from the county and state and was provided with an assistant. While little seems to have been taught in the lower grades beyond the three Rs, the school acquired some local renown and students came to it from several other counties.[24] Josiah Combs, one of the Settlement's first graduates who went on to earn a Ph.D. in French literature at the Sorbonne, was a student for nine years in the Clarke establishment prior to the opening of the Settlement school. His reminiscence may be biased but it is the most direct evidence available on the education offered at Hindman prior to the arrival of Pettit and Stone. He wrote:

> I was put in the village school…and the curriculum extended scarcely beyond the "three r's." I must have gone through the "common school branches" so often that I could have reproduced them, word for word, had they suddenly become lost to the world. When one of these texts was "finished" for the first time, we would go right through it again, ad infinitum. This was the Professor's system.[25]

According to Combs, exams were unknown and repetition, rote memorization and drill were the hallmarks of the school's approach. Not surprisingly, a popular name for such schools was "blab schools."

Clarke's school was the location of the Teacher's Institute in 1900 and 1901 which Pettit and Stone attended as part of their summer work. Pettit's comments on the Clarke school in her journal are more favorable than those penned by Combs. But nearly two hundred students were served by only two male teachers. Pettit described them both as, "of very good education, with some progressive ideas" but she noted the difficulty of teaching a hundred children of all ages. By the time Clark sold his school it had two hundred, thirty-four students so the women had a good base on which to build.

Clarke left Hindman for four years but then returned and started another school. It offered subscription courses designed for teacher certification and remained open until 1914 when it burned down. He left after this to establish a similar school elsewhere.[26]

Unquestionably, other than their own experiences, the greatest influence on the development of settlement work at Hindman was Jane Addams and Hull House in Chicago. Both women were deeply influenced by Addams' view of education which declared its impatience with

> schools which lay all stress on reading and writing, suspecting them to rest upon the assumption that all knowledge and interest must be brought to the children through the medium of books. Such an assumption fails to give the child any clew [sic.] to the life about him or any power to usefully or intelligently connect himself with it.[27]

Aside from advice from the Hull House workers, Katherine and May prepared for the opening of their own social settlement by several months residence at Louisville's most important social settlement institution, Neighborhood House. They also toured other educational institutions, including Berea College and Tuskegee Institute, to see how they were operated. Pettit probably always subscribed to the "cleanliness is next to godliness credo" but from Tuskegee, she acquired an absolute faith that scrubbing every inch of the institution's buildings once a week was a moral exercise as well as an hygienic imperative. It figured large in the routines at both Hindman and Pine Mountain.

A combination of industrial and practical education, combined with academic preparation, characterized the school from the beginning. It also reflected the general social settlement model first introduced at Hull House in 1889 which spread to more than one hundred settlement institutions in the following decade. For example, Hull House offered kindergarten for toddlers, clubs for both youths and adults, classes in proper diet, drama and singing groups, courses in cooking, dressmaking, child care and manual arts. So did the Hindman Settlement School. Where Hindman and Hull House diverged rested more on the difference between urban and rural needs than on any difference of philosophy. The stated purpose of the Hindman Settlement School, reiterated many times, was, "to educate the children back to their homes instead of away from them."[28]

The annual letters reveal how they went about implementing these goals after the school opened in August, 1902. The letter of January, 1904, highlights some of the curriculum changes immediately introduced into the school. Besides common school (primary grades) there were now kindergarten classes and classes in basketry, sewing, cooking, gardening and carpentry. Pettit and Stone were the first to introduce these features into a public school in the state. The first building, added in 1903, was a log workshop housing the manual training. Two years later they built a weaving cabin. They stressed practical lessons, both for the children at the school and the adults in the larger community.

The journals make clear that both women respected and admired central elements of the culture they found. Pettit especially valued the older, traditional ways of the mountain people–the hospitality and stress on family and kinship ties–for its strength and simplicity. As early as Camp Industrial she commented negatively on the side effects of "progress." Her first observation upon returning to Hindman after a year's absence was to rue the "ugly new frame houses" now obstructing the beautiful view from their hillside. John Campbell said that, from the outset, Pettit had doubts about placing the school in a town although its population density provided a wider audience for educational and settlement activities. This hostility to the impact of town life, led, within a decade after the Hindman School's founding, to Pettit's decision to establish the Pine Mountain School at a spot remote enough (on the isolated far side of Pine Mountain in Harlan County) to be free of these problems. She would learn quickly, however, that physical isolation brought its own problems. And physical isolation did not rid her of her chief nemesis, the railroad.

Admiration for the traditional culture had its limits, especially as it pertained to the life of many mountain women. The Cedar Grove journal is very critical of the conditions of women's lives. And, in a letter written in 1899, Pettit wrote to a friend that:

> It is the deplorable condition of the women that appeals so strongly to me. Their condition is truly wretched. The domestic life of the mountaineer is crude. They know absolutely nothing of decent living. How can they when the women who should be fitted for housekeepers and homemakers are doing the work of men, who think their duty consists in hunting, fishing and sitting on the fence talking politics. While the women hurriedly cook their meals and spend the rest of the time in cultivating crops, building fences and milking cows.[29]

Pettit was hardly the only one to comment on the hard life of women. Lucy Furman wove this theme into her novels and had a principal character in *The Glass Window* say, "we jest got to take what comes–specially if we're womenfolks. 'Pears like they're a sight more predestyned than men!"[30]

Furman's other three novels about the school, *Mothering on Perilous*, (1913); *Sight to the Blind*, (1914); and *The Quare Women*, (1923); also delineate in great detail the patriarchal mountain culture. While Stone and Pettit were often sharply critical in letters to friends, they were careful about making negative public statements about mountain culture for they recognized that the mountaineers were very proud. Rather than criticizing, they adopted a "teaching" attitude hoping to encourage change by having people learn by observation. This approach prevailed from the earliest summer camps.

Rhonda England observed that the settlement curriculum "was an active participation in the life of the community and...changed or adjusted to meet the needs of the participants."[31]

Another central idea of Progressive social thought that was naturally employed at the settlement was a belief in using the real life experience of people as a basis for learning. The "quare women" attacked the problem of the status and conditions of women by trying to provide them with better homemaking skills and better health and hygiene. Such changes provided immediate help and also exposed mountain women to new possibilities in their daily lives.

The low status of women extended to the fotched-on women themselves. They noted that "there has been some prejudice because it is a 'wimmen's school' and some of the mountain people have said 'no woman is fit to teach school'." They gradually overcame this bias, again largely by allowing observation to prove their case. They noted a major breakthrough in their acceptance when many men expressed admiration for the log ice-house they built. They recorded the grudging admission that, "if them wimmen could teach school as well as they could build log houses they were alright."[32]

For more than a decade Katherine and May were partners in a path-breaking experiment at Hindman. Their school opened on August 5, 1902, with one hundred ninety students, five of whom were boarders. They first called it the Log Cabin Settlement School but shortly afterward, changed the name to the WCTU Settlement School, reflecting the fact that the land and buildings of the school were the property of the WCTU and the organization provided the majority of financial assistance.[33]

Many factors were necessary for success, not the least the faith and determination of Pettit and Stone. Another, certainly, was the early financial support of the WCTU which made rapid expansion of their programs possible. The organization paid four of the seven teachers' salaries during the second year of operation. Two others were underwritten by friends in the Northeast. Francis Beauchamp, head of the state WCTU, volunteered for a month every summer and taught them to build fences, lay road and sidewalks. By mail she directed the crop planting on the rented farm for many years.[34]

The WCTU tie eventually became a mixed blessing. Although it would seem most likely that it was Pettit's link to the organization which had led to the sponsorship, it has been said that one of Pettit's concerns which figured in her decision to found the Pine Mountain School was her opposition to the WCTU affiliation. What appears to have happened is that over the first decade the school grew so rapidly that the financial contribution of the WCTU shrank in comparison to the school's needs. When the decision to become independent was taken in 1916, the explanation given was that the affiliation hampered the broader base of fundraising now required. It may have been that, with the national prohibition campaign heating up, the affiliation was more controversial than it had been earlier. For its part, the WCTU accepted a friendly separation and transferred its Hindman property and the endowment fund to the new Executive Board. Francis Beauchamp, President of the WCTU, remained as a director.[35]

With two schools needing aid from the same body of supporters a serious financial crisis resulted at both institutions. At Hindman it probably forced the affiliation issue and led May Stone to have the Hindman Settlement School incorporated by the town as an independent school. While no one can say that the school would not have survived without the WCTU's support in its early years, its rapid expansion into both a new and wider curriculum and into community social settlement work could not have occurred without the funds provided by this relationship.

If reading the narratives of the three summer camps raises our admiration for Pettit and Stone for their ability to overcome all kinds of adversity, the first decade of social settlement work at Hindman shows that they continued to overcome substantial obstacles, some imposed by natural calamity.

The first school year opened with four teachers. By the second year, the staff had expanded to seven teachers. The school was supported by the county as Clarke's had been and for six months of the year it was a regular public school. Three subscription months followed for a nine month school term. All students took the same curriculum and the boarding, or "home" students, shared responsibility for maintaining the school, its grounds, and farm. By year two the school was already selling baskets and furniture crafted by the boarders working for their tuition. Some of this handiwork was exhibited at the 1905 World's Fair.

In these first years the boarders and teachers all lived in what was described as a "rough, open plank house...very cold and much too small" for eighteen.[36] An appeal for funds for a larger building was successful and a large log house with twenty eight rooms was built in 1905 at great effort. It had Pettit traipsing up ravines and across mountains to select trees and have them cut and hauled to the campus. Lucy Furman fictionalized this effort in *The Glass Window*.

Only two months after opening the log house, the first of several disastrous fires struck the school. It destroyed the entire campus including the loghouse, the manual training shop, and the school with its library of 2,000 books. Only the original cottage was left standing since it was located across Troublesome Creek. The teachers carried on for the remainder of the year in two local churches and the masonic lodge without books or supplies. Pettit and Stone sent out urgent appeals for help and started rebuilding.

Some forms of adversity were not quite so life threatening but almost equally discouraging. A case in point was the marauding hogs. Let Lucy Furman tell the story in her own words from a 1907 newsletter which appealed for funds for a fence. Furman was not only housemother to the boys but also responsible for all of the outdoor work and the farm. She wrote:

Our troubles began at the very start. The fence all around the place was in a tumble-down condition. It had never been strong…positively inviting the numerous hogs of the neighborhood to come in and visit. All they had to do was to root under the light panel a little, lift it up and enter. They strolled in and out at pleasure, helping themselves to our potatoes, corn, onions, peas, lettuce and tomatoes….It seemed to me that day and night for weeks at a time I never had hogs off of my mind. I would get up at all hours of the night to run them out, and the little boys were kept at it all day. Of course we did what we could to mend the fence by nailing slabs and old planks all around the bottom….

By this time, however, the hogs were persuaded that they had rights of possession and were determined to enjoy them. If they could not come in under the fence they would some other way. So they began on the gates, which were also decrepit, tearing them off the rusty hinges, and breaking every latch we could devise. Not content with this, some of them learned to trip daintily over the stile at the back of our place, and one would mount the horse block out in front of the Cottage, force the palings apart at the top, and jump through….Last year the hogs made the discovery that the palings were so thin, weak and rotten that by battering them sufficiently at any one point, they could break in anywhere. And since then we have had troubles indeed…and this old sow has been especially successful as a battering ram (I have several times caught her in the act, about bed time at night and just before day in the morning) and it has become a common thing to hear Kelly or Ishmael or French or Nelson call out while I am dressing, "That air ole sow's done broke in a new place and fotched several with her," or, "I run nine out of the corn this morning."

We have also had trouble with the town cows jumping over our front fence, to get at the blue grass and clover which this year has certainly looked tempting. So with the cows in front of us,

Troublesome to the rear of us, and hogs all around us, the nerve strain may be imagined.[37]

Funny as the story is, with a tight school budget, the damage done by the neighbors' hogs and cows was clearly no small matter. No wonder Furman compared her tribulations to that of Mary Tudor, noting, "If, like Queen Mary of England, one word should be found written on my heart after death, that word at present would be 'Hogs.'"[38]

Lucy, her boys, and the school got their fence but fundraising did not always keep pace with the needs of rapid expansion and the extraordinary demand for places for children from all around the region. For the first time in 1908 the annual letter warned that they had not been able to pay all due bills during the year. The next few years do not indicate any financial crisis but clearly fundraising was being turned into a fine art in the letters and pamphlets that flowed from the school. In addition both Stone and Pettit spent considerable time on the lecture circuit in the East. Meanwhile serious plans for raising an endowment began. This work weighed heavily on May Stone who had responsibility for financial and business affairs. In 1910, Lucy Furman described the situation as a "crushing weight."

If the daily strain of meeting bills was not enough, a second great fire occurred the very month that Furman wrote the letter quoted above. Everything except for the boy's cottage, the workshop, power house and small hospital was again destroyed including the two main structures, Settlement House and the school house. Pettit estimated the loss at $25,000 while the school carried only $14,000 insurance. Both Stone and Pettit were away when the calamity struck and it is clear that Pettit, at least, was reluctant to start over again at Hindman.

The town leaders rushed to pledge their support to a rebuilding effort, fearing not only the impact of this loss on the education of their children but on the economy of the town as well. They quickly subscribed $6,000 and elicited other pledges, one from the county for sixty-five additional acres to allow adequate spacing for buildings on the campus to avoid a repeat of the total destruction which had accompanied the earlier fires. The outpouring of assistance led them to agree to stay and rebuild.[39] But Pettit remained convinced that her ideals could not be fully realized at Hindman where the majority were day students and where town attractions competed with the school for influence over the impressionable children. Many volunteers noted the difference in the behavior of the boarding and town students. Moreover, since it was a public school for six months of the year, no selection of students was possible. So, despite her pledge to stay, Pettit soon began plans for a new school at Pine Mountain.

As part of the agreement for the dissolution of their partnership, Pettit agreed to help Stone raise a $100,000 endowment for the school prior to establishing her own institution. Despite several years of effort only $40,000 was raised. With fourteen buildings to maintain serving three hundred students, one hundred of whom now boarded, the financial operations of the Hindman School were extensive–and precarious. The endowment was insufficient and financial crisis in 1915-1916 forced the lay-off of several instructors for the first time in the school's history. After becoming an independent institution, the school's financial situation began to improve.

One of the important ideas of Progressive social thought, embodied in the Settlement House movement, was the belief that the social environment rather than the individual was the critical starting point for change. Consequently, the routines and schedules established for every hour of the day at Hindman and Pine Mountain were a vital component in the achievement of the school's goals.

The annual letters set forth the rigorous routine established for the live-in students. Children spent six hours in classes with an extra one and one half hours of study at night. Each child also worked four and a half hours a day and six on Saturday at the chores that kept the school operating.

They rose at 5:30, cleaned their living quarters and did morning chores on the farm or in the kitchen and dormitories. Breakfast came at 6:30, followed between 7 and 8 with work. For the boys this was mostly outdoors on the farm or on the road. For the girls, it involved dishwashing, food preparation, housekeeping and similar activities. Between 8 and 11:30 students were in class, then came dinner with thirty minutes of play-time afterward. Afternoon classes lasted until 3, additional chores took until 5:30, then came dinner and another play period from 6 to 7. The next hour was devoted to study. During the last part of the evening, before bedtime, the children gathered in their individual dormitories with their housemothers for stories, singing, popcorn and similar recreation. Lights were out for everyone, including the teachers, by 9:30.

On Saturday major work included the washing and ironing of all the clothing and bedding for the week, scrubbing down of the floors of all buildings, turning of mattresses and changing sheets. Outdoor work involved fencing, working on the road which always needed mending, attending to farm work and general repairs. Afternoons were generally devoted to clubs and organized activities. "Socials" were often the highlight of the week, held on either Friday or Saturday evenings. Sunday saw the school and its faculty in church and Sunday School and then there was free time in the afternoon and a "picnic" supper which many former students remember with great fondness as the most special of all the meals of the week.[40]

It wasn't just the strenuous daily schedule but the insistence on total self-sufficiency which characterized the Hindman Settlement School. The school routine provided constant practical lessons in proper homemaking for the girls and farm and manual skills for the boys. Moreover, the routine was expected to instill an understanding of the necessity of work and a team spirit of cooperation and responsibility. The emphasis in all activities was always on "learning by doing."

Students, under the supervision of their teachers and housemothers, raised almost all of their vegetables and flowers, their meat, milk, corn and flour. Sometimes the school traded clothing and items donated by supporters for additional supplies from neighbors. The Fireside Industries, established the year after the school opened, helped fund the tuition for the non-public school months for many students. The blankets, baskets, woven goods and furniture that was made not only supplied the school but the excess became a source of funds for its operation. Quickly, the Fireside Industries became an important social settlement activity reaching beyond the school. Local artisans sold their crafts to the school which were advertised and resold across the nation. It helped the local economy and was also intended to preserve regional crafts. Not surprisingly, many of the mountain women saw the work primarily as an economic endeavor while Pettit and Stone saw it primarily as preserving a cultural tradition. The clash of views was apparent when Pettit and Stone express dismay that their artisan suppliers preferred to use commercial dyes rather than the older, more laboriously prepared, natural ones.

When Pettit opened her Pine Mountain School its remoteness seemed ideal for her goal of giving "mountain people a chance to have good industrial schools before the railroad comes." Ironically, in the 1920s a logging railroad, whose right of way had been purchased across Pine Mountain long before the school arrived, chugged its way through the campus only a few feet from her front porch.[41]

The activities and routines at Pine Mountain were largely identical to Hindman. The school was private, however, and all students boarded. Although social settlement activities were undertaken, the school's principal biographer, James Greene, says that the stress was on the school. As at Hindman, many of the teachers and volunteers came from the eastern women's colleges and almost all the faculty and workers were women. Perhaps because of the railroad or the proximity to Harlan, Pettit grew increasingly troubled by the expansion of the coal industry and tried to interest local churches in setting up social settlements in the company mining camps which were mushrooming everywhere.[42] Little was done, however. When she retired from Pine Mountain in 1930 and the Great Depression hit, she spent much of the time during her final years attempting to help families living in the camps to return to the land. She still believed that subsistence farming could provide a living if better agricultural techniques were used. She also served as an intermediary in the sale of handicraft goods which sustained many families in these desperate times. Two years after her retirement from Pine Mountain she received the Algernon Sidney Sullivan award for outstanding service to the people of Kentucky. She died of cancer in 1936 at the age of sixty-eight in Lexington. Lucy Furman, her life-long friend, wrote of her that, "no living person has worked so long in the southern mountains and nobody so well understands the problems of the mountains. Furthermore, no Kentucky woman has ever done such service to her state."[43]

It is easy to assume that these schools served only children and youth. While they were certainly model educational institutions, Hindman, especially, was a true social settlement as well and had a substantial impact upon the entire surrounding region.

The settlement work, as distinct from the schooling of the children, was important right from the start. A brief discussion of only a few of the major activities provides a sense of the enormous impact of this work. Perhaps the greatest concern of Pettit and Stone was the poor health and hygiene they found everywhere in the region. Changing that situation became a high priority. From the beginning they often did home nursing, attended the sick and sometimes the dying. Training others to do this work and training the mountaineers themselves in simple techniques of modern hygiene, nursing and medicine led to "home nursing" courses. Usually a day-long session, they covered everything from how to read a thermometer and how to change a bed with a patient in it, to how to cook for the sick and how to deal with contagious diseases.

Other health work which Stone and Pettit took on at the outset of their camps was finding places for sick or handicapped children at institutions in the Bluegrass where they could receive help or training. In the Camp Industrial and Sassafras journals, Katherine reported that they had acquired scholarships for several of the most promising children and also places for several who were blind and deaf at special schools and hospitals in Lexington and Louisville. More than forty were aided in the first few years. The Settlement worked on another endemic health problem in the region, hookworm, holding clinics and instituting an educational program to help eradicate it. There can be no doubt that these activities made a real difference in the health of the people of the surrounding region.

Improved agriculture figured importantly as a concern of their social settlement program and the school quickly welcomed cooperative ventures with the University of Kentucky's agricultural extension services. Forage plots were established on the school land to see what would grow best on the steep mountain slopes. In 1910, the school sponsored the first County Fair to exhibit produce, animals, and crafts and to make their neighbors more aware of better farming methods. Pettit was especially involved with this kind of work and earned the name, the "Blossom Lady," for her distribution of flower and vegetable seeds, a practice she began during her first trip to the mountains.[45]

The Fireside Industries represent still another major program intended to preserve traditional crafts and provide cash income for mountain families. Their baskets and coverlids often translated into a new cow for the farm, windows for their homes and other comforts. In the first three years of operation, local people earned sixteen hundred dollars this way. Through widely distributed printed pamphlets (which went to organizations like the DAR) orders for goods came from far afield.[46] The interest in handicrafts was not unique since it was also an important aspect of urban social settlement programs. Hull House was known for encouragement of crafts for both cultural and economic reasons.

Preservation of the local arts and crafts was a special labor of love for Katherine and May who remained fascinated with the beauty of the quilts and woven goods they found in nearly every dwelling. The buildings of the campus were filled with crafts and furniture made by the students in the training programs at the school. Pettit and Stone also shared a strong determination to preserve the oral culture of the mountaineers through the collection of ballads, hymns, and other musical traditions. Becoming familiar with this heritage became an integral part of the school's curriculum. The beauty of the ballads and their haunting minor key music was mentioned first in the Cedar Grove narrative and Katherine collected the words of many ballads (some of which were contemporary) during the Camp Industrial summer and included them in a separate addenda to her report. In 1907, she published a collection of these lyrics in the *Journal of American Folklore*.[47] Publication stimulated ballad collectors to visit the Appalachian region and the Hindman and Pine Mountain schools served as centers for their efforts. Both institutions were magnets for collectors such as Cecil Smith, Olive Dame Campbell, Josephine McGill, and others. They spent time at the schools, listened to the children sing the old songs and used the school's resources to locate individuals who were knowledgeable in the many versions of the old ballads.

At Hindman the school came to play a central role in town life. It became a community center, not only for its lending library and games but for the twice-weekly socials and the many clubs formed for youth and adults. For example, a mother's club dispensed practical training in the care of infants and probably helped reduce the local infant mortality rate. Other types of clubs headquartered at the school included an adult literary club, a current events club and a drama club. In addition to their regular activities, they often engaged in projects for town improvements. The school provided the town with electricity from its power plant and the money generated for this service paid for the engineer. The Practice Home established on the campus served a dual purpose. While older students lived in it to train in the daily activities of modern housekeeping, it was also open to any passerby who might want to stop and learn the latest in up-to-date homemaking.

The educational influence of the school reached well beyond Troublesome Creek after a few years. Almost as soon as the school had trained its first girls in industrial classes and social settlement work, they went out to teach special classes at district schools. In 1907, two were sponsored by women's groups who provided salaries as well as the books, materials for manual training, maps, globes, flags and other school supplies. Soon the work was expanded to additional schools.[48]

These varied programs of help and self-help endeared the school's founders to neighbors who at first had been suspicious of them. Their mountain friends sought to repay them when possible, often through hospitality which they received everywhere they went. There is a long piece in the archive describing how the school's first graduate, Mallie Baker, won the position of district school teacher at Sassafras. It is a lesson in the importance which many placed on the work that Katherine Pettit and May Stone had done for these communities over the years. Mallie won the job against nearly insurmountable odds. The school system operated on the basis of cronyism with the elected school trustees treating the local district school more or less like a private fiefdom. Her rival for the position was a kinsman of a trustee of the school. Normally Mallie would have had no chance despite far better qualifications. But the fact that conflict between the rival and supporters of Mallie occurred and, indeed, threatened to break out into a feud, illustrates the changes which institutions such as the settlement school were bringing to the area. Chief among Mallie's supporters was Judge Combs, a prominent figure in the narrative of the Sassafras summer. He explained the unusual outcome of the conflict this way, "if we'd a let Miss Mallie here go back home without gettin this school, after all the good those ladies did over here on Montgomery [Creek], why, it would have been the worst kind of ingratitude."[49]

Such successes might seem small but Pettit urged other workers who might feel discouraged at their progress to do as she had done. She suggested, "take a trip within fifty miles and visit the homes of the boys and girls you taught in the early days. You must see what good homes they have, what well trained children they are bringing up and what good fathers and mothers they make."[50] If they did this, all of their doubts would soon disappear.

One final thing might be noted in assessing the importance of the establishment of the Hindman Settlement School by Katherine Pettit and May Stone. Cratis Williams, in his exhaustive study, *The Southern Mountaineer in Fact and Fiction*, noted that the success of the Hindman Settlement School produced a, "far-flung effort to establish similar schools and centers throughout the mountain region." So Hindman was not only a pathbreaker but a model. And he concluded,

> "There can be no doubt as to the effectiveness of these institutions in meeting the needs of the mountain people at a time when the commercial invasion of the highlands was bringing them into social and cultural conflict with the outside forces accompanying industrialization."[51]

So, from an initial six week excursion came one of the most influential and creative institutions founded in the mountain region of Kentucky during the Progressive era, founded by two improbable reformers not yet out of their 20s. Why they went–and especially–what they found, is the story told by the "Quare Women's Journals."

First settlement at Hindman, Kentucky, 1900

Settlement home built 1906

W. C. T. U. SETTLEMENT SCHOOL

IN THE KENTUCKY MOUNTAINS   45 MILES FROM THE RAILROAD

"Aunt Aislie first heard the news from her son's wife...'Maw, there's a passel of quare women come in from furrin parts and set 'em up some cloth houses there on the p'int above the court house, and carrying on some of the outlandishest doings ever you heard of.'"

Opening of The Quare Women *by Lucy Furman*

Camp Cedar Grove at Hazard, Kentucky Summer of 1899

Early in Spring of 1899 the Rev. J. T. Mitchell, a Presbyterian minister of Hazard, Perry County, Kentucky, wrote a letter to Mrs. C. P. Barnes, Chairman of the Traveling Library Committee in the mountains of Kentucky. After telling her of the library in his care, he wrote:

> Cannot the State Federation send us a woman, a gentle, womanly woman, a dear old fashioned woman, young or old, who can win woman's true rights in that conquest, that in itself is simply being a woman? What do I want of a woman? I want her a few weeks of the coming Summer to assist in the conduct of meetings of wives, mothers, housekeepers, young ladies and little girls. Lectures and lessons in cooking and home-making should be made particularly enthusiastic and then the intellectual and moral features can be made interesting.[1]

When this letter was read at the annual meeting of the State Federation of Women's Clubs in Frankfort, on June 2, it met with an earnest and substantial response. Money to carry out such work was immediately subscribed and Miss Katherine R. Pettit, of Lexington, asked to take charge of it, which she gladly consented to do.

The first of August, the Committee, consisting of four members, went to Hazard and established a Camp for six weeks, to work along the lines suggested in Mr. Mitchell's letter. Hazard is the county seat of Perry County, a town of six hundred people, located in the North Fork of the Kentucky River, about forty miles from Jackson, the nearest railroad point. This meant a journey of forty miles in a wagon over very rough mountain travel, besides a night spent in a mountain home on the way.

The Camp was pitched in an ideal place, about half a mile from Hazard, in the midst of a cedar grove on a beautiful knoll, surrounded by mountains. The tent was made as clean, neat and attractive as possible. It was decorated with flags, bunting of stars and stripes, Japanese lanterns and pictures. A bookcase was made of a box, with an embroidered cover, a dressing table of a box, covered with white cotton, put on with brass tacks. The cots were covered with white spreads and pillows. Outside were hammocks, steamer chairs, and a table with flowers and books. The kitchen was under the trees with a cover of oilcloth.

The novelty of the tent and the life there attracted people in large numbers. The first afternoon, before things were gotten in order, a young girl from town came up and admired a hemstitched muslin necktie worn by a member of the camp, and asked where she could get one. The young lady told her, if she would bring some muslin, she would show her how to make one like it. The girl went home and in a little while returned with six others and material for ties. Everything was stopped to teach these girls to hemstitch and the next Sunday morning, the seven girls appeared at church, wearing the neckties. When it came time to get supper, they asked if they could help. They were allowed to do so and told that we should be glad to have them come up any day, bring their materials with them and let us all get dinner or supper together. This met with approval by them and so they were interested to come and learn, without knowing that it was our chief object to instruct them. We always made the table as attractive as possible with a white tablecloth and flowers in the center.

One of the girls said: "I never heard of puttin' flowers on a eatin' table. I never thought of it before, but things do eat better when they look nice."[2]

This lesson was a good one, learned merely by observation.

After a little while, the work was in good running order along many lines. Three afternoons a week we had the young girls from fifteen to eighteen years old for cooking lessons, other days these same girls for sewing or reading. Every afternoon some very little children came for kindergarten, which one little girl called "Mckinley garden," and one young man, a school teacher, an hour a day for shorthand.

One day we asked twelve little girls from the country to spend the day and dress dolls, while twelve little town girls got the dinner. The children began to come by six o'clock in the morning. They were intensely interested in the sewing and did it very nicely. They could hardly be persuaded to stop for dinner. How happy they were that afternoon, when each little girl took home her doll! Several had never owned a doll before. We had some small boys out to read to Sunday afternoons, and had religious services at the Camp several times.

The people all seemed to enjoy reading and were glad to get the books, papers and magazines that we gave them. They were everywhere very cordial and glad to help us in any way. We had company from six in the morning till six in the evening, often twenty and twenty-five people to dinner and supper.

One day two of us were in a store in town, when we saw a tired-looking woman sitting there counting the teeth in a long comb-like affair. We spoke to her and asked what she had in her hand. She explained that it was a slade (sley)[3] to use in her loom in weaving. We found her very interesting and asked her to go home with us to dinner. After a little hesitation, she went. She told us she had left home, 15 miles away, at the peep o' day and come to town mule-back to do some tradin'. She had her mule loaded with her purchases

Within a year of opening, the school was planning for its own certified nurse, paid for by one of its supporters. The nurse, Margaret Butler, came on staff in the fall of 1904. Not long after they added a small hospital and then a larger one which served both the school and the community for decades. Within fifteen years, due to their efforts, there was a traveling district nurse headquartered at the school. In addition, the Settlement served as a training ground in rural nursing for organizations such as the Red Cross.

The trachoma clinics held twice yearly from 1911 on and run by Dr. Stucky drew hundreds of sufferers and received national attention. Their success led to the establishment by the Federal government of several trachoma hospitals in the mountains. "Sore eyes," which was how mountaineers described the disease, often led to blindness and was endemic when the Pettit and Stone first arrived. The government estimated eight to ten percent of the populace was afflicted. The settlement's efforts helped eradicate it. Lucy Furman use the trachoma campaign as the theme for her second novel, *Sight To the Blind*, published in 1914.[44]

Mary Stacy and Rhoda tending the sheep, in this case sowing salt from a gourd.

and rode out to the Camp while we walked by her side. She had a headache, so we asked her to lie in the hammock and rest till dinner time. She had never seen a hammock and was afraid o' spillin' out, but got in for a few minutes. She saw some girls learning to hem-stitch handkerchiefs, so she asked to be taught too and she was very apt. When she had done a part of one side, she said she knew how and would take it home and finish it. Then she went out to the kitchen to see what was going on there. She learned to make beaten biscuit[4] and said she would make some when she went home. She left after dinner in order to get home by dark. We gave her books, pictures and magazines. When she started, she said: "I never seed any quare wimmen like ye all before and I have seed sich a good time today. I never seed sich a fine time in my life before."

There was a Perry County Teacher's Institute while we were there. One afternoon we had about sixty teachers out for a reception and gave them lemonade and cake. Many of them had never seen a lemon. Each teacher was given a picture of George Washington and two flags for his schoolroom. We put up pictures and flags in every school house we passed. Another day we had about twenty district teachers to lunch.

We hear a great deal of the sturdy, strong mountaineers, but we saw few of them. Most of the people are tall, thin, sallow and far from vigorous. How can we expect them to be otherwise, when we know the conditions in which they live? We visited as much as we could, in the homes of the people. The houses are mostly one and two room log cabins, often containing families of ten or twelve. In Hazard there were some two story houses and some weatherboarded. They all look better from the outside than on the inside. We were impressed by the bare, unattractive rooms and the quantity of dirt. The floors are bare; the furniture consists usually of a bed in each corner, a few chairs, a table and a stove. In rare cases the beds are made up, but they are generally left just as the family got out of them and present anything but an inviting appearance.

Many houses in the country have no windows at all. One cabin I remember especially. It was made of rough, round logs with the bark on them and not very well chinked. There was one long, narrow room with no sign of a window and only a low, narrow door. Inside I could hardly see anything, though it was a bright, sunny, summer morning and the door open. After a few minutes, I could dimly make out a large, empty fireplace, two or three beds and some broken chairs. In this house live the father, mother and five or six children, the youngest a boy of four, blind from his birth.

Another thing that strikes us is the bad cooking, if we chance to try to take a meal with the people. They live on fat bacon, corn bread and a few vegetables, all cooked in the most unwholesome way. Everything is fried in as much grease as they can get. Our efforts in the line of cooking were to teach them to make good bread, to cook the vegetables in as many ways as possible, and the meat without so much grease; in every way to make the best use of the material they have.

Add to bad air, dirt and bad cooking, the use of tobacco by men, women and even children as soon as they can walk and talk, and how can we expect good health? And without any regard to the laws of health, how can the people be strong, mentally or morally?

Most of the mountain men do little or no work. The chief occupations are logging, illicit distilling and country storekeeping. The women and children do all the work. They plow the fields or hoe them, when the hillsides are too steep for plowing, put in the crops, tend them, build and repair the fences, make the garden, keep the house, cook, wash, milk, sew and everything else done at all. Many of the women still spin and weave coverlids, blankets and cloth for their own use. We always asked to see these things and they take great pride in showing them. This and quilt making is the only development of their aesthetic nature.

One charm of the people is their lack of self-consciousness. After an hour's acquaintance, many told us their whole life's history.

They are very frank and the first questions they asked us were: "How old be ye?" "Be ye married? Why not?" When asked how old we were, we inquired how old they thought us and the response was very flattering to us. No one took us to be over eighteen or twenty years old, and would not believe it when we told them we were older. When we saw how old the women there looked, we were not so much surprised. Those eighteen and twenty looked thirty, those twenty-five looked thirty-five, and those over thirty looked as old as they ever get. We never saw a single old maid in the mountains, only one girl over twenty. When told we were not married, they seemed really sorry for us and asked why not. One young lady said: "I have not found anybody down my way that wants me." The mountain woman took pity on her and said: "If you will go home with me, I can get you married in a week to a widower with five children."

The native preachers are very illiterate. We had an opportunity to hear them at a funeral we attended about six miles down the river from Hazard. It is quite common to have these funerals held long after the death occurs. Sometimes the roads are impassable and the favorite preacher may be many miles away. One of our neighbors invited us to go with her to her grandfather's funeral. He had been dead several years. We accepted, of course, and had a new experience, which none of us can ever forget. Our neighbor discussed with us the question of a suitable dress for herself. At last she decided on a black calico wrapper with white beading. We insisted on leaving off the beading, but she "aimed to be jest as well dressed as any other grand-daughter." The main glory of her apparel was the apron, a blue and red checked one. No woman was well dressed that day who did not wear an apron and yarn mitts. We all went in a large road wagon, with a white cotton cover. Our seats were chairs and over the rough roads it required our constant attention to keep in the wagon at all. It was an all day trip. We started at six in the morning and got home a little before dark. The services were held under the trees on the river bank, a very beautiful spot. There were five or six preachers, each giving us a sermon, some two or three. The hymns were lined out[5] and all sung to the same tune. One of us took the sermons down in shorthand and I quote a fair sample of the style:

> The old ship of Zion, yes, ah, how long will it be, yes ah, before she struts out, yes ah, for that land of glory, yes ah? Your money is paid, yes ah. Come and get on, yes ah. Christ is gwine to come, yes ah. This is the day of Christ's post-mortem, yes ah, and angels after angels, and potentates after potentates, yes ah, in robes of white, yes ah, with palms of victory, yes ah. Come on brothers and sisters, let's ride, yes ah, with brother _____ yes ah, and Jesus, yes ah. Let's ride with the cheribums and the seraphims, yes ah, let's ride with the Ibims and the Timtims, yes ah.

The last night we were there, about one hundred people came up to tell us good-bye. We had the Camp lighted with Japanese lanterns and a big campfire. The scene was the most affecting of all. Men, women and children, all seemed loath to say good-bye. They hung about us, wept, begged us all to write to them and to promise to come back next summer. One man said: "You don't know what your being with us has done for us, and you may never know. But after a long while, when you may have forgotten you have ever been here, we will not forget and the good you have done will live with us."

HINDMAN
SETTLEMENT
SCHOOL

INCORPORATED

DEPENDENT UPON VOLUNTARY
SUBSCRIPTIONS

HINDMAN, KENTUCKY

EXECUTIVE COMMITTEE

MISS MAY STONE

MISS RUTH HUNTINGTON

Hindman, Ky. 1900. "We consider that no better field could have been chosen for our work than Hindman."

Camp Industrial at Hindman, Knott County, Kentucky June 12 to August 31, 1900

On June 12, a party of six, Miss Katherine R. Pettit, Miss Curry Breckenridge and Miss Katherine Christian of Lexington, Miss Laura Campbell of Philadelphia, Miss Eva W. Bruner and Miss May Stone of Louisville, started to Hindman, Knott County, Kentucky, to establish a Social Settlement there, under the auspices of the Kentucky Federation of Women's Clubs. All the winter before, two of us had been busy planning for the work, getting the necessary helpers as well as materials for the different classes.

The journey from Louisville to Hindman occupied three days and was full of incident and interest. The first day we went nearly two hundred miles on the railroad to Jackson and the other two days were spent going forty-five miles over a very rough, mountain road. We had quite a caravan, three large wagons, heavily loaded with supplies, and two so-called hacks, rather two-seated, covered spring wagons, in which rode the members of the party. The rate of travel was never more than two and one-half miles an hour, but often less; so that we had a good chance to observe the scenery along the way. Our drivers were very communicative and pointed out all the points of interest. All mountain roads follow the streams, except where it is necessary to cross a mountain. We went first on one side of a creek, then along in the bed of it, then on the other side and so back and forth. We were on as many as eleven different streams, following one as far as twelve miles, and we crossed four mountains.

From Jackson we went three miles up the North Fork of the Kentucky River, a half mile on Quicksand, one mile on the South Fork of Quicksand, two and a half on Smith's Branch, then crossed the first mountain, called Smith's Branch Mountain, 1150 feet above the sea. On the other side of this, we followed Riley Creek three quarters of a mile to the second mountain, Clayhole Mountain, 1150 above the sea. After one mile on Clayhole Branch, we came to Troublesome Creek, which we followed for six miles and then left it, till we got within two miles of Hindman. We next went up Buckhorn Creek from its mouth to its head, twelve miles in all. Most of this distance, the road was right in the creek bed and for roughness and deep holes it cannot be excelled. At the end of the first day, we had gone about twenty-five miles, when we reached the appointed resting place about eight o'clock. Here we were met with the cheering news, that they had received no word of our coming and could not take us in, as they had about twenty-five lumber men there spending the night. We had about resigned ourselves to spending ours in the wagon, for it was too dark to go further, when two of the men came out and offered to give us their room, which we gladly accepted. We spent the evening sitting on the front porch in the moonlight, while the young men sang a number of old English ballads never heard by us and only preserved now in the remote mountain districts where they have been handed down by tradition. We took down the words of as many of them as we could get, but the music is equally as unusual as the words. The people then asked us to sing and we tried to give them some of our patriotic songs, which they had never heard. We regret to say that we could not remember nearly all the words, but we promised to learn them while we were gone and sing them for them when we stopped there on our return. This promise we kept. On our way home, we gave them the songs with all the words and also with the accompaniment on the organ, which we had with us. After a very good sleep, three in a bed, we were on our way again by five o'clock in the morning, journeying up Buckhorn Creek, at the head of which we had to cross the third mountain, Buckhorn Mountain, 1350 feet above the sea level, the longest, roughest, steepest and most danger-ous one on our way. We then followed Ball Creek a mile and Trace Fork of Ball a mile, before we crossed the last mountain, 1450 feet above the sea. It is called Ogden Mountain, but correctly Audubon Mountain, for the great naturalist of that name, who passed over it on one of his journeys. It is a long trip over this mountain, but it winds around so that it is not so steep as some of the others. We went down Audubon Branch about two miles, when we came again to Trouble-some Creek for two miles, before we reached the little town of Hind-man, nestled in a very narrow valley among the high hills.

The whole of the second day we had traveled in a pouring rain and were drenched to the skin, when we got to Hindman about three o'clock in the afternoon of Thursday, June 14.

Circuit Court was in session, the Court House was crowded with men listening to a political speech, when a boy ran in and called, "The women, who are to live in the tents all summer, are coming over the hill." The minister explained to the people, who we were and why we were coming, when one man cried, "That's the best news we have ever heard in Hindman," and he received more ap-plause than the political speaker. When we rode up in front of the hotel we were met very cordially. Everybody was expecting us and welcomed us heartily. One baggage wagon went along with us, but the other two were delayed by rain, high waters and logs in the creeks and did not get to Hindman until Saturday night.

One of the drivers, a Knott County teacher writes:

Mallie, Ky., June 27, 1900.

On June the 12, 1900, I arrived at Jackson, Kentucky, for the purpose of meeting 1/2 dozen ladies and to carry their goods to Hindman, Kentucky, a distance of about fourty miles. Two of the ladies met me and my partner at the Depot the next morning at

6:30 o'clock for the purpose of seeing their goods put carefully on our wagons and at 10:30 o'clock we started for Hindman, Kentucky. We had lots of rain and by being water bound and the overflow and drift of logs we did not get to Hindman till the 16th. We had to wade water to get the logs out of the way of our wagons and we had double teams in order that we might get through the mud and sand that was thrown up by the flud of water.

Jno. S. Mullins

So we spent the first five days at the hotel, getting acquainted and planning the work. The very first evening, after supper, as we were sitting on the porch of the Stacy House, we made a beginning with the children. Miss Bruner, who had charge of the kindergarten work, saw about half a dozen little children playing out in the street and went out to speak to them. In a few minutes she was seated on the porch with the little ones in her lap and standing by her, while she told them stories and sang to them. They listened with wide open eyes and mouths. From this time there was kindergarten every day. We had the use of two rooms in the new dormitory. Here we stored our things, unpacked, put camp stools in an empty room and had the children come every day to sing, play, make chains, etc. They could hardly be persuaded to go home to dinner, until they were promised that they might come back in the afternoon. Here we received many callers and talked to the grown people as well as the children about what we hoped to do.

It was not until Tuesday that we got our tents pitched and our possessions in order, so that we could move up onto the hill, and this moving was an interesting but slow operation. The mountain, on the side of which we camped, was at its highest point 1750 feet above the sea level, and 750 feet above the creek. The tents were about 250 feet above the level of the town and the ascent was very steep. There was no way a wagon could go up and indeed only a footpath. Every article had to be carried up by hand, and there were many willing

hands offered. Every piece of lumber for floors, tables, shelves, the
five tents, poles and all were taken up in this manner. Then dishes,
groceries and supplies were unpacked at the dormitory and carried
up in small quantities. Only the stove was put on a slide and dragged
up by a horse. Nearly every man, woman and child helped us and
not one would accept a cent for service rendered. One kindergarten
boy, five years old, said: "I wan me a bucket to pack you something
up in." A number of men worked hard leveling places for the tents,
making floors, pitching the tents, putting up boxes for china closets,
pantries, chicken coops, making kitchen and kindergarten tables,
bookcases, dressing tables, various shelves and dairy. When all was
in order, the Camp was very attractive. We had five stories: cellar,
kitchen, dining room, sleeping tents and sitting room and kindergarten table on the top of the hill. The cellar consisted of a dairy, dug
out of the side of the hill, covered with rock and earth and with a
door of sliding plank. The whole was fenced with a high rail fence to
keep out hogs.

The kitchen was on the first terrace or bench of the hillside in the
midst of a grove of thirteen different kinds of trees; sourwood, paw-
paw, hickory, walnut, chestnut, persimmon, basket-oak, black-oak,
dogwood, redbud, wild grapes, sassafras, and sugar-maple. Here
there was always shade and always a breeze. Near the kitchen tent
was a table, twelve feet long and four feet wide, with shelves above.
The whole was covered with oilcloth. On these shelves were kept all
the kitchen utensils and tinware and at this table all the cooking was
prepared. Convenient to the kitchen were several washstand shelves
for the members of the cooking classes, visitors and also the little
children. Not far away were our two chicken coops, boxes nailed to
the trees, with slats on top and in front. Just above the kitchen, on
another terrace was the dining room. This was in the midst of the
trees but had a roof of white oilcloth. In the center was the table and
on either end, nailed to the trees were our china closets, boxes with
shelves, covered on back, sides and front with oilcloth, which fas-

tened down with buttons and buttonholes.

Still higher up by fifty or sixty feet, was a third terrace, our upstairs. Here there were three tents arranged around an open fly.[1] The front tents were the bedrooms. They had plank floors and rugs. Each bedroom contained three cots, which were covered with bright spreads and sofa pillows. In one tent, in two corners were boxes of our clothes covered with embroidered table covers. In the third corner was the organ with the song books on it. In the fourth corner was a Women's Christian Temperance Union Circulating Library and a large gourd which we used for a waste basket. At the back of the tent were hung three large linen bags, full of pockets for our various toilet articles. In front of the end pole was the dressing table with three shelves. This was covered with figured silkoline, and a white scarf on top. All the walls and most of the roof were covered with pictures and calendars. The rope below the ridge pole was hung with Japanese lanterns and sunbonnets. There were also many flags crossed on the walls. The other bedroom was equally as much decorated. The back tent was a store room. In it were wooden boxes of household, kindergarten and sewing supplies. On the pole were hung dresses, wraps and umbrellas. The space enclosed by these three tents was covered by an extra fly and formed the sitting room. At the back against the center pole was the book case, a tall box with three shelves of books. The back and sides were covered with red cheese cloth, plaited on with brass tacks, a cover of red and sliding curtains of the same in front. On top of it was a book rack filled with educational games. Above this was the word "Welcome," in large letters, making the visitor feel at home at once. The ropes from pole to pole were draped with red cheese cloth and suspended from the ropes were Japanese lanterns. The walls were covered with pictures and flags.

On every side of the tents, which were surrounded with trees, were hammocks, swings and steamer chairs.

The view from the Camp was a magnificent one, consisting of knobs, hills, winding valleys and roads, with here and there a little home. Looking down over three points, beyond the town was the very beautiful Valley of Troublesome. On each side of the creek, the hillsides were cleared of trees, some even to the top covered with corn. The natural beauty of the scene is varied by an occasional white house. The beautiful sunrises and sunsets, the light of the full moon, the magnificent storms and the rising of the mists will long be remembered by all the members of Camp Industrial.

By the end of the first week, the work was well organized and the classes in good running order.

The people understood exactly why we were there and seemed eager and anxious to learn everything that we could teach them. Many of the old people said they have never had a chance, but they rejoiced that their children could now have a chance to "larn somethin'." One man asked us to please "larn my children some manners." Sometimes families of children would come in from the country to spend the day and join all the classes, and several girls who lived too far to come in every day, came in to stay so they could be with us all day. One country mother said: "My gal likes clean livin' and purty fixin's and I 'low to send her to larn of ye."

When the people came from the country, we would have to show them "the sights." Every department and our possessions were carefully examined and commented upon. Pictures and magazines were also given to the country people. We were constantly surprised at the number of the visitors from the country who could not read. When we handed them a hymnbook, many of them would say, "I hain't got no larnin'. I never had no chance to larn, but I like the pictures."

Entire families "tended" the corn crop in the fields. Girls from seven years old spent all day hoeing. One woman sixty-six years old hoed several days in sight of the camp.

Mr. Hicks, a Baptist preacher, fifty years old, told us he never went to school but three days in this life. After he was nineteen, he learned to read by himself. He was at times rather eloquent and very flowery. He lived at the head of a branch about three miles from town. He was the father of seventeen children, five dead, five married and seven at home. This was a one room log house, with a small kitchen adjoining. The one room was probably fifteen feet square, with a big old-fashioned fireplace and no window. Until just before our visit, another son and his wife had made their home there too and a married daughter and her husband were there on a visit. Four girls from this family come regularly to our classes.

There were classes in singing by Miss Campbell and four of us taught in Sunday School every Sunday over sixty children. In a class of twenty-one boys none knew the Ten Commandments and only one the Lord's Prayer. Very few had Bibles, but they were keen to purchase the Testaments that we had for sale and were proud to bring them to class. The lesson that impressed them most was the "Transfiguration," or as they called it, the "Three Tents on the Hill." In a class of eleven girls, six knew the Lord's Prayer. Only one had no Bible in her home. One of the Hindman girls helped Miss Bruner in the primary class, so that she could be able to take charge of it afterwards. She writes that she is getting on nicely and is so thankful for the assistance she received in the summer.

We often had religious services at the Camp on Sunday afternoons.

One girl spent a week with us, another two weeks, simply to learn all they could. They came by five o'clock in the morning, helped with any work to be done, cooking, setting table, washing dishes, sewing and all, that they might learn what we had to teach.

It was very encouraging to have the half-grown boys come every day to read, play games or sing and discuss various questions. They asked much about the way we lived. They would unblushingly tell how many times they had been drunk and would not hesitate to say that they could not do without liquor. We gave them pledge cards, asked them to read them every day and think about it. Some of them signed them before we left and others have signed and returned them in letters since. The boys became very dear to us. They were always on hand to help in every way possible and we felt free to call on them for everything.

The people were unusually kind to us. Mr. Sam Kilgore, one of the lawyers, sent a cow for us to use. Monroe Maggard, our boy, said that he could not milk, that boys and men did not milk in the mountains. But we did not intend to set any such example to the women, so we told Monroe that he must learn. Miss Breckenridge went to one of the neighbors to learn and then undertook to teach him. At first the cow refused to let a boy milk her, but we all gathered around her and kept her in place, while Monroe learned. One had to keep the flies from her head, one hold the bucket, while the boy milked. In a short while he could milk her alone, but he never was a success and whenever we wanted an extra supply of milk, Arminta, the maid, would help him. Many people from the country would look on in amazement to see a boy milk and were much more surprised when we told them that the men milked in the level country and that women did not work in the field. (We finally had to put a skirt on the boy to fool the cow.)

A neighbor woman pastured our cow for us, so that we had all the rich milk and cream we needed, without it costing us anything. One man loaned us a good cooking stove, another lumber to floor the tents, the sheriff a table from the Court House, which served as our dining table.

One of the workers was sick one day and a boy came and said: "Whar's the sick lady? I brung her an onion head." Whereupon he put his dirty hand into his dirty pocket and produced the onion head. Not only did they come to see us and bring us things, but they were most cordial and hospitable in inviting us to their homes, and we visited as much as we had time for, every home in town and many for miles in the country. One trip taken by three of us, I am sure will never be forgotten. It was an all day trip, as we walked from Hindman four miles to the head of Perkins Branch, visiting on the way thirteen homes, where there lived ninety-six people, sixty-seven of them being children. Many of them afterwards came to our classes.

At every home Miss Bruner sang and told stories to the children and made pin wheels for them. We saw a great many pretty quilts and drew off some of the patterns, with names like: Waves of Ocean, Sun Flower, Catch Me If You Can, and Democratic Banner. These quilts were made of the solid yellow, red and green calico put together with white.

Our little organ was a source of great delight to all. Some spoke of it as the brass band. Soon after we got there, we were invited to "take part" in a Fourth of July picnic to be given in Carr, eleven miles from Hindman. We began at once training the girls to sing patriotic songs. When the great day arrived we went, twelve in a wagon, to the picnic grounds. This was a trip of eleven miles, but it took us four hours to go, we spent four hours there, and then took five hours to get home.

On the way to the picnic, we passed a "Blind Tiger" on the road. It was a very tiny log structure, and no one was visible about it. But at a small window, when the requisite sum of money was deposited, a bottle of whiskey was found ready for the purchaser. The young boys that were on horseback procured some of the liquor and the bottle could be seen passed around from crowd to crowd and soon the pistol shots rang out along the road in front of us. The spot selected for the picnic was a wide valley under beautiful large trees. There was no platform, but we chose a central place, put up flags and placed the organ. There were about two hundred people present and we had patriotic speeches, recitations, the reading of the Declaration of Independence and singing of patriotic songs. One of the teachers gave a fine address on Christian Citizenship, much of the material for which he had secured from a book on that subject, that we had given him. This picnic gave us a good chance to meet the people, many of whom afterwards came to see us.

We met a young bride of three weeks, who wore a bright blue cashmere dress trimmed with white lace and red ribbon. She said she bought the lace from a peddler, and you could not buy any fine, wide lace like that at any of the stores. This was her wedding dress.

For her wedding, she had made a white dress and this blue one, as "blue and white were the only colors suitable for marriage clothes." If it was a bright day she would wear the white, but if rainy, the blue. The day was cloudy, so she wore the blue because "she did not want to go to his house all drabbled up."

From this time we began to look forward to the Teachers' Institute, which was held in Hindman the first of August. During the week of the Institute we gave up all class work at the Camp and attended the meetings. We had offered to decorate the College Chapel[2] and the result of our work was very much appreciated by the teachers.

The room was quite large and light, having two windows in each end and four or five on each side. There was a platform about ten feet wide across one whole end. In the front of this were two upright pillars and one across the top of them near the ceiling. Across this top were three pairs of large flags crossed. In the center under the large flags were two small ones crossed with a Japanese lantern between. On each of the two pillars were seven pairs of small flags, one below the other. Over every window there were two large flags with Japanese lanterns between. Kindergarten chains of bright colored papers were festooned above the platform from window to window all around the room. The stoves were covered with green branches, the pipes covered with small flags and Japanese lanterns. The walls of the room were decorated with colored Sunday School charts and a great many pretty pictures. On the back of the platform above the blackboard in the center, were the pictures of George and Martha Washington and Miss Willard.[3] On the top of each stove, table and the organ were cans of ferns, covered with various colored tissue papers. The Secretary's table on the platform had a white cover on it and some pretty ferns. The effect of the whole was very good. The girls said that they had never thought of doing anything like that before, but hereafter they would always decorate for the Institute. We also washed the windows after the school began, as it did not occur to the teacher to have it done.

By our decorations, we hoped to inspire the teachers to go home and do likewise, and when they left, we gave them flags, pictures and charts for their school rooms.

The first night of the Institute, we gave an entertainment to start a fund for an organ for the Methodist Church and made $12.00. We had been training the boys and girls for weeks and they did remarkably well. They sang temperance songs and gave temperance recitations and marches.

The older girls had a flag drill which was a great success. We were a little amused and disconcerted that two girls, who were not expected, announced that they would recite. One said "The Curfew" and the other "The Maniac"[4] in a very forlorn way.

The crowning success was the tableau of "The Old Oaken Bucket" by the young men and women. They had the sweep and well on the platform and sang very softly. It was a beautiful picture.

Shortly after school began, one afternoon, one of the settlementers was in the school house and upon hearing singing went upstairs and found the children marching and singing temperance songs and going through with their part of the entertainment. And they write that they are still doing it.

The Institute was very interesting, the teachers bright and alert and glad to get any new ideas and suggestions. In discussing the question, how to keep order, a sixteen year old boy said, "I shame em some. I am young yet and hain't whipped much." In answer to the question, "Why attend school," one said, "To learn how not to do the things that we are engaged in most of the time, to better the mind."

The teachers discussed the subject of "district and school libraries." They said they were much needed in the country, but that they did not see any way to get literature into the homes of the people. We told them of the Traveling Libraries of the State Federation and the Circulating Libraries of the Women's Christian Temperance Union and offered to try to send them some. Twenty-one teachers asked to have libraries sent to them just as soon as possible and most of the sixty-seven asked to have periodicals mailed to them regularly. One teacher gave the name of his post office as "Witch," and said, "Have you ever heard tell of the witches that were burned at Salem? Well, I named the post office for them witches."

One afternoon we gave a reception to the teachers and others, about one hundred in all. We played games and served ponora and cake. The costume of one teacher was worthy of note. At the Institute she had on a black woolen skirt, white cross-barred shirt waist with very large bishop sleeves with gathered ruffle four inches wide at the hand, and six inches wide around the neck, falling over the shoulders. Her necktie was of ashes of roses ribbon, tied in a flat bow in front, a watch guard of narrow one-half inch black lace. Around the gathers of the sleeve at the hand, inch-wide pink gauze ribbon was tied around the wrist with a double bow on top. Her belt was black satin ribbon, four inches wide. She wore also circular gold ear-rings, black cotton finger gloves, hat of brown straw, with black and white checked ribbon, brown gauze ribbon, and poppies and green leaves and, crowning glory, a bright green barege veil. At the reception at the Camp, she wore a skirt of mingled reddish-brown and black woolen, waist of tan brown wool, large mutton-leg sleeves, double ruffle over the shoulders of navy blue silk, edged with narrow white lace, a full front of black velvet, edged with a plaiting of narrow pink gauze ribbon, black ribbon belt, narrow black lace watch guard, white linen collar and ashes of roses ribbon necktie.

The last day of the Institute, when the resolution of thanks and appreciation of the "helpful influence and work of the ladies on the hill" was read, one of the teachers said: "I move you that this resolution be accepted, as we each and all appreciate to a superlative degree everything that has been done from their presence here; the beautiful decoration of the room, the nice reception, the gift of pictures and flags for our schools and the offer to send libraries and periodicals."

After they adjourned, many of them followed us to the dormitory to get *Youths' Companion*[5] and magazines to take to their pupils, and as we stood on the bridge at the forks of the Troublesome and told them goodbye, as they started to walk five, ten, fifteen or twenty miles to their various schools with this literature in bags and calico pillow cases (they had borrowed from friends) over their shoulders and their arms full, we thought if our friends at home could see them, they would be glad to mail their periodicals to the mountains.

One of the teachers, who carried saddle pockets full to her school twenty miles over "in the Yellow Mountain country," said that "the children fairly fit [fight] over the magazines so that she had to tear them in two to make them go around."

We left some papers on the desks at one country school while the teacher and pupils were having their pictures taken. The oldest girl hurried in and gathered up all the papers and put them in her desk. When we passed that way the next day the children told us that the teacher had whipped this girl for stealing their papers.

Three members of the Camp went one day to visit a school in the country. They found it clean, the walls filled with pictures that we had given the teacher, a large flag over the pictures of George and Martha Washington. He had a clean newspaper on the table and a can of ferns covered with white paper just as he had seen us fix the colored paper on them. He was especially anxious to have the children taught new games.

While we were at the station at Jackson, having the wagons loaded, one of the teamsters looked up and said, "Beant you the women that passed through the mountains last Summer and gave out party picture books?" On being told that we had distributed some magazines on the way home from Hazard, he said: "I live fifty miles back in the sight of Big Black Mountain, but me and my gal wuz in a wagon a comin' to Jackson, and you give her a book that she still has and wouldn't take its weight in gold fur today." We left a magazine or paper at every house we passed in going from Jackson to Hindman, and it was interesting to see the eagerness with which the boys on the road held out their hands for the papers and immediately sat down on the roadside to read them, and then how the patient faces of the women would light up, as they came with outstretched hands for the magazines we gave them. We were very thankful for the boxes and barrels of reading matter and the two Circulating Libraries that we had with us. The girl in the post office said she was so glad that we had brought some books, that the country people were always asking her for things to read, but that she never had anything to give them. We left one of the libraries with her and the next day she told us that the first book she gave out was to a man who lived five miles in the country. As he left he said to her, "Wall, they'll be no sleeping at our house tonight; hit's been so long since we have had anything to read, that everybody will stay up to hear this read."

Hindman is surrounded by a very thickly settled country, there being two hundred ninety children in that school district. The school began three weeks before we left and they had already nearly two hundred enrolled. There were only two teachers, both men of very good education, with some progressive ideas and earnestly striving to do their best with the children under their charge, but it is very difficult for one teacher to instruct one hundred children of all ages and in all grades.

We had with us for a month Mrs. Cora A. Smith of New York, who was sent by the Board of Reformed Church to spend several months in the Kentucky Mountains seeking a good location for an Industrial School. The people of Hindman were very anxious to secure the school. The citizens closed their stores and all came to the Court House one afternoon to discuss the needs of Hindman for a good school. The lawyers and business men spoke and made an earnest plea for industrial and educational training. They spoke of the noble qualities of the mountain people, their ambition and capacity. They offered money, lumber and assistance and one woman said that she would give $100 if she had to "sang" it out.[6] But, after looking about a good deal, Mrs. Smith has finally located her school at

McKee, Jackson County.

One Sunday morning we attended a "funeral occasion" that had been "norated"[7] for many months. The funerals of four people were preached, a man, his two sons and a daughter. The first died in 1890, the last in 1899. It was a remarkable service and long drawn out. There were four sermons, prayers, hymns lined out and sung to a strange tune and at the end much shouting with something almost like a savage religious dance. A widow of two or three weeks was dressed in a green plaid calico dress, with a red bandanna on her head, but she shouted vigorously. The people sat around under the beautiful forest trees on sharp-edged rails and on the fences over the graves. One of the men was discussing a preacher and said he had no use for him, because he would "horse swap and listen to banjo picking any day." We asked why the funerals were so long delayed and they said they "could not fix to get ready any quicker." But all the fixing we could hear of was scrubbing, making pies, and borrowing some knives and forks. The real thing was to get as many preachers together as possible.

Another day we went to the funeral of a baby girl, one year old. A neighbor had made a muslin dress of tucks and lace for her to be buried in. The casket was a rough box covered with light figured cretonne and had silver handles. The mother was lying on the bed in a black dress and sun bonnet. We all stood around in the dirty room, most of the people spitting on the floor, while Mr. Rainey conducted the service. Then we all walked up behind the coffin to the grave, which was just below our Camp. It was very shallow and the men had to look some time before they could find a shovel to fill up the grave with and when that was done, they spent quite a time searching over the field for stones to put up at the head and foot. There was not one flower.

Early one morning two men, whom we had never seen, came to the Camp to propose that we give a picnic on our hill and invite all the country school teachers to come and bring their pupils. They said it would give all the country people a chance to meet us and that many of them had never been to town. We at once adopted the suggestion, wrote to every teacher to come with his pupils and when the next Saturday arrived we had about three hundred people with us, a great many we had not seen before. They brought good dinner in abundance, and all seemed to enjoy it. Some of the dinner brought consisted of corn bread, done up in a red bandanna kerchief. We played games in the morning and in the afternoon we had a short religious service, then songs by the children and several fine speeches. The children of the sewing class were very anxious to sew and twenty-one of them gathered in groups around the teacher and sewed quietly while the speaking was going on. Strange to say, the two men who had suggested the picnic neither came nor sent any excuse for staying away.

The last Saturday we were there, we were invited to the District Teachers' Association on Trace Fork of Ball, about seven miles from town. We were asked to take the organ and conduct the singing. So we and the organ took a three hours' ride in a wagon, having to cross Audubon Mountain. There were probably one hundred fifty people there. The teacher gave an interesting program of talks on school work with recitations, and we furnished the music. Some of the teachers were drinking and while a paper on the Cigarette Evil was being read, there was shooting on the outskirts of the crowd.

There was a bountiful lunch provided for all. Before we started home, we visited the school house near there, decorated it with kindergarten chains, flags and pictures. On our way home from Hindman to Jackson, we stopped at every school house to put up pictures and flags. We came to one dreary school room when it was nearly dark and of course no one was there, but the door was hospitably open, so we went in, put up our pictures and flags, left some reading matter on the teacher's desk and departed. There must have been some wonder and surprise the next morning. Another place, the door was locked, so we put a package of flags, pictures and books in at the window, with the hope that they would be used in the right way.

Two of us made a visit of two days in Perry County with Mrs. Simon B. Stacy, a friend whom we had met at Hazard the summer before. Shortly after we reached Hindman, she came to see us and at once asked if we could show her how to make rice pudding. Miss Christian had a full class but she took her in and she said she "larned a sight." Her quaint expressions and childish delight at seeing the things that we did not have last year was simply charming. One of us helped her to gear up her mule, the same one she rode on to see us at Hazard. We filled a pillow case with colored paper, pictures, magazines, ribbons and quilt pieces, tied it with a twine string to her saddle and watched her go over the hill. We promised to go to see her on July 24th and stay all night. When that day came, we took the sixteen mile trip in "Mr. Bailey's hack." Mrs. Stacy lives at the mouth of Montgomery, where it comes into Carr's Fork, not far from the North Fork of the Kentucky River. Her home was a perfect delight to us. Everything was clean, neat and really artistic. The yard was green with grass and bright with flowers. There was a good well, a nice cellar, the three rooms had bare, clean floors, the walls were covered with pictures, many of them large advertisements, but they had all the effect of the modern posters. She had made a bookcase like the one we had in our tent at Hazard, and had the magazines and books we had sent her on the shelves, and pictures, flag and Testament on top. She had used everything we had given her to decorate the house. She had a number of cans of plants and cut flowers, covered with colored papers. On her dinner table, she had a white table cloth, flowers in the center and the table set just as we did it. She told us that she had tried to cook everything like we had taught her and that she had learned from the cookbook we sent her. She had a rice pudding with blackberries around it, just as we had served it the day she was with us. She said she had taught her friends our way of cooking and that she had made beaten biscuit for many weddings. One thing of great interest to us was the loom, where Mrs. Stacy made the most beautiful blankets we saw in the Mountains. She raises her own sheep, shears them, cards the wool, spins it, dyes it and weaves it into blankets and cloth for her own and her husband's winter clothes.

We were up and through breakfast the next morning by four-thirty o'clock, and on our way up Montgomery Creek to see Mattie and Ida Combs, the girls we had been asked the summer before to adopt. They are now being sent to the Marlan school by the Women's Club of Lexington. Mrs. Combs, their grandmother, over eighty years old, had spent the night with us at Mrs. Stacy's and walked with us a mile up the Creek to her home. She said she had been journeying up that stream for more than sixty years and she had many interesting things to tell us of the "olden times."

When we reached Judge Combs' house we found, lying on the porch on a dirty quilt and pillow a fourteen year old boy, suffering agony from a copperhead snake's bite. He tramped on it coming through the weeds and it bit him on the big toe. He had a rising[8] also on that foot. The doctor had sent some iodine, which they put on. An old towel was tied very tight above his ankle and the rising was running. Three women and a grown boy were standing around talking about snake bites, but doing nothing to make him comfortable. He was covered with flies, so we got some water, bathed his foot and sat down by him to keep the flies off. We rubbed his head, painted his foot with iodine and tried to comfort him. He was dreadfully frightened and said he would die if we left him. In a few days he was well again and some of his people wanted us to bring him home with us and try to help him get an education.

On our way home from Mrs. Stacy's, we took dinner with her father and mother, Mr. and Mrs. Rob Cornet and one glance at the surroundings showed us why Mrs. Stacy was so thrifty. Mr. Cornet was born in this same house, seventy-four years ago. His father came there from Virginia, "because he was a mighty hunter and there was so much game." We did so enjoy the quaint room, with the immense fireplace and mantel, the tall clock made by his grandfather and still keeping time, the beds with the beautiful coverlids, the spinning wheel and the walls hung with wool. Mr. Cornet played "meetin' house songs" on the dulcimer that he made forty years ago.

We found that many of the older women still spin and weave, but the young ones are not keeping it up and unless some new interest in it is revived, this great industry will die out.

The coverlids and blankets made there are not found now except in the remote mountain districts. Some of them are rarely beautiful and artistic. The most common colors in the coverlids are indigo blue and madder red with white. The names of the patterns are very odd: A Chariot Wheels and Church Windows, Dogwood Blossom and Running Vine, Cat-Track, Snail-Trail and Cat-Track, Log Cabin, Governor's Garden, Blooming Leaf, Pine Bloom, Doors and Windows, Young Man's Fancy, Rose in the Wilderness, Castle City, Flowers of Edinburgh, Ladies' Delight and Lonely Heart.

Some women also weave table cloths and towels which are beautiful. Another industry we found was weaving baskets of willow withes, but this was very rare. The boys make their own marbles of what they call black limestone.

They get a piece of stone as round as possible by knocking it against another stone, then make a hole in a large rock and put the small stone in the end of a split stick and work it around and around in the large rock, until it is perfectly smooth and round. It takes about six hours to make one marble.

Very little wheat is raised in the mountains and it is generally threshed with a flail, the same kind used in Bible times. It is made of hickory, so bruised and twisted as to be swung easily and with much force.

Three of us had a five mile horseback ride over to Whitesburg to see Mrs. Henry Escott. We went through a very primitive part of the state. That night Mrs. Escott was called up to go and sing to a dying woman and the next morning she took us there. We never witnessed such a scene. They had attempted to clean the room by sprinkling water on the dirt. The straw tick the woman died on was being burned in front of the door. She was partially dressed, had on black woolen, fingered gloves and was lying on a cot with a soiled sheet over her. The husband, unwashed, uncombed and ragged, sat around with a baby in his arms in the same condition. Three little girls stood by the dead mother as if they were dazed. A girl and two boys, of fourteen, fifteen and sixteen years of age, were screaming in a frantic way, "How I do love my dear old mother, ah, how can I live without her ah, Lord have mercy on me ah, how wish I could go with my dear old mother ah." They walked around almost bent double while they were saying this in the regular old Baptist preacher style.[9] We had a little prayer service, which seemed to quiet them.

In the afternoon, seventeen of us, mounted on horses, rode six miles through a beautiful valley up the North Fork of the Kentucky River to the foot of Pine Mountain. Half way up the mountain we left the horses and climbed to the top. It was a long steep climb. A very deep hole interested us very much. It was five hundred feet deep to where it turned and had been explored by Mr. Wilson Fields' grandfather fifty years before. He thought the Kuklux ran the cattle into it, so he went down to see, but found no traces of them, only the opening to a great cave. On the top was a solid formation of "high rocks" for two miles, at the end of which was a lake. We ate supper on the rocks and sang "America." Willie Fugate repeated the Lord's Prayer by sign. The view from that point was superb. Big Black Mountain, which separates Kentucky from Virginia, towered above us and we seemed miles above the Kentucky ridges. The sun was shining on the valley of the Kentucky River, but had left the head waters of the Cumberland. The moon shone over the Big Black Mountain, flooding the dark valley of the Cumberland with its silvery light, while the sun was shining on the ridges in the Kentucky Valley. When we reached the horses, the moon had not risen and the sun had not set.

We consider that no better field could have been chosen for our work than Hindman. It is a town of probably four hundred people, built in the narrow valley at the Forks of the Troublesome.

The people were especially communicative and told us all of their family affairs, and many sad stories we heard, how the father drank and "whooped" the mother, or of some member of the family who was in the penitentiary or had been murdered. One woman said that her father and two brothers had been killed and whiskey was the cause of it. She said when she grew up, "they never had any schools or churches, no outside people ever came in, no one ever went out and they were shut in and never knew nuthin'." She rejoiced now "that times is a growin' better and the young folks will have more of a chance than she did."

Many of the good people were afraid the bad boys of the town would disturb us, that they would rock or shoot at the tents at night, when they were drinking. Although there was much shooting on the street, it never came our way and we were not disturbed in any way. Indeed these very bad boys were our protection and swore at and threatened to shoot anyone that would disturb us.

The Kuklux Band is very strongly organized, containing many of the best citizens. The Police Judge told us that most of the men teachers belonged to it. It has proved very degrading for the boys. Several of our "protectors" were taken away to an adjoining county to be tried, a short time before we left.

Whenever there was a big crowd in town, the women and sometimes the boys would come up and say we had the only safe place in town, that they were so tired of the drinking, fighting and shooting that were going on in the street. At times there was fearful fighting among the prisoners in the jail.

Some of the people thought it was wrong to have any kind of music, but "meetin' house songs." We forgot that and asked a boy to bring his banjo and give us some mountain music. A good sister hastened to urge us not to have "banjo pickin'" and said only wicked folks would allow it and that some of the people were saying that we could not be good if we liked it. We asked one teacher to get the words of "Barbara Allen" for us. He said, after much persuading, he got his mother to repeat them to him, just as she used to sing them when she was a girl, but she made him promise not to tell anybody that she said such "wicked words" now.

One woman, weighing three hundred pounds, came to see us regularly from the country and said the climb up the hill did not "weary" her much. One day at the dinner table, she pushed down her stocking and showed us the scrofulous condition of her leg.

So many of the people had stomach trouble and risings. Nearly all the children have these dreadful sores and, as their parents did not seem to do anything for them, we offered to help. One day, while one of us was bathing a place on one little boy's head, he looked up and said, "Miss Pettit, who heals all the little boys' sore heads at your home, when you hain't there?"

We planted ferns in tin cans, covered with tissue paper, tied a scripture text on them with white ribbon and sent them to any who were sick. All seemed to appreciate them.

One woman walked in ten miles from the country with two grown, barefoot girls, who seemed very shy and we were at a loss to know how to entertain them. A copy of "Sweet Songster"[10] was brought out and they thawed at once and began to sing in their shrill, long-drawn-out way, "Come all ye young people" and various other popular hymns.

At first we wondered and wondered where so many children came from, but as soon as we had a chance to visit in the country we wondered no longer, for we found all the windowless, one room log cabins filled with children.

We were much discouraged by the prevailing use of tobacco. Men, women and children chewed and smoked. One girl five years old would frequently take her grandmother's pipe and smoke it. Visitors often asked us if we smoked or chewed. One day a country woman asked one of us to have a chew and when the offer was declined, she said, "Now do have some, which will you have home made or manufact? I can give you either." She put her hand into her pocket and brought forth the two kinds. After the paper on the Tobacco Habit was read at the Teachers' Association, two women sent us word that they "didn't aim to use no more tobac'."

We gave a bright, attractive looking girl the triple pledge[11] and asked her if she could sign it. She read it and said, "Lord God, yes I can."

Very many of the men, women and children swore and when we talked to the children about it and asked them not to say Our Father's name or Jesus' name unless they did it very softly and reverently, they would say: "Well, I'll aim to quit." Profanity was in the air and they simply could not help it.

One day there was a political speaking at the Court House by one of the numerous candidates for Congress from an adjoining county. Some of the lawyers asked us the day before to come and we told them that some of us would try to do so. We were so busy with the class work that we did not think anything more about it. But after the ringing of the second bell, they sent word that they were waiting on us and as the candidate had to hurry on to another appointment, for us to come on, so some of us had to stop work and go to hear the speaking.

"Air ye goin' to Sarah Dukes' prayer meetin'?" was often asked us. Mrs. Duke held this prayer meeting at the Methodist Church every Saturday afternoon. It seemed to us that exactly the same things were said by the same persons every time. The children would run up and down the aisle and play games or fight and oftentimes receive a cuff on the side of the head by a mother who was praying. The shouting was tremendous. The women would sometimes shout until they were quite stiff and the children would stand about with eyes and mouths open, watching them. Some nights we went to sleep while the sounds of the shouting would reach us from the church and the pistol shots from the street. One of the mountain preachers advised the young people of his congregation to "come to meetin' with your best behavior and most morality." The song service at the Camp on those dreamy Sunday afternoons was very sweet.

One of the most interesting women in Hindman was Mrs. Mallie Bailey. We found a post office and many children named for her. Her husband was a fine lawyer but very dissipated. He had spent a good deal of money on a rambling hotel, known as Bailey's Folly and never completed. He owned a fine $10,000 Law Library. In contrast to this was their home, a small house of two rooms, on the side of a steep hill. Her son, Robert, eleven years old, would not allow any whiskey on the place. He found a jug of whiskey one day under the bed and immediately broke it. Mrs. Bailey went to school only eighteen months, yet she had a first class certificate to teach. She was a niece of Mr. French who was one of the leaders in the famous French-Eversole feud.[12] During that noted war she used to ride horse-back, at night and alone, from Hindman to Hazard, a distance of twenty-five miles, to warn her uncle of any conspiracy to kill him.

A very unique character is Uncle Solomon Everidge.[13] He is seventy-eight years old, goes barefoot all the time and never wears a hat. Late one evening three of us called at this house, a mile from town. Uncle Solomon, after hoeing in the corn field all day, had just gotten home. He greeted us cordially and invited us in, saying, "I am plumb tuckered out." His costume consisted of clean white cotton under drawers and shirt, for which he made no apology at the time, but did one day at our dinner table.

We have certainly never seen brighter children anywhere than in Hindman. They are wide awake, quick and ambitious. We believe that our work was a real help and benefit to them. The teachers said there was a noticeable difference in them after we came. They did not use profane language as formerly, were more obedient and easily managed.

The children themselves were very appreciative in all our classes.

One little girl said: "Since you all have been here I've quit saying, I'll make ma do this or that and quit using bad words and say always, yes sir and yes ma'am." A girl who spent only one day with us said when she left: "If you folks don't get to see me before you leave these parts, I hope we'll be blessed to meet again."

Two of the children wrote the following letter:

Hindman, Ky., Aug. 19, 1900

My dear girls and Boys of the Danville Gleaners:

Hit's a sight in this world how we Delight in the pictures and Books that you sent us by Miss Pettit when she came up here in June. She and five other girls are living up here on the mountain over town in tents all summer and larned us sewing lessons and cooking lessons and singing and Kindergarden. Miss Bruner is gone and we are so sorry for she larned the little children to stop swearing and to make pretty paper chains and many things that we did not know before. Don't make fun of sech ugly writin' and we was all well pleased with the papers. 250 children in the classes up here at the tents. 98 in the sewing class, over 30 of them boys. Miss Pettit drawed my attention and I quit using tobacco. And I don't aim to use it no more. It's a pretty sight to see us boys and girls sitting on the steep mountain side every day. I have heard the people say that these women made a great change in this town. Before they came, every breath of some of the children was swearin' and now it hain't.

We live in the forks of the Troublesome creek and its troublous times we have when theys a tide comes. They have such pretty meetin's up here on Sundays. We don't have meetin' at the church-house but once a month. Miss Pettit thinks we say such funny things in the sewing class. When I handed her my needle full of thread and asked her to jerk a knot in its tail she laughed so. I am a little girl and my father is Judge Baker an my mother loaned Miss Pettit and the Camp a cooking stove and the little boy who wrote some of this letter is Harrison Maggard eleven years old. His father is a miller but a mighty good man. He made Miss Pettit some marbles like we children have up here.

My friends, I aim to close. Write to us.

> Your little Mountain friends,
> Mallie Baker
> Harrison Maggard

One woman said: "I like you, you jest seems so natural, jest as plain and common as the rest of us, not but what I like all you women folks." Another said: "You all are the friendliest ladies I mighty nigh ever saw." A man said: "If you all go away from here and my girls never see any of you again, they'll never forgit you nor what you've larned 'em."

It was with deep regret that we left this place, which, with its friendly people, had become so dear to us. None of us could bear to look back on the hill after the tents were taken down.

The last night we invited everybody up to a campfire and probably about one hundred fifty came. We had prayer and singing of "Blest Be the Tie that Binds," and a number of the most appreciative speeches. The words of praise for us and our work among them were really embarrassing and we felt that a response must be made, so one member of the Camp, who said she had never made a speech in her life, arose and made a very good one, thanking our mountain friends for all they had done for us.

We asked the children if they would be up the next morning to tell us goodbye, and the teacher said they would all be on hand to see us off, for school would not begin till we had gone. We had our last breakfast almost at daybreak, so that we could start by nine o'clock. When we got down into the village to climb into our wagons, the whole town was assembled to say goodbye. All seemed sorry to have us go and begged us to come back.

We feel after three month's work at Hindman, that the settlement plan is the best way of reaching and helping these people. But instead of a few month's work each summer, we hope to see before long a well established, permanent Social Settlement and Industrial School, located in one of these mountain towns.

To live among the people, in as near a model home as we can get, to show them by example the advantages of cleanliness, neatness, order, study along both literary and industrial lines, and to inspire them to use pure language and to lead pure, Christian lives; these should be our efforts, if we wish to elevate and uplift them; and they stand ready, willing and waiting to do their part, if we do ours.

The cry of the mountaineer is, "I have not had a chance. I would be so glad if my children could have a chance."

The total cost of the Summer work was $296.00.

REPORTS FROM CAMP INDUSTRIAL

The Sewing Class

I had a sewing class of one hundred ten children, thirty-six of them boys. Just as soon as we were settled in Camp I began work with them by asking several little girls of ten or twelve, with whom I had gotten acquainted, to come up on the hill a certain afternoon, if they would like to learn to sew. That day I had ten girls and three boys. We had wondered among ourselves what we could teach the boys in the way of industrial work and wished for someone skilled in Sloyd,[14] but the problem easily solved itself. Those three bright boys came to me and said: "Miss Stone, why can't we sew too? We want to learn everything the girls do." Of course, I was delighted and took them in. The class increased every day, the boys taking as much interest as the girls, some of them doing as good and even better work than any of the girls. I took all the children over eight years old, with two or three younger. They varied in age from six to eighteen years. Many came from four and five miles in the country. I told them to come every day from two to four in the afternoon, but they would begin coming by twelve o'clock and as soon as I was through with my dinner I let them sew. Very few were willing to stop at four and most of them would stay until the "sun ball went down behind the mountain." Some who started in later would come early in the morning, bring a lunch with them and sew all day to catch up with those ahead of them.

It was interesting to watch the eager, earnest faces of the little workers as they gathered in groups on the steep hill side, seated on camp stools, straw mats and on the ground. Rain did not keep them away and on such occasions we often had as many as twenty-five crowded into the tents. Cots were put one on top of another and the children were satisfied to sit any way, if only they were allowed to sew. Sometimes the little ones would be frightened by the storm, for fear the tents might blow over. Then we would talk or read to them, pray with them and often get out the organ and sing, till their fears were quieted.

When the class was small and they were busy, it was very interesting to listen to the conversation among them. One little girl threw her sewing down very carelessly, when she got up another about eight years old said: "Dally, is that the way to sarve your sewin'?" "Hit's a sight what I'm learnin," said one boy. "She's a sight good teacher." Another asked: "How much do you like o' being' 'round the edge?" and the answer was "I like a bushel." One little girl said to me one day: "Please jerk a knot in the tail of this thread." Many aimed to complete the whole set of ten models and make them into a book like mine. About six did this. I told them in the beginning that I wanted to make two books of models of their work, one for Miss

Pettit and one for myself, and whoever made the best of each model was to make one for me, trying to ask no child for more than one. They were delighted to give us their work and many extra pieces were presented. The little girl who made one of the bags brought it to me when she had finished it and said: "Here's Miss Pettit's bag, but it ain't much pretty."

One little boy, who had been coming regularly, was absent several times and I was wondering if he had lost interest, when Miss Pettit saw him and asked why he didn't come. He had been trying to learn to hem on the third model and as his eyes were not very good he found the little stitches quite hard to do. He told her he couldn't do them and asked if she thought I would excuse him from it. She told him to come back and she would see about it. When he came he said: "Miss Pettit said she'd ask you to excuse me from makin' this 'em. These little stitches jist ruin me." I gave him the next model, the bag, but when he came to the hem he said: "Now, I'm afeard this is goin' to ruin me agin." The same boy went home one day and asked his mother to get out his winter overcoat so he could sew the buttons on it. I was much pleased with the interest and attention of the children and proud of the progress.

The last three weeks we were there the school was in session, so I went down there every afternoon from three to five to teach the sewing class, having often between fifty and sixty children at one time. One boy, perhaps fifteen or sixteen, not in my class, gave me some trouble one day by teasing the little ones and making a noise. The father of this boy had asked us especially to get some hold on him if we could as he was so bad. I asked him if he would like to join the sewing class but he declined. I asked him to be quiet or leave the room, which he also declined. But this was only one day. Then he came to me and said: "Miss Stone, I want to sew too," and the rest of the time he sewed patiently and quietly.

I have had letters from many of them. They told me before I left that they were going to keep up the sewing class, the girls who had finished the course to teach the others. I gave them all the material I had left and my patterns. They write that they have a room at the dormitory, which they have decorated with pictures and kindergarten chains and where they meet every day after school to sew. Of course, I do not know how much good it will do them but it shows the interest they take in it. They promise to send me some samples of their work.

One boy wrote: "i lost mi soen for about a week. Bartram had hit. i was trubled about it and he foch it back home."

One girl writes: "The patchin' was sich a help to me."

May Stone

Report of the Kindergarten Work in the Kentucky Mountains

The members of Camp Industrial arrived in Hindman June the fourteenth, ready to work, but deterred by the fact that the baggage had not arrived. After the rain ceased, we sat after supper on the piazza of the hotel, and there toled in several small children who were playing in the street. Then and there began the kindergarten work. The children were intensely interested in the stories, "tales," and songs, and remained a rapt audience until escorted home. One of these little girls told her father all about it that evening, and awakened him the next morning by repeating the songs and stories. Each day found the children congregated about the teacher, listening to what she had to say, looking forward eagerly to the time when we could make pretty things. In a few days I took them to a large, incomplete building where we were given a room for our own use, and taught the children to make chains, to play games and to sing. They took hold of the work readily. They seemed to enjoy the singing, that is, in listening to the teacher sing, but it was difficult to get them to join in. It was found that the children did not take up the songs readily. They learned them in time but only after great effort. The only reason that I can assign is that they are unaccustomed to singing except "long metre" hymns and certain tuneless ballads. They were not accustomed to bright singing from birth. One morning we had the rain song, and afterward I asked, "Don't you think that's a pretty song?" "No," replied a frank little boy, "I don't think it's pretty, but I like to hear you sing it." Unconscious flatterer!

The interest in the stories was keen. They constantly begged for more, and were very positive in their likes and dislikes. One boy of five took a violent fancy to the story of "Little Red Hen." The first morning in Sunday School that I said I was going to tell a story, meaning the story of the lesson, "Little Red Hen?" asked Troy. He was hardly satisfied when I told him that this was a story from the Bible. In a short time Troy got up to leave the room and I attempted to draw him back with the promise of another story. "Little Red Hen?" he asked again, and receiving a negative reply, Troy took his departure not to be tempted by all the tales found in the Good Book.

The word "story" was new to these children. Every story is a tale, and the teacher was one day made the object of ridicule by a play on the word. It was near the close of summer. One morning this same bright little boy of five said: "I know a tale, Miss Bruner." "What is it?' I asked, all the kindergartner's enthusiasm bubbling over in an endeavor to draw the child out. "Cow's tail," said Troy, and the teacher was forced to join in the gale of merriment that swept over the children and visitors.

After camp was pitched, there was a cessation in the kindergarten work, due to the necessity of all hands helping to "get settled." Later kindergarten reopened on a shaded terrace above the Camp, a long steep climb for the baby legs. The class was not large. Forty were enrolled, with an average attendance of fifteen. A long plank table was built under the trees, with a bench on each side for the children to sit on. For the circle we used the ground and sat on straw mats. An old horseshoe and a pair of scissors supplied the needs of triangle and striker. Splinters of wood from the carpenter shop served as caste sticks, and Mason jar tops for paste dishes. There were a few difficulties not found in ideal kindergartens. The terrace was so sloping that our games were necessarily played up and down hill. A wail often arose from a child who had stepped on a briar overlooked in the general cleaning up. And alas! One child had an excuse for his repeated absence that he didn't want to come up on the hill for there were so many chiggers there. I thought he was quite sensible, but was glad when he overcame his dislike of the creatures sufficiently to attend regularly.

The older children manifested the keenest interest in the work of the little ones, and would willingly have joined their class. Indeed, a rousing kindergarten could have been organized among children from ten to fifteen. They drank in the songs and stories, and were very happy if allowed to do some of the work. After holding kindergarten at the large building in town one rainy morning, some of the older girls afterwards collected the scraps of "silk paper" and took them home to play with. As near as I could find out, the term "silk" was applied to any bright colored paper. It was pathetic to see how hungry they were for color.

An older child decorated her home with chains made of newspaper. Her mother said she swept up a bushel of scraps after the child finished.

It was somewhat discouraging at first to find that to have a full kindergarten, it was necessary to send out for the children each morning. Repeatedly we drummed [up] a crowd for the morning hours. The people of that country have little appreciation of time or the obligation of an engagement. Therefore, many a day found us with only a handful of children until they were sent for, and again the log near our breakfast table would be covered from end to end like a roost full of chickens or a log full of watchful frogs as early as our seven o'clock meal. An earnest invitation was sent out to the mothers to come to a mother's meeting. The time came, and with it half a dozen mothers. The others had all betaken themselves to see a dear sick baby who was well enough for her mother to attend prayer meeting. The next time the mothers were invited, they went off instead to see a sick woman. After that, irregular attendance on the part of the children ceased to cause wonder.

The play life of the mountain children is poor. They do not live in such a world of make believe as we see in this part of the country. On the forty-five mile trip over the mountains, we saw only three sets of children playing. One group of boys was engaged in a game of marbles. Another was swinging a single rope. At one house, a large boy was racing round and round the house dragging a tiny cart. At the other places the children came out of doors and [ar]ranged themselves in rows watching our cavalcade, for all the world as if they were posing for a picture. We saw few toys in the mountains. There were dolls, for the Presbyterian Sunday School had distributed dolls throughout one portion of the country. We saw the dolls, but never in the arms of the children. In every home they were hung on nails on the walls, ornaments reminding one of the idols in pagan temples. In one family where there was a large family of girls, we counted six dolls disposed on the walls cruelly out of reach of the children. Their dolls were object of beauty only, not living, breathing, loving babies to be carefully dressed and cared for and punished.

The traditional games do not hold the sway that I expected. The children knew William McTrimity and "Pussy Wants a Corner." They called the child left without a corner "beggar." They had never heard of Drop the Handkerchief. They need more of the traditional games and more imaginative play. Through the country the children are early put to work hoeing, and until the "crap is laid by" have little time for fun. Numbers of children were prevented from joining the classes at first because they were needed in the field.

That they are thoroughly capable of enjoying a play life is proved by the interest they took in the games and plays, the enjoyment found in working with the gay material, the appreciation they felt of the toys they made in kindergarten work.

In the town the children do little work and play almost constantly on the street. Here they chase one another up and down falling in the dust and caring little for dirt. In the midst of men all day they hear profane language until it becomes second nature to them. The first morning the Camp was pitched, one of the children came up to one member of our party who readily detected the signs of mulberries on his round face. "Troy, aren't you going to bring me some mulberries?" she asked. "Well, I'll be God damned if I don't," cried the irrepressible Troy as he darted off for the purple fruit. The same child's lack of reverence was displayed the same day. The gray-haired minister ran a race with the child and then thoughtlessly boasted of beating him. "That's a dag-goned lie!" cried Troy.

Smoking and chewing were among the evil habits of the village and these found advocates even among the children. One day going into the gate of the hotel, a small urchin of five followed me in, and what was my amazement to see him puffing a huge cigar. In bewilderment I asked him how many years he had been smoking. He didn't know, and as a crowd of men was around ready to make sport, the child was not questioned then. Later, after the crowd had gone, I went out on the porch and found Wesley still solemnly smoking. The cigar look disgustingly large in proportion to the child.

"Wesley, why do you smoke?" I asked.

"Because it's good." he replied.

"What makes it good?"

"It's sweet," he answered.

"What is sweet?"

"The smoke," was his prompt response.

"Aren't you afraid it will spoil your teeth?

"How will it spoil them? he asked, surprised.

"It will make them yellow."

"I'll make them white again," he readily responded.

"How?"

"Get new ones and put in."

One day when the children were crowded around for stories, Wesley was chewing tobacco. I told him that a gentlemen would not chew where there were ladies, and suggested that he throw away the weed. He complied very readily, tho' upon leaving the presence of the ladies he picked the quid from the grass and enjoyed it at his leisure. For a long time this boy could not be enticed to the kindergarten on the hill. Eventually he enjoyed it every day, but only after bribes and much persuasion had gotten him up there several times. One morning another little five year old boy was helping to cut down the underbrush to make a place for our kindergarten. He was eager to help and really did wonderfully well. Each stroke of the hammer was accompanied by what I supposed was a grunt, but which proved to be the word, God. I talked to him quite seriously about the evil of using the name of the Lord, and the little fellow promised to refrain. In a few minutes I hear the same sound. "What did you say Bartram?" I asked. "God." "But you said you weren't going to say that again." "I had to that time, Miss Bruner." "Why?" "Because this wood wouldn't cut." This boy has earnest Christian parents, and I cannot believe that he hears such language at home. In the town one does not have to go the length of the town to hear an oath. If the children do not use the genuine oaths, they make use of expressions as "dad-burn-it," with the frequency and strength of feeling that characterizes the older sinners of the town. Even the little girls were often guilty. One little girl, (daughter of a preacher) was capable of using the most profane language. Yet she was an ardent stickler for the customs and services of the church. One morning in kindergarten we heard the court house bell and at one Annie said, very emphatically, "Well I must go."

"Why" asked the children.

"Cause there's going to be meetin'."

Oh no, that's just the court house bell," I told her.

"Can't help it. Going to meetin'," she argued, but the fascinations of chains prevented her trailing down the hill to the business meeting at the court house.

Soon after camp was pitched we gave a candy pulling to the children. Before producing the candy, the organ was brought out and all joined in singing gospel hymns. Troy, with a greater appreciation of sweets than of religious song, said, "Say, when meetin' broke will you have the candy?"

At first the children called the kindergarten "meetin'." They also spoke of that part of the hillside where we worked as "Miss Bruner's tent."

The day of the candy pulling, a generous citizen sent up a large quantity of lemonade. The little boys had all been served, when someone asked for a cup of lemonade for Charlie Stergil. Quickly Troy asked, "Let me have a cup for Charlie Stergil's brother." "Who is Charlie Stergil's brother?" "Me," promptly replied Troy, and for his brightness was given the coveted drink.

By the different people throughout the country, various modes of address were given the workers at Camp Industrial. Some called us "the ladies," other "them women," and a few "the gals."

One day little Chester Allen came up on the hill with a donation of straws for our work. In inquiring for his teacher, he asked, "Where's the woman that teaches us how?" Robert Bailey's usual cheery salutation was, "Good morning, children," with such a bright contagious smile that one was glad to be a child again with him. Troy one day describing his teacher, said: "She's the one who teaches us how to make everything in the world," and another child went so far as to assert that the kindergarten teacher was the prettiest of all the women.

The names of people in the mountains are very fanciful. Everyone hunts for odd and unusual names. They disdain the old fashioned names, just as a generation ago people in our own country loved the Violets and Maries and looked askance upon the names of their ancestors. Here are some of the names we learned to know in the mountains "Lonnie, Nonnie, Dallie, Sylvany, Imozel, Bernice, Troy, Wesley, Beatrice, Thurman, Carol (a boy's name), Tryphina,

Arminta, Viola, Pearl (boy's name), Sally Ally Fair, Narcissa, and Hettie Viola. One little new baby was named Xina Lake, the Lake taken from Lake Erie. Another child received the name of Shannon while we were there. Helen was pronounced He-len, and Gladys, Gla-dys. One child said to Miss Pettit: "Why do you let them call you Katherine? It's such an old fashioned name."

Did the work pay among the children? I think it did. There was less profanity when the party left. The children seemed happy and well satisfied after the summer's work. They were responsive to suggestion. One morning in kindergarten a small bird was discovered under the oak tree near our table. The boys rushed pell mell to the bird with the boy's usual interest in something alive, an interest which does not always manifest itself in kindness. Seizing the opportunity we sang the pretty little song of the nest in the old oak tree, and spoke of the poor little bird falling from its cradle in our own oak tree. What would the poor mother do without her baby? The suggestion was made that we leave the baby bird at the foot of the tree where the mother could find it after kindergarten. One of the most thoughtless and carelessly cruel boys in the crowd gladly laid the bird down and gathering dry leaves made a nest for it near the roots of the tree. The next morning all looked for the bird, not finding it, were happy to think that the mother had taken the tiny one back to the nest.

The work in the kindergarten was continued after the second month by Miss Curry Breckinridge of Lexington, who is connected with the Free Kindergarten system of that city. Under her able care the class flourished until the party left town. School having opened at the time she took charge, Miss Breckinridge held her class in an unused room of the public school. The interest in the work grew, and the numbers increased rapidly. In answer to the query, "Did it pay?" I will quote the teachers in the public school. They stated that the children were more easily controlled than in any preceding year, and there was refinement among the children. There was less profanity, greater politeness, more consideration. Here are some extracts f rom a letter written to me by four little five year old boys soon after my return. Miss Pettit acted as scribe. They were sitting on the hillside near the camp, watching the moon, and composing their first letter.

"What a pretty moon hit's to where Miss Bruner is, hain't it?" wrote one boy. "Miss Bruner, I hain't chewed tobacco but three times since you went away, and smoked but two cigars. I hain't said no swear words, but I throwed rocks. I want to see you. I am aiming to come over to see you and make some chains." These were Wesley's words: "I want to make chains when you come back. "I like you & chains too," was Bartram's impartial statement. Troy told of his first experiences in school. Said he, "I went to school & learned ox & box & ax & a & o & nothin' else. I hain't forgot the Lord's Prayer. We just said it to Miss Pettit. Pon my honor! I will have to go home. It's getting dark & paw will whip me. Please write to me. I love you."

It was hard for Wesley to realize that I was really gone. He said, "I have been a hunting for you all day. I thought you was over to the post office." Bartram, the irrepressible, wrote, "I like you to death, Miss Bruner. I want to make chains awful bad." Also, "I liked that donkey tail." Another, "I want to hear that old gray horse tale, Miss B. Come over & tell me." "I liked the little red hen," said another. Wesley says, "I aim to quit smoking & chewing tobacco, & I don't already swear." And in another place the same boy says, "I loved you last Sunday, Miss B." That last Sunday of my stay there was the first that we could get Wesley to Sunday School. They concluded by saying, "We are all coming up in the morning with a nice clean face to kiss Miss Pettit for you."

Such an appreciative letter was ample reward for my summer's work among the children. There is no doubt the work pays. These children are so bright, so responsive, so eager and greedy for the new ideas and interests that even in so short a time one is filled with encouragement. They are full of native ability, latent talent, which needs only the proper cultivation to make the mountain children rivals of the children of more prosperous lands. What they need is a chance.

Eva W. Bruner,
Crescent Hill, Louisville, Kentucky

Cooking Class

Miss Christian had charge of the cooking department. Her classes were held from nine to twelve every morning. Seventy-eight received instruction from her in classes of six or seven. Of these seventeen were boys and many married women. The children were always alert and responsive to instruction. One little boy of ten was a particularly interested pupil. After taking a lesson in biscuit making, he attempted some at home. He compounded them, as he thought, properly and put them into the oven, when it occurred to him that he had omitted the lard; so opening the stove door, he took the biscuit out and with a spoon, very carefully made an opening in each one, into which he put a little lard. While this did not rectify the mistake, it showed he was trying and thinking and most likely he would not forget another time.

Many walked from six miles in the country and many more from two to three miles, bringing something with them to contribute to the meal, and after three hours' work, would walk home again. A cook book of simple recipes was given to all the members of the class, which they seemed very glad to receive.

It has been said that the Mountain people do not like our way of cooking, and I do not wonder that they refused the croquets, chicken salad, and chocolate cake of some, but we found that they did like our simple way of cooking. They proved how much they liked it by the amount they ate. We tried to show them how to use the material they had in a hygienic way. Aside from the bacon they put lard in the beans and expressed great surprise that we did not do it. But they soon learned to like our way. They cooked the vegetables one way only and were pleased to know that they could be prepared in different ways. The class would set the table, and then help to wash the dishes and put the kitchen in order. One day while two girls were setting the table a visitor asked them what they were doing. One of them replied, "Setting the table just like they do in pictures." They soon became interested in gathering fresh ferns for the center of the table and wild strawberry leaves to garnish the dishes.

Then they would say, "Hit's a sight in this world, how them wimmin folks do spend time washin' dishes." They had not thought it necessary to rinse and dry them.

Very often they would ask to make the same thing they had made last time, so they could be sure that they had done it right. And the girls often told us how much the folks at home liked to eat what they cooked. One girl said they could never eat rice until she learned how to cook it from us. They were constantly telling us how much they had learned and how glad they were to have a chance to know how we did things.

One afternoon we were making a visit, while the supper was being cooked and it seemed that more lard was used for that one meal than we had used all summer.

BALLADS

Barbara Allen

All in the late season of the year,
The yellow leaves were falling.
Sweet William, he took sick,
All for the love of Barbara Allen.

As she was walking through the street,
She heard the death bells ringing,

She thought she heard her true-love say,
"Come here, Barbara Allen."

When she came to his bedside,
She said, "Young man, you are dying."
"Yes, I am low, low indeed,
All for the love of Barbara Allen."

The more she looked, the more she grieved,
She busted out a-crying,
"Take away, take away this young man,
For he is a-dying."

He turned his pale face to the wall.
"Adieu! adieu!" He turned his back upon her.
"Adieu to my friends all,
Adieu to Barbara Allen."

"Oh, Mother, Mother, go fix my bed,
Go make it soft and narrow;
My true-love has died for me,
I'll die for him tomorrow."

They took them to the new churchyard
And there they did bury them;
They buried his true love by his side,
Her name was Barbara Allen.

Out of his grave, there grew a rose,
Out of hers a brier;
They lapped and tied in a true love-knot,
A rose around the brier.

Loving Hanner

Loving Hanner, loving Hanner,
Come give me your right hand,
Say if you ever marry,
That I shall be the man.
(Sing the last line 3 times, then repeat last 2 lines)

I rode to church last Sunday,
My true-love passed me by.
I knew her mind was changing
By the movements of her eye.

When the parents saw me coming
They flew in an angry rage.
 "You must not steal my daughter,
For she is under age."

"Kind sir, to steal your daughter
I never yet did try,
But court her in some bride room
I never shall deny."

"Go on at your own exposion
And court just who you please.
When you think my poor heart is broken,
I am living at my ease."

Her hair is black as a raven,
Her eyes as black as a crow,
Her cheeks as red as a rosy,
That blooms in the morning glow.

My true-love is both neat and proper
And she is very small,

And she is good-looking,
And that's the best of all.

I wish I were on some sea
Or in some foreign town.
I'd put my foot in a bonny boat
And sail the world around.
I'd sail all o'er the ocean,
I'd sail all o'er the deep;
When I'd think of loving Hanner,
And then set down and weep.

Hiram Hubbard

A sad and mournful story
Unto you now I'll tell,
(repeat first two lines)
Concerning of Hiram Hubbard
And the way he now has fell.

He was traveling through this country
And through Kentucky came.
He was trying to raise his family,
He had no other aim.

He was traveling through this country
Through sorrow and distress.
The rebels overhauled him,
With chains they bound him fast.

They drove him on before them,
They drove him through the mud,
They drove him on before them,
Till the road's all stained with blood.

They drove him to Cumberland River
To try him for his life;
They swore so hard against him
They took his precious life.

They drove him up the hollow,
They drove him up the hill,
At the place he was executed,
He begged them to write his will.

"Come all my friends and neighbors,
Who all I love so well,
I leave this letter with you,
For it is my last farewell.

"Come all my friends and neighbors,
Likewise my wife and child,
I leave this letter with you,
For I am going to die."

They lashed these cords around him,
They chained him to a tree,
Eleven balls shot through him,
His body sank away.

Hiram Hubbard was not guilty,
I've heard a great many say.
He was not in this country,
But ninety miles away.

Little Oma

"You promised to meet me,
At Adams' spring,

Some money you would bring me
Or some other fine thing."

"No money, no money,
To flatter the case,
Sing if we get married,
It will be no disgrace."

"Come jump up behind me,
And away we will ride,
To yonder fair city, I
Will make you my bride."

She jumped on behind him,
And away they did go,
To the banks of deep waters
Where they never overflow.

"Oh, Oma; Oh, Oma;
I will tell you my mind.
My mind is to drown you
And leave you behind."

"Oh, pity; Oh, pity;
Do spare me my life,
And let me go home begging,
If I can't be your wife."

"No pity, no pity
Have I.
In yonder deep water
Your body shall lie."

He beat her and whipped her,
Till she could scarcely stand,
And threw her in the water,
Below the mill dam.

Little Oma was missing,
And could not be found,
Her friends they all gathered
And hunted around.

Up stepped old Miss Mother,
These words she did say:
"James Luther has killed Oma
And he has run away."

"He has got to Elk River,
So I understand,
They have got him in prison
For killing a man."

"They have got him in Ireland
Bound to the ground,
And he wrote his confession
And sent it around."

"Go hang me or kill me,
For I am the man,
That drowned little Oma
Below the mill dam.

I Wished I Were Some Little Sparrow

Come all ye young and tender ladies,
Take warning how to court, young man,

They're light a bright star in the summer morning,
They'll first appear and then they're gone.

They'll tell to you some lovely story,
And tell to you, their love is true;
Straightway to some other girl and court her,
And that's the love they have for you.

I wish I were a little sparrow,
Had sparrow wings and I could fly,
I would fly away to my false true-love,
And while he would talk, I would deny.

But as I am not a little sparrow,
Got no wings, nor I can't fly,
I will sit right down in grief and sorrow,
And try to pass my troubles by.

If I had knowed before I courted,
That love had been so hard to win,
I'd locked my heart with the keys of golden,
And pinned it down with a silver pin.

Ellen Smith

Come all you young people,
Who live far and near,
I'll relate to you the history
Of June last year.

I never knew she's shot
I never knew she's found,
She's shot in the body,
Lying cold on the ground.

Ellen Smith is dead
With her hands ascrost her breast
The sheriff and the high town
Will give me no rest.

I've been at home,
Praying all the time,
Praying for the man,
That committed this crime.

If I was back at home,
A free man today,
I would strew roses
On sweet Ellen's grave.

On last Monday morning,
About the break of day,
They came and carried
Poor Ellen away.

They sent me down to Frankfort,
They locked me in the pen,
I couldn't see nothing
But niggers and white men.

I'll go back at home
And live if I can
And try to be
A law-abiding man.

Pretty Polly

I set up with dead Ellen, the livelong night,
Got up the next morning before daylight.

He led her over the hills and valleys so deep,
(Repeat, third line three times)
Till the poor girl she began to weep.

"Sweet William, Sweet William, you're leading me astray,
On purpose, my life to take away."
"Oh yes, Pretty Polly, you're guessing just right
Been digging your grave the best part of last night."

They went on a piece further, a chance to spy,
Saw the grave was dug and the spade a-stickin' by,
She threw her arms around him, saying "Suffer no fear,
How can you kill a poor girl, who loves you so dear?"

He opened her bosom, as white as any snow
He stabbed her to the heart, the blood did flow,
And in the cold grave, her poor body must go.

He threw some dust over her, returned to go home,
Leaving nobody but the birds to mourn.
"Oh, where is Pretty Polly? Oh, yonder she stands
Gold rings on her fingers and her lily white hands."

Lord Daniels' Wife

The first came down all dressed in red,
The next came down in green,
The next came down, Lord Daniels' wife,
She's as fine as any queen.
(Repeat: Queen, she's fine as any queen.)

"Come and go home with me, little Galy," he said,
"Come and go home with me tonight,

For I know by the rings on your fingers,
Your are Lord Daniels' wife."

He had sixteen mile to go,
And ten of them he run,
He rode till he came to the broken-down bridge,
He held his breath and swum.

He swum till he come, where the grass grown green,
He turned to his heels and run,
He run till he come to Lord Daniels' gate,
He rattled those bells and rung.

He traveled over hills and valleys,
Till he come to his staff, stand still.
He placed his bugle on his mouth
And blew most loud and shrill.

(Last verse)

He took little Galy by the hand
And led her through the hall.
He took off his sword and cut off her head,
And kicked it agin' the wall.

The Drunkard's Dream

Oh, Edward, you look healthy now,
Your clothes look neat and clean,
I never saw you drink a drop,
Pray tell me where you have been.

Your wife and children, are they well?
You used to treat them strange,

But have you to them kindly grown?
What caused this happy change?

It was a dream, a warning dream,
That heaven sent to me to warn me
Of a drunkard's grave of woe and misery.

I dreamed I staggered home one night,
There seemed a dismal gloom,
I missed my wife, where could she be?
And strangers in her room.

My little children standing 'round.
"Oh, Father dear," they said,
"My mother has been crying so,
Because we have no bread."

I heard them say, "Poor thing, she's dead,
She lived a wretched life,
Grief and woe have broken her heart,
Who is a drunkard's wife."

"She is not dead," I madly cried,
And rushed to where she lay,
And pressed a kiss on her own warm lips,
And they was cold as clay.

"Wake up, dear Mary," I faintly cried,
"'Tis Edward's voice you hear."
And when I woke, my Mary dear,
Was kneeling at my side.

I pressed her to by breast,
And joyous tears did stream,

And ever since, I have heaven blest
For sending me such dreams.

William Hall

There was a brisk and gay young farmer,
Who lived near Domesse town.
He courted a brisk and gay young lady
Who lived near Pershelvy town.

And when their parents came for to know it,
It did grieve their poor troubled souls,
They said they would send him afar on the ocean,
Where he couldn't see his true-love no more.

He sailed and he sailed all over the ocean
He sailed till he came to his own sea side,
Saying "If Mary is alive and I can find her,
I'll make her to be my lawful bride."

So he was walking the streets one morning,
And his true-love came walking along,
Saying, "Good morning, good morning, ye fair pretty lady
And its will you fancy me?"

"Oh no, my fancy is on a farmer,
Who has lately crossed the sea,
And his life is as sweet as sugar dandy,
And no one but him suits me."

"Describe him, describe him, ye fair pretty lady,
Describe him, describe him to me,
For perhaps I have seen some sword go through him
While I was a-sailing on the sea."

"Oh, he was meek and he was modest,
An oh, them pretty blue eyes isn't all,
He had black hair and he wore it curly,
And his name was William Hall."

"Oh, yes, I saw a French ball go through him,
And by death I saw him fall.
He had black hair and he wore it curly,
And his name was William Hall."

"Oh, love it is great and love it is charming,
When we have it in our view,
But now we are parted and broken-hearted,
Oh, Good Lord, what shall I do?"

"Cheer up, cheer up, ye fair pretty lady,
Cheer up, cheer up, for I am he,
And for to convince you of this matter,
Here is a gold ring that you gave me."

Oh, there they joined themselves together,
And straightway to church did go,
And there they joined their right hands together,
Whether their parents were willing or no.

Ballad

I heard the soft wind blowing
Through every bush and tree,
Where my poor mother is lying,
Away from home and me.
(Last line 3 times, then repeat last 2 lines)

I saw the pale moon shining
Through Mother's new tombstone,
The rose bush around here twining
Just looks like me alone.

She is not like me a-weeping
Cold tear drops on her brow;
She is gone from earth to heaven,
I have not mother now.

I heard the trumpet a-sounding,
All on the mountain low,
Saying give up your old Mother,
For you know she is bound to go.

If I could see my mother,
I'd take her by the hand,
I'd say, God bless you Mother,
We'll march to social band.

Ballad

Oh, bury me not on the lone prairie,
Those words came low and mournfully,
I oft wish to be buried, when I die,
By my father's grave, beneath the green hill-side,
By my father's grave, oh, let it be,
Oh, bury me not on the lone prairie.

Where the wild cows and the buffaloes roam,
The wind of the west support my tomb,
In the narrow grave just six by three,
Oh, bury me not on the lone prairie.
(Repeat last 2 lines)

Where the dew drops fall and the butterflies rest,
Where the wild flowers bloom on the Prairie crest,
In the narrow tomb, just six by three,
Oh, we buried our boy on the lone prairie.

EXTRACTS FROM LETTERS

Letters of the Hindman People to us since our return [home]

Miss Pettit,

I feel it my duty to thank you for the kindness you have shown my children. I'm sure I appreciate it very much. I must say your visit to the mountains has been a great benefit to the people and hope you'll spend another summer here. Wishing you success in all your undertakings, I am your friend,

Mrs. Salyer.

We miss you all very much, hoping you will come back and spend next summer with us. The hill without your tent looks like the ruins at Jamestown. Miss D____ is attending school now. I guess she feels like the lost sheep of Israel since you all left here. I have held faithful so far about my pledge and I am going to hold out faithful through life.

Roy Baker

I am so glad you are giving your best efforts to establish a permanent Home Industrial School in some part of the mountains and if the letter which I intend to write you has any effect in getting the funds, I shall be one of the happiest fellows on earth. I have had so many chances, which the other Mountain children haven't had, that I want to do something to help them. My mind goes with the poor Mountain people all the time and if it is God's will that I should spend my life trying to help them, I will do it.

Your true and sincere friend,
[He is a deaf and dumb boy, who recently graduated at Danville with the valedictory of his class. He is now attending the College for Deaf and Dumb at Washington City. He came from a very poor home in Perry County and has grown sisters who cannot read. He is very anxious to help educate his younger brothers and sisters.]

I have been studing about sining mie name to that card. It looks lonesome up on the hill. I have been cooking a little. I have got ever thing that you give me in a little box.

Robert Bailey

I have quit sitting hump back and I have quite smoking segrets and always will.

Mr. James Begley
(About 10 years old)

I have quit drinking and trying to quit swearing. I no I can if I will try. I don't carry any pistol and don't expect to. I don't get much time to read my testiment much. I work the most of the time, but I read a verse or to every night.

Yours truly friend as ever,
Joseph fitzuo Patric Draughon

Some how when I left you standing in the road, I thought I would see your sweet, friendly face again. When I looked back and saw you standing, looking a me, O, I can't tell how good and kind and nice you did look to me. I have made some chains and hung them up and they are nice. I wish you knew how much company all the reding is to me that you gave me. Goodby.

If ever there was a friend,
Mary B. Stacy

"I and Dally is a teaching Kindergarten. We have decorated the room all up jist as you uns would." I would be pleased to see you. I have felt so sad since you have leaft Hears. I wish you would come back agin. I hated to see you go of, more than you hated to go. It felt like some of my own people had leaft. You was so much help to me. That patching was so much help to me. I don't want it to be long till you come back.

Your friend,
Dellia Hays

I am going to school every day and going to sunday school. I wish you was here to teach are sunday school lesson. We girls are teaching sewing. We have got a room in the dormitory and have got pictures up in it and chains, it is pretty, I wish you could see it. I am looking upon that lonely hill and thinking what a good time we had. I wish you would come back here. The town looks so ode without you women. I try to keep from crying but I cant. We read are Bibles and say are prayers of a night. From your hindman girl, a big kiss, your friend,

Rachel Everidge

I am going to school and sunday school every Sunday and say my prayers and read the Bible. i wish you was here and teach Sunday school. by by, ty ty, your friend,

Mary Everidge

Do you guess you will ever come back here? We hain't never been up on the hill yet. Where are you going to camp next summer?

Ida Combs

I am so thankful that you ever came to Hindman, as you have been the means of my sweet child being where she is now. If there is anything in the world that I can do for you, please don't hesitate to call on me, for I feel that I owe you a life long service for what you have done for me. May God bless you and crown your efforts with success.

Your kind letter received and read with joy and unspeakable to know that my precious child can be cured.

I do hope that you will all come back next summer. I feel very closely attached to you and when I receive a letter from you, it seems almost like getting a letter from one of my own family.

Yours lovingly,
Sarah J. Howard

EXPRESSIONS HEARD

One man said he loved for a rainy day to come so he could sit all day and "hate peas." [eat peas]

Maiden hair fern called Never Still and Blackbird's foot.

Where do you live when you're at home?

Come, go up, come go home with me. Can't I reckon.

I went to school jist a little grain, but I aim to go a big grain this year.

Air ye aimin' to have meetin' this morning?

I must go home to get some sand to put on the floors to keep the fleas from hoppin'.

Ain't it a sight? It's a sight in this world.

I ain't been no often.

I aim to eat me a piece of pie now.

Miss Bruner, Here's a flower pot I brought you (meaning a bouquet of flowers).

Hit keeps a woman plumb busy.

I jist slept till the sun ball was way up.

Knock 'em up (meaning to beat eggs).

I'm a little grain better.

He's the illest boy (meaning cross).

Rattle snakes is heap pizener than copper heads, but they ain't so ill.

That hill worried me (meaning wearied).

Yon-side, tother side.

"Atter" for "after."

I think so.

And it is too. It is pretty too.

"Panther" called "painter." One child asked, "Does it eat paint?"

A woman asked, when she heard one of us had been to Europe, "Well now, did ye see that creeter, half-fish and half-woman?"

I fotch it.

Mr. Hicks in a prayer, "May we come a leapin' and a skippin' over the dead faculties of our souls."

I hain't got no larnin'.

Hain't her and her man parted?

I had to mind the flies offen the baby.

Well, what about that anyway.

Hit looks pint blank like hit's goin' to rain.

Air any of you women kin? Any of you married? How old air ye?

I'm allers sayin' sumpin' awkerd.

Her and her man was parted. When he found she was fiftified, her man left her.

They have sech pretty meetins on Ball.

I aim to go home to help ma make peach pie.

Dr. Duke is the best doctor and the feelingest.

Hit's a sight how they do larn 'em to sing.

She larns to beat any thing that ever was.

I told ma I'd look for you 'uns.

Are there many people in town? I seed a might fine chance of 'em.

Father has shingled his moustache and I hardly know him from another man.

I staid as long as I handy could.

I 'lowed you warn't aimin' to get supper.

Did you 'uns took that air picture?

Betty Troublesome Branch.

Push Back Branch.

Plumb straight.

Pint blank like it.

I've got me three children dead.

I'm all tore up in my mind.

I followed teachin'. He followed going to Jackson.

Pearly is so frowny.

I've seed 'em make reddinin combs that way.

Narcissa holpe me at a workin' yesterday, (meaning chopping trees and bushes for corn).

I like Miss Pettit best because she drawed my attention to using tobacco.

It hain't been much long since we heard.

As much of a crop as I can handy tend.

The reason the mist rises at night is because the sun don't have no impression to drive it away.

Laura is powerful terrifying about going any place. Alza is not so terrifying as Laura.

Are you sleepy? I'm about it.

Set it out or catch it out, (meaning to set on fire).

Eva just wanted to slap its jaws, its so much like you.

You're before me, (meaning ahead of me).

If I had a knowed you women wuz here, I would a brung her.

I was hitched up all night, (meaning nursing the sick).

I put it in a poke.

He fell away 18 pound.

When I was just a chunk of a boy.

Church house always for church.

Poppy dolls: what children call store dolls because they have red cheeks like poppies.

"Slips" for "drawers."

I traded a lot for a nag and a yearlin' and $12.00.

CLASS & GUEST LIST

List of Members of the Sewing Class

May Howard
Maggie Howard
Ida Draughon
Ida Combs
May Everidge Robert
Bailey Blanche Salyer
Helen Salyer
Eva Baker
Arminta Cody
Chester Stacy Greene
Maggard Dally Bailey
Joe Combs
Matt Combs
Harrison Maggard
Blanche Combs
Flossie Cody
Bill Gibson
Robert Sturdivant
Lonnie Bailey
James Jones
Ella Combs
Mattie Draughon
Bent Mullins
John Mullins
Joe Kilgore
Mary Gibson
Ella Caudill
Mary Mullins
Minnie Jones
Ida Hays
Narcissa Hays
Laura Maggard
Lizzie Cody
Jane Duke
Mattie Jones
Maryland Maggard

Minta Calhoun
Lina Calhoun
Nonnie Jones
Pearly Maggard
Roncie Maggard
Mallie Baker
Learlie Perkins
Martha Slone
Jessie Combs
Sallie Stamper
Lucinda Collins
Robert Allen
Arminta Collins
Liberty Hays
Grover Perkins
Viola Gibson
Mallie Pigman
Angelina Dobson
Melissa Collins
Wana Allen
Judy Gayhart
Hattie Tignor
George Denny Combs
Lottie Baker
Arminta Stamper
Alta Dickinson
Nonnie Everidge
Dan Gibson
Bent Newland
Sarah Tignor
Maggie Dickinson
Hattie Sturgill
Sherman Collins
Sarah Hicks
Cosby Hicks
Lurania Hicks

Hester Newland
Nettie Calhoun
Roscoe Combs
Cora Gayhart
Jimmie Bagley
Crettie Collins
Cattie Gayhart
Minerva Collins
Ellen Collins
Callie Perkins
Giddy Hays
Martha Risner
Rachel Everidge
Guernie Baker
Nancy Collins
Mary Dickinson
Virgie Perkins
Allie Perkins
I. B. Slone
Nellie Dyer
Charlie Combs
Maggie Slone
John Everidge
Rachel Slone
Pearly Perkins
Wiley Dyer
Joe Hays
Willie Gayhart
Willie Hays
Dycie Hays
Pearl Combs
Richmind Baker
Dellie Hays
Charlie Perkins
Orley Davison

Members of Kindergarten

Carrol Howard	Annie Hall	Nonnie Everidge	Lurania Hicks
Lulie Howard	Wesley Combs	Cecil Everidge	Clara Amburgy
Beatrice Baker	Troy Sturgill	Barnam Gayhart	Allie Perkins
Bill Baker	Chester Allen	Odis Smith	Della Baker
Ishmael Wallin	Estill Fugate	Curtis Smith	Mollie Gayhart
Arthur Draughon	Maggie Slone	Sarah Calhoun	Claudia Fugate
Mary Mullins	Bernice Napier	Cora Gayhart	Ruba Childers
Jessie Combs	Marie Sturgill	Blanche Combs	Dora Combs
Gladys Smith	Viola Gibson	Maggie Calhoun	Liberty Hays
Mabel Smith	Grant Combs	Edna Hays	Nancy Collins
John Duke	Mary Gibson	Myrtle Combs	Annie Combs
Siebert Gibson	Nellie Dyer	Rachel Slone	Rank Brewer
Bartram Johnson	Crettie Collins	Naomi Dickinson	Maggie Baker
Maude Bailey	French Baker	Rubie Hays	Hobart Allen
Sylvanie Hudson	Dexter Hays	Hester Nowland	Guernie Baker

Members of the Cooking Class

Flossie Gibson	Hettie Calhoun	Narcissa Hays	Pearl Combs
Sarah Tignor	Cosby Hicks	Maryland Maggard	Ida Horton
Dan Gibson	Sarah Hicks	Mallie Pigman	Elza Maggard
Joe Combs	Jane Duke	Pearly Perkins	Callie Perkins
Ida Draughon	Bent Mullins	Mrs. John M. Baker	Mrs. Irvine Stacy
Blanche Salyer	John Mullins	Lucinda Everidge	Mrs. Cora Smith
Dally Bailey	Eva Baker	Sarah Baker	Dora Smith
Greene Maggard	Pearly Maggard	Chester Combs	Mallie Newland
Pearl Gibson	Roncie Maggard	Grant Combs	Mary Gibson
Hester Newland	Ella Combs	Hulda Jane Slone	Vicie Hicks
Matt Combs	Lonnie Bailey	Maggie Dickinson	Nonnie Jones
May Howard	Harrison Maggard	Alta Dickinson	
Ella Caudill	Chester Stacy	Arminta Duke	
Mary Everidge	Helen Salyer	Mrs. Henry Maggard	
Ida Combs	Robert Sturdivant	Arminta Cody	
Monroe Maggard	Mrs. Simon Stacy	Arminta Stamper	
Roscoe Kilgore	Mrs. Caudill	Rachel Smith	
Robert Bailey	Lizzie Cody	Electra Newland	
Minnie Jones	Laura Maggard	Polly Newland	
Mattie Jones	Caroline Terry	Rachel Everidge	
Blanche Combs	Celia Terry	Mrs. Boyd Baker	
Minta Calhoun	Line Calhoun	Mrs. George Clarke	

Guests at Camp Industrial

H. C. Rainey
Mr. and Mrs. Tom Johnson
Willie Fugate, Yerkes, Perry County
Richard Duke
Mrs. Betsy Hughes
Mrs. Sturtevant
Ballard Salyer
Roy Baker
Mary Jane Calhoun
Maggie Gibson
Dewitt Perkins
Sue Lee Howard
Mr. and Mrs. Granville Howard
Mrs. Polly Hays, 80 years old
Dr. John Wesley Duke
Mrs. Nancy Duke
Mr. and Mrs. Will Duke
Mr. and Mrs. Irvine Stacy
Ida M. Horton
Mr. and Mrs. Shade Combs
Mrs. Sexton
Dr. Amburgy
Sarah Mullins
Diana Amburgy
John S. Mullins
Mrs. Marion Stamper
Mr. and Mrs. Napeir
Mr. and Mrs. W. W. Wallin
Prof. and Mrs. George Clarke
Mr. and Mrs. John Parks
Eva Parks and Fannie Parks
Mr. Reuben Hicks
Mr. and Mrs. Jessie Hicks
Mrs. Edgar Mullins
Lizzie Maggard
Allie Combs
Maggie Sturtevant
Belle Salyer
Mr. and Mrs. John M. Baker

Judge and Mrs. Will Baker
French Combs
Judge G. P. Combs, Sassafras
Mattie and Ida Combs, Sassafras
John C. Combs, Sassafras
Mr. and Mrs. Wesley Hall
Lillie May Issacs
Mr. and Mrs. H. C. Phillips
Lila Cook
Mrs. Pigman
Hattie Allen
Mr. and Mrs. Chic Allen
Mr. and Mrs. Troy Perkins
Mr. and Mrs. Maggard
Arminta Perkins
Mr. and Mrs. Carew Smith
Mr. and Mrs. Sam Kilgore
Lela Pratt
Ferris Hays
Katherine Hays
Mrs. George Hays
Mr. and Mrs. Henry Maggard
Mr. and Mrs. Daniel Hays
Mrs. Austin Combs
Hillard Smith
Blaine Combs
Fannie Everidge
Mr. Griggs, Mt. Sterling
Mrs. Sib Combs
Dr. and Mrs. Kelley
Mr. and Mrs. Johnie Miller
Willie Begley
Mrs. Elza Maggard, over 80 years
Tryphena Pratt
Mr. Madison Collins, 76 years old
Mr. Polly Hughes
Mrs. Sandy Martin
Ashland Martin
Mr. and Mrs. John A. Bailey

Mr. Will Mullins
Mr. Kinnard Tillie
Mrs. and Mrs. Simon Stacy, Sassafras
Elizabeth Madden
Rufus Davis, Hazard
Uncle Noah Spencer, Jackson
Mrs. Fanny Combs
Dally Combs
Robert Lee Pigman
Christopher and Bertha Pigman
Taulbee Tignor
Uncle Soloman Everidge and Wife
Patrick Sturtevant
Daniel Hays
Mrs. Coon Everidge
Hattie Viola Collins
Sally Ally Fair Collins
Mrs. Whittaker
Miss Huff
Mrs. Giddy Hays
Mr. Lucas
Cicero Perkins
Mrs. Newson
Miss Collins
Mrs. Gunnell
Mr. Tyler, Methodist preacher
Kate Bolling
Anderson Gayhart
Fannie Patton
Mr. and Mrs. Horace Click, age 17 & 14
Jennie Hughes
Mrs. Martha Ann Gayhart, Vest coverlids
Mrs. Messer
Mrs. Risener
Mrs. Williams
Mr. Mosely
Mr. Grigsby
Mrs. Riley Cornet
Mrs. France
Joseph Draughon
Mr. and Mrs. J. B. Fugate

Willie and George Senters
Arlena and Dora Collins
Mrs. Pratt
Mrs. Tilda Thacker
Henry Combs
Mrs. Perry
Tom Triplett
Arthur Holiday
Mr. and Mrs. Jim Hughes
Mr. Tic Bailey
Will Nickells
Captain Hall
Mrs. Nancy Jane Coubolt
Mrs. Susanna F. Greer, baskets
Mrs. Ransom Baker
Mrs. Leonard Perkins
Adam Hays, Vest
Mrs. Henderson Baker
Mr. and Mrs. Boyd Baker
Mrs. Jasper Baker
Mrs. Ben Newland
Becy Ann Messer, 11, Vest
Polly Jane Messer, 7, Vest
Mrs. Elijah Combs
Mr. Richart
Mr. Kelley and three children, Sassafras
Jasper Patton
Bird and Willie Stamper
Ronnie Draughon
Mrs. Thacker and Mandy Thacker
Mrs. Moore, an old lady, grand-
mother of Senters boys
Mrs. Dyer
Alex Stewart and George Stewart
Joe Vermilim, Hazard
Professor V. W. Shipp, Winchester
Professor March, Berea
Lee Stewart
Dr. Humbel, West Virginia
Mrs. Frankie Hughes, Pine Top
Mrs. Martha Ann Nice, Pine Top

Mrs. Huff and Alice Huff
Miss Martha Cornet, Cornetsville, Perry County
Mrs. Slone
Mrs. Margaret Triplett, Keger, Knott County
Nancy and Melissa Triplett, Kegor
Mr. Huff
Mr. and Mrs. Owen Childers
Mrs. Dr. Stewart
Mrs. Young

Photo Essay;
The Social Settlement Summers

Lucy Furman, in her book, *Mothering on Perilous*, noted that "while at the big house talking with the head workers yesterday, they showed me some albums of photographs made in the beginnings of their work here, before the school was even thought of, and when they came up from the Blue Grass only in the summers, and lived in tents" Most of the pictures in the following essay are the ones she saw. There are a number from the first summer at Cedar Grove while the majority were taken during the summer at Sassafras.

Furman had her main character in the novel, The Quare Women, *describe the tent city on the hill above Hindman this way: "Aunt Ailsie's eyes were instantly drawn to the tent itself, the roof of which was festooned with red cheese cloth and many-colored paper chains, a great flag being draped at one end, while every remaining foot of roof-space and wall-space was covered with bright pictures."*

The tent facilities became more elaborate each summer. Pettit wrote that their Sassafras tents were "covered with bright pictures" with "bookshelves filled with interesting books and periodicals" and "pretty covered boxes filled with pictures to give away," with "sewing and kindergarten supplies, a sofa, screen, organ, steamer chairs, camp stools, straw mats, stereoscope, sea shells, educational games and scrapbooks."

Some of the young children who visited the camp.

Giving out books and magazines brought many to the camp as this group shown here.

This unidentified group may be some of the district school teachers whom Katherine and May met at Hindman as well as some of the settlement workers. The woman, second from the left in the first row, appears to be Katherine Pettit.

This is a good view of the open-air dining facilities at the camp.

Written on this photo is, "Town of Hindman saying goodbye to the women, Aug 29, 1900."

During the wagon trip over the mountains, in a wagon much like the one here, the interest of their mountaineer hosts in these outsiders sometimes produced humorous encounters.

For example, when a mountain woman in whose home they were staying watched them get ready for bed by putting on nightgowns, she asked, "Do ye all do this every night before ye go to bed?" When told they did, she responded, "Ye all must be a lot of trouble to yerselves."

This picture shows typical female attire of the day; long back dresses with deep brimmed, cotton sunbonnets. The woman on the left is holding a turkey wing fan.

Here are some of the Hindman children who turned out to greet them on their return visit during the Sassafras summer. Third from the left in the front row is Wesley Combs, a five year old Hindman boy who Pettit and Stone attempted to reform the previous summer. It doesn't appear to have worked since, on their return visit, they mentioned seeing him with a whiskey bottle in his pocket and reported that he was often seen drunk.

THE BOY

EVERYTHING 's predestĩned,
   So the Preachers say —
Wisht I 'd been predestĩned
   To be my brother Clay.

He 's the only man-child
   Mammy ever bore.
Four of us that 's older,
   Sev'ral young-uns more.

Eats with Pop and Grandsir',
   While we women wait.
Has his wings and drumsticks
   Waiting, if he 's late.

Rides behind with Poppy,
   When he goes to mill,
Fun'ral-meetings, anywhar
   Hit suits his little will.

Folks delight to sarve him,
   Let him come and go, —

In this patriarchal culture, males of any age were deemed superior to all females. Ann Cobb captured this view in her poem, "The Boy" as well as reflecting on what many females must have felt as a result of this bias.

Another example of female dress is shown on this young girl wearing a type of headgear common in the mountains, a crocheted fascinator.

This building, Buckner Academy, was the one in which George Clarke held school during the summers when the social settlement workers visited Hindman. It was sold to the Women's Christian Temperance Union when Pettit and Stone agreed to establish the settlement school at Hindman.

During the summer at Sassafras, Katherine and May had their headquarters at Mary Stacy's home , pictured here.

One of the important social as well as religious events in mountain culture on which Pettit and Stone commented extensively was the "gatherings" or funeral meetings. At Sassafras they heard Uncle Ira Combs, one of the region's most noted preachers, who was later memorialized by James Still's poem, "Epitaph for Uncle Ira Combs, Mountain Preacher." Above, a gathering; below, a preacher at work.

The Sassafras camp, shown here, was pitched next to the branch of the river.

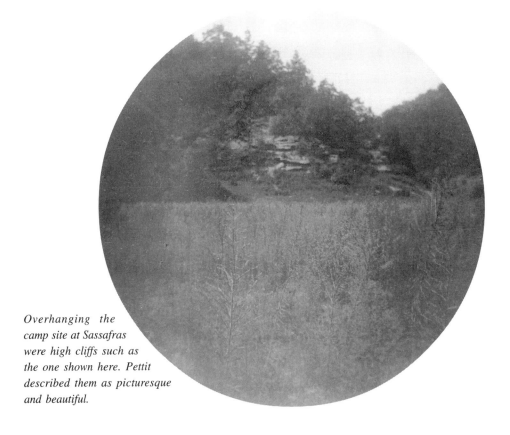

Overhanging the camp site at Sassafras were high cliffs such as the one shown here. Pettit described them as picturesque and beautiful.

Here is the Sassafras School where Sunday School was held and sewing and other classes took place after the school year opened. Fifty people were waiting for them on their first Sunday, many of whom had never attended a Sunday School before.

Pictured here are the kindergarten and sewing classes with Rae McNab, the kindergarten teacher. Pettit came upon the sewing class one day and called it "a picture of delight. . . to see the children seated in a circle on the hill side working away so industriously".

Rae McNab taught the children organized games, something few had participated in before. Boys as old as sixteen joined the kindergarten group for these and other activities.

The clothes were washed near the creek. Pictured here is one of the black washerwomen they employed with several of her children. The other young woman may be Rhoda, Mary Stacy's helper.

Crossing the creek to Sunday School, shown here, could be quite an adventure like the time when the women had to jump from rock to rock and then balance on a rail over water so swift it made them dizzy.

The women took a portable organ to their Sunday School meetings. Pictured here is a group return-ing from Sunday School, including Jasper Mullins, the young man hired to be their assistant during the Sassafras summer. He has the organ on a mule. Jasper and most of the local people were fasci-nated by the organ which he called the "little new cupboard."

This group is having a "social" at the camp. Much of the recreation of the area involved drinking, shooting and swearing so the women gave several parties to show the young people that it was possible to have fun without these things.

George's Branch schoolhouse, pictured here, was another location where they held Sunday School although, in actuality, on Saturday afternoon. At first the trustees would not allow its use, not believing in Sunday School; but they later relented.

Dr. Roarke was someone the women saw regularly during the Sassafras summer. He passed back and forth dressed in a black Prince Albert coat and high silk hat. When they visited his home, Pettit expressed surprise at the dirt and she also noted that he talked "in a very learned way of the vast medical knowledge he had received in Louisville." Pictured here are Dr. Roarke and his home on Montgomery branch.

Dr. Roarke's eleven-year-old daughter, Della, seen here, was described as quick and alert, wearing her hair in a tight knot and dressed in a pink calico shirt waist and long black skirt. She told the fotched-on women that she could "rein a nag as well as any man."

Crossing the creeks was part of the normal daily activity. As one can see from this picture, several methods were employed including stepping from rock to rock or removing the shoes and wading.

Mary Ritchie was the blind daughter of a Hindman storekeeper. She accompanied the women on their return trip to Jackson to attend a school for the blind.

Nannie Green and Louisa Summer, shown here, were both about fifteen years old that summer and were two of the "bad girls" of the neighborhood whose various scrapes were recounted in the Sassafras diary.

This is a fairly typical example of the one-room mountain homes that Katherine and May visited.

Here is one of the many families they visited during the Sassafras summer.

The women attended a log raising up Scuddy branch where a new home was built for Kenton Cornet and his young wife on the only ground level enough on their farm for a home site. Eighteen men helped with the work while the women brought supplies and cooked. Pettit noted, "this was a gala day as a working' in the mountains is a social time for all."

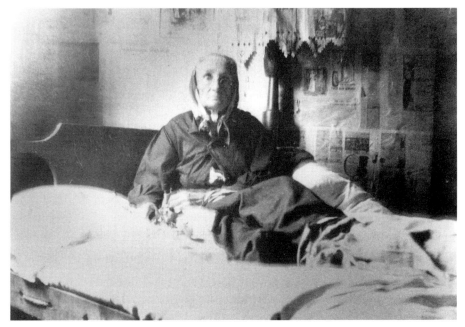

This is a rare picture of the interior of a home. It was common for newspapers or magazine pages to be hung on the walls to brighten them up. The woman is unidentified.

The women visited Mrs. Brashears, pictured outside of her cabin with other family members, in hopes of buying some blankets from her.

A scene of men logging. The coming of the timber industry was the first major economic change for the region and had already reached Sassafras. One day, as the women held their classes in the Sassafras school they noted that, "all the time we were there we could hear the great crash of the trees falling on the mountain nearby, where men were getting out poplar timber.

Here is the sawmill where Pettit and Stone went to buy lumber for a floor for their tent.

Pictured here is the water mill. Friday was mill day and when its whistle sounded people would appear along the road on horseback or mule with bags of corn to be ground into meal. Since they passed right by the camp, Friday became an especially busy day at the settlement.

A common activity shown here is a woman picking geese whose feathers were used in the mattresses and pillows in many homes.

Everyone helped on the farm and life revolved around its needs. For example, school closed for two weeks during foddering season when the winter food supply for the animals was harvested. Seen here, children pulling a sled, commonly used to transport items on the steep hillsides.

Mary Stacy and her assistant, Rhoda, spent a great deal of their "free" time preparing wool and cotton from their own sheep and the farm. There were many tasks involved in carding, spinning and weaving. Shown here: 1) sizing cotton, 2) reeling wool into hanks, and 3) spooling cotton and quilling flax.

An event recorded in the Sassafras diary was attendance at a local court session held out-of-doors under the trees on George's Branch on August 8. Pictured here is Squire Gent, the chief magistrate. The judicial outcome was not entirely satisfactory. The squire sat at a table with a big law book open before him. Two lawyers had come the fifteen miles from Hazard. But as the cases were called, neither prisoners nor witnesses appeared. In the end the warrants were dismissed.

The return trip to Jackson by boat included Mary Ritchie, the blind girl, and Tilford Beverly, a young boy afflicted with severe rheumatism. The boat itself left much to be desired and was described as "very dirty" and it had to be bailed constantly. Nonetheless, it got them to Jackson, or, at least, a mile from the town.

Rhoda washing wool in a basket in the creek. *"She held up her dress, showing her red linsey skirt, while she pressed the wool in the basket with her feet....It was hard to realize that we were not living in the time of our great-grandmothers."*

Daily Record of the Social
Settlement in the Mountains of Kentucky

SASSAFRAS, KNOTT COUNTY
JUNE 25-OCTOBER 4, 1901

At the meeting of the State Federation of Women's Clubs June 6, 1901, when the report of the past summer's settlement was given, it was decided to have the third Social Settlement in the mountains. $262.00 were given by the various clubs and individuals and Misses Mary McCartney, Rae MacNab, May Stone and Katherine Pettit were appointed to take charge of the work.

June 25.   Jackson, Kentucky.   A day's journey on the train from Louisville brought us to this mountain town, the terminus of the Louisville and Nashville Railroad.

June 26.   En Route. We spent last night at the Arlington in Jackson and were up early and at the station two hours and a half, getting together the thirty pieces of luggage from the freight cars and packing room, and seeing them loaded into the wagons, that had come from Perry County to meet us. We left Jackson at 9:30 in one of Mr. Taulbee's covered spring wagons, with Uncle Noah Spencer, who always drives us.   The old road was washed away so we had to go out of town another way and across an extra mountain.   A mile out, in winding up a steep mountain side, the horses were trying to pull out of a tremendous mud hole, when one of them slipped over the bank and rolled down and over three times.   The harness had to be cut off and the fact that the wagon was mired kept it from going over. A man and two boys helped us out of this difficulty but we had to walk much of the way.   We came to a hill, where it seemed absolutely impossible for a wagon to go up.   I went on ahead to try to get a man and horse.   He was up the creek a mile fishing.   A little boy ran after him, he came but no nag could we secure.   When we reached the wagon, found they had unloaded it, carried the things up the hill and, with the help of a small boy, had gotten the wagon up.   Another time the wagon was fastened on a large rock in the middle of the road and had to be prized off with fence rails.   We met Mr. Parks, our teamster of last summer, who stopped with us for luncheon, which we ate on the bank of the Quicksand while he told us the Knott County news.   Early in the afternoon we began to realize that it would not be possible to reach Mr. Jim Hays' for the night, and this is the only place in the forty-five miles between Jackson and Hindman where one can spend a comfortable night.   At half past seven we came to Mr. Alfred Allen's at the mouth of Buckhorn.   We were careful to have supper from the lunch baskets before we stopped for the night. Miss McNab soon had the many children about her teaching them kindergarten songs and stories.   A number of men and half grown boys and girls were around "watching at the quare wimmen folks," while we all sat on the porch rejoicing in the wonderful moonlight scene before us.   Uncle Noah reminded us that we must start early tomorrow, so we sang a hymn and had prayers before going to bed.

June 27.   En Route. A "sorry" time we had last night. We were fortunate to have a room to ourselves, which is not often the case. There was only one light in the house, an old, dirty, greasy, smoky tin lamp, without a chimney, which a girl held while we undressed. She said that the rest went to "lay down" in the dark. In the midst of it a tall old woman with a long brown cloak on, suddenly appeared in the doorway and asked us to come and see the pictures on her wall. She had an attractive, comparatively clean room with homespun coverlid and blankets on the bed. She showed us her loom and promised us to teach her granddaughter to spin and weave. She proved to be "Granny Allen" who was "Kinder quare" and would not eat with the rest of the family. We were glad for the sheets we had with us, which we put on the undersirable beds after the girl had disappeared with the smoky lamp. Tired as we were, there was not much chance for sleep. In the middle of the night, a loud voice was heard from the road calling for Aunt Poll. As she got up and went away with him, we supposed that she was the doctor of the neighborhood. We were on the way by "peep of day" this morning, did not even wait for breakfast, but were ready for what we had in the lunch basket. Then began the journey up the Buckhorn for twelve miles. The road, or rather the bed of the stream, was rough and we were out of the wagon more than we were in it. We left a magazine, paper and picture at every home we passed. The women would often drop everything and run out for them. At one home, where there was a fifteen year old deaf and dumb girl, we talked very earnestly to the parents about sending her to the school for the deaf and they promised to try to send her. They did not know that a deaf person could be taught. While we were having luncheon on a log by the wayside, a woman from the little cabin nearby asked many questions but we were interrupted by a great wind storm, so we let the curtains down and hurried on. At least we found some friends of last summer waiting for us. Mr. Richie, the store keeper, who started us on the way home last summer with a bucket of honey was waiting for us with another. He had his blind girl eleven years old, who told us that she was going home with us to go to the school for the blind.

Soon after we left Jackson yesterday we met a man who said "war is on ahead." Then he told us that the day before two men had followed another man to a corn field and "shot him down dead just for nothin'. Now the people were a gathering and there would be trouble." This morning while we were talking to Eva Hays at her home, two young men came out of the house with shotguns on their shoulders and went into the dense woods. She told us that they were the murderers of the day before, that they had kept them last night, but as the people were a gathering across the mountain to hunt them, they were going to "lay out in the woods."

Just before we started to cross Audubon Mountain, which the mountaineer calls Ogden, Uncle Noah hesitated between two roads, and took the wrong one, for in an instant the wagon was up to the hubs in the quicksand, the horses to their knees and one of them down. Miss Stone waded out and Uncle Noah carried Miss McNab, Miss McCartney and I were walking at the time. She hurried on ahead and I went back, both of us to get aid, for Uncle Noah was helpless. I walked a mile and half back, found a man who said he would come and sent a boy further back to get a mule. When we got back, a long log was filled with women and children, while several men and boys were wading nearly to their waists unloading the wagon. Rails were put under the wheels and mules hitched to a chain which was put to the back of the wagon. After a great effort on the part of both men and mules it was pulled out and up the hill backwards by jerks and jumps. Then we reloaded and walked two and one half miles across Audubon Mountain, while the moon rose over the hill and we thought surely there was nothing more to happen this day. The bed of Audubon Branch was the roughest of any road yet and a great log in it stopped the wagon. Fence rails were once more secured and we prized the wagon up, while Uncle Noah pulled the log out. The horse was cut on the ankle and the stream was colored with blood, which made us very anxious about the horses, as the trip had been very hard on them. Progress was again stopped by a large stump in the road and the wagon had to be lifted off with fence rails. We drove into Hindman by moonlight, which helped us to follow the narrow rough road. At that late hour our friends were waiting to greet us and the hearty welcome repaid us for all the effort we had made to reach them.

June 28.   Hindman. A comfortable night spent with Mrs. Salyer. The children began to come early and later many of the grown people. Some of the mothers told us that the boys had been dressed up all week waiting for us, had them to wash their shirts and collars, and one boy, whose mother was sick, washed and ironed his own shirt so as to be ready to receive us. Miss McNab gathered the children around her and put them to work making paper chains. This afternoon we went to see the sick friends and many were the sad stories we heard of the trouble that had come to them in the past year. One of the boys had been murdered, husbands and wives had separated, a government still had been started just outside of town, so that the boys were well supplied liquor. But there was a glad story also. The leader of the Kuklux Band had gone to the Philippines and there was general rejoicing. Then there had been conversions in the town. A sick friend said:

> Law, hit's a sight what conversions we had. A preacher came and he preached the awfullest that ever wuz; Monroe, he was converted and Fanny, she married the preacher and she got renewed again. Lizzie, my gal, wuz renewed again also. A preacher came to build a Baptist church but he spent so much time a sparkin' that Paw Maggard said he wished the preachers would quit a sparkin' and go to preaching. But he went to raising a crap and is now going to marry Belle.

We were so pleased to meet Miss Granger, the Bible teacher sent from New York by the Northern Presbyterian Church. Mr. Bailey has given her the use of his library, which she uses as a reading and sewing room. She said that the lessons in sewing that Miss Stone had given them last summer had been a great help to the girls. They all begged us to stay at Hindman and the boys said they would make a good road up the hill and help us in every way if we would stay. Late this evening we climbed up to the old camp ground to see the moon rise over the hill, which brought back memories of last summer. Some of the children followed us and we had a quiet talk with them about what the year had brought to them. Only the dairy was found just as we had left it. Even our favorite view of the valley of the Troublesome was changed by the ugly new farm houses that were dotted here and there.

June 29.   Hindman. We are faring well as to rooms but the meals are impossible. Mr. Ritchie's honey helps out considerable. We were receiving friends all morning and visiting in the afternoon. Had the pleasure of seeing Miss McNab get on a horse for the first time. As she has never spent a day in the country before this trip, she is very green as we must explain to our mountain friends. We went to Miss Granger's sewing class which seemed quite like old times with our same girls just a year older. There were no boys and Miss Granger said that she had not been able to get a hold on them. She had a quantity of good kindergarten material which she did not know how to use. Miss McNab called in some children and had a class to show her. Wesley Combs, the five year old kindergarten boy, whom we had tried last year to persuade to give up chewing, smoking and drinking, was there with a whiskey bottle in his pocket and we hear that he is often drunk now. Dug Hays, a murderer and ex-convict, sits next to me at the table, and has kindly offered to help us in every way possible. He has taken the place of the Combs boys in the Kuklux Band, and is also a revenue officer. He gave me a piece of copper still that he had broken up over on Elkhorn in Pike County and said the people there were the roughest in all the mountains, that the men wore long hair and carried shotguns buckled to them as they worked in the fields. He told in a very pathetic way of the death of his comrade, Rufus Mooten, who was shot last winter when they were out on a Kuklux raid. There were tears in his eyes as he told how lonely it was in the dark night on the road side, as his friend lay dying begging him not to let go his hand until all was over.

All this time we had been anxious to know what our friends, the Dukes thought of the account in Sunday's *Courier Journal* of last summer's work, which had the pictures of Minta Duke and French Combs side by side with Blaine Combs' name under French Combs' picture. As the name of Blaine Combs means everything that is bad and lawless, we felt the Duke boys would resent bitterly having their sister's name connected with his. As nothing had been said, at last I asked her what they thought of it. She was very nice about it but had a long story to tell of the comment it had caused in town, how the paper had been passed around, read and discussed. To be sure they did not like it, but accepted our explanation, and were just as friendly and cordial as before.

After supper the Maggard boys came with a cornet, harp and tambourine to play for us. We had heard much of the Maggard band and of the "pretty music they made." I asked Harrison where they got the instruments and how they learned. He said they saw them advertised in a book, sent off for them and, just as soon as they came, went to playing right on them and had been playing ever since.

June 30. Hindman. Mr. Rainey had a jolt wagon[1] all ready to take us four miles up Troublesome to Jonas Chapel for Sunday School and preaching. The friends there all seemed so pleased to see us. Each of us had a class. Immediately after dinner we went up on the hill for our favorite view and a quiet Sabbath afternoon, but the young people followed and we read to them. At twilight we were left alone with Roscoe, Roy and Daniel. Daniel–who last year told me that it was no use to give him the triple pledge–said that he had stopped using tobacco entirely. Roy said that he had often wished that he had given it up when we asked him, that now it was hurting him and he had to have it all the time. We talked about it and Roscoe and Roy–to our surprise–took out a "poke" of tobacco and cigarette papers. We burned them while they sang, "We don't like tobacco, do you know what we think, that the boys who will use it are quite sure to drink." It really was impressive and the boys were affected. I do think that we have influenced them and if we could be with them all the time, that it would be for good. We had lunch and then went down to church. After church we met a man whom I had met years ago in Bell County. He was a mountain preacher, but is now an insurance agent. I told him that I thought that he used to be a preacher but he said that he guessed that he "was not much to hurt."

July 1.   Sassafras. We were up early this morning. Our old friend, Joe Drough, who is fifteen years old and very small, but one of the best teamsters in the county, was at the door with two strong mules and a jolt wagon. We went up the main fork of the Trouble-some to Betty Troublesome, across Dead Man's Branch to Irishman mountain and across it and down Irishman Creek to Carr's Fork and five miles down to the mouth of Montgomery, where we are to pitch our tent. Here in this somber depths of Carr's Fork Valley we seem no end of miles from anything else but wilderness and thick forest. The laurel and rhododendron line up close and thick along the road and the beautiful pink blossoms are in great masses. It is bright frame for the low roofed log cabin home. And we are in the most remote spot in all the southern mountains, sixty miles from Jackson and just over the hill the mail goes via Norton, Virginia. Perry, Letcher and Knott Counties unite here, so we hope to reach people in all three counties. We are fifteen miles from Hazard, Hindman and Whitesburg, but they say it is thickly settled round about here. Sassafras is a mile and a half away, and simply a county post office located in a private home. We found Mrs. Stacy making a goodly supply of pies and cakes. The house was in perfect order and her childish delight at seeing us was charming. She made us feel very welcome. Rhoda and Mr. Stacy were up on the mountain hoeing corn. The little room that Mrs. Stacy had emptied for us had a large feather bed, spinning wheel and reel and a shelf full of "bed kivers" left in it. There were nails all along the wall up against the ceiling and hanging high up all the way around the room were very brilliantly striped linsey skirts. Our supplies, thirty pieces, were all in this room, but we had to get them out to make room for the four cots. Joe helped us to lift them out into one corner of the yard and just as we got them covered with the tent there came a great wind and rain storm. After an early supper we had prayer and are ready for bed at eight o'clock.

July 2. Sassafras. Mrs. Stacy was up at three o'clock this morning and the big farm bell right at our window rang loud for breakfast at fifteen minutes before four. It did not occur to her that we should not follow their custom of getting out of bed, washing our faces and coming right in for breakfast, but as we had to bathe and dress we kept breakfast waiting a bit. The family would not eat with us at first, but we insisted and very reluctantly they all sat down. Immediately after breakfast, Jasper Mullins, the boy we had engaged to help pitch the tents, came with the word that no lumber could be gotten for the tent floor. As nothing could be done without the lumber, Miss Stone and I started to the saw mill to see if we could purchase, rent or borrow some. Jasper led us along the side of a beautiful but steep and dangerous cliff, where we were so interested in gathering the laurel and rhododendron that we came near forgetting the lumber. Mr. Stacy ("Simon's Pap") was not there but we looked around, found what we wanted and left word for him to send it to us, although Jasper, and Mr. Stacy ("Our Simon") pitched the tents. Neither of them had done anything like this before and Jasper had never seen a tent. They went to work with energy and with our direction and judgement soon had them up. For the first time our Camp is in a valley right on the bank of the creek and although we may miss the extended view from the mountain top, the picturesque one of hanging cliffs on every side is beautiful. Mrs. Stacy ("Our Mary") asked us to take entire charge of her house and arrange things just as we like. First we asked her to take down all the linsey skirts and gave her one of our boxes to pack them in, and succeeded in getting the spinning wheel and reel out. We put closet hooks on the walls and made cheese cloth curtains to hang over the clothes. The cots were very pretty with cretonne covers and sofa pillows. We changed the kitchen into a dining room by moving the stove out into the yard under an oil cloth covering. We fixed a china closet and nailed boxes on the walls for tinware. We put up muslin curtains in front of them and the windows, which made a cool, attractive dining room. The rest of the day has been spent in unpacking, washing and putting in place china and kitchen supplies.

Miss McCartney started out alone at six-thirty A.M. to make visits and returned at three. She went up two branches and made seven calls. At one place she helped them make the clothes and dress a child for burial. In the same little room there were ten people and an immense fire cooking dinner. She held the burial services, which they appreciated, as they are not in the habit of having one. Up one creek there were four negro families. In one home a young white woman was living as the mistress of a big burly negro man.

July 3.   We were up at three forty-five this morning and after breakfast, unpacked the groceries and stored them away in the cellar and dining room and then went to work to furnish the tent. Jasper was here to help. He swore so much that I asked him not to and since then we have not heard another oath. He would have us stop every little while to play a tune on the "little new cupboard" as he called the organ. He thinks it is the greatest thing he ever heard. Early in the afternoon Martha, Maggie and Robert Stacy came, so we had to unpack all the songs and sing for several hours. They joined in heartily. Robert is so anxious to go to school, so Miss McCartney is writing to the Boy's Farm School at Asheville to know if he can get in. Just before dark a great wind and rain storm came, which caused a tide in Montgomery that was wonderful to see. Miss McCartney made four visits this morning and had to wade across the creek.

July 4.   In honor of the day Mrs. Stacy did not call us until daylight. We had planned to go ten miles to the head of Macy's Creek to a fourth of July picnic, but the rise in the streams made it impossible. We worked all morning covering boxes and putting in shelves for book cases. Some of the boys came and helped us pin pictures on the walls of the tent. One seven year old boy came and Miss McNab began her kindergarten with him. Miss McCartney made light bread[2] which we are glad to have. Mrs. Stacy is a good cook, keeps a nice clean table and we fare very well. After a busy day we are now going to bed before early candle light.

July 5.   We were up just at dawn. I had to hurry to work the butter for breakfast which Rhoda churned. We have persuaded Mrs. Stacy to milk twice a day, so now we have good cream for the cereals. The milk is kept cool by hanging in the well. I made cottage cheese, the first they had ever seen. If they just knew how, they could make so much better use of what they have. After the butter is churned, they just wash it once and stir it with a spoon. Mr. Stacy is to make me a cedar paddle and I am to have charge of the butter. Mrs. Stacy asked me how she is to cook everything and how to set the table. A mother came with two little boys and grandmother Stacy with Willie, so that Miss McNab soon had a class of three. They were so interested and intense. As they were leaving one boy said, "Mammy, I want to learn everything!" Some young people came and we had singing, going over and over the songs so that they could learn them. A short story and the Sabbath School lesson were read to them and they played the bird game. One of the young men took the first book from the Circulating Library. He had a lame hand, with the bullet showing plainly in the wrist, where he had shot himself when he was drunk. He was the boy who had charge of the Sunday School that Mr. Rainey organized at the Sassafras School house. Their plan had been to have the young people meet and then go off the rest of the day "to frolic," and they let it be known that they did not want any old people to come. So the Sunday School broke up in disrepute. They hail with delight the news that we are to have one there for young and old. We have "Caused it to be norated about" that we shall organize one at Sassafras school house at nine o'clock Sunday morning and at Montgomery school house at four o'clock in the afternoon. Some of the mothers say that they will come, Monday afternoon with their little children for the kindergarten while they join the sewing class. Some of the mothers are to come Tuesday to learn to make light bread. One woman is very anxious to know, because her husband has indigestion and cannot eat the hot bread they have. Early supper and a quiet twilight while we listened to the reading of *Black Rock*.[3]

July 6.   Spent the morning putting the finishing touches to the tent. It is now quite the most attractive one we have ever had. The walls are covered with bright pictures. The book shelves filled with interesting books and periodicals which are to be given away and loaned, prettily covered boxes filled with pictures to give away, and with sewing and kindergarten supplies, a sofa and screen (where we have visions of resting if there is ever time), an organ, steamer chairs, camp stools and straw mats. We are provided with a stereoscope and pictures, sea shells, educational games and scrap books to entertain our visitors. Three girls from up Montgomery came. We taught them some songs, showed them the things and gave them pictures and papers. They each borrowed a book. Diana, ten years old, told me that her mother died at her birth and that she had a grown sister who had left home and they did not know where she was. That is a very common story here. After dinner Mrs. Stacy and I started walking to make some visits. We went around the cliff to the boat and called to grandmother Stacy to come take us across. Then we went to Uncle Rob Cornet's. A rain storm came, we stopped under a great rock house for a while and then trudged on in the pouring rain, mud and quicksand. Uncle Rob, Mrs. Stacy's father, is a very interesting old man, whose father came from Virginia and settled at this place more than one hundred years ago. The house is over seventy-five years old and has may quaint things in it. The beds are covered with beautiful coverlids, a tall old clock in the corner still keeping time. He plays "meetin'-house" songs on a dulcimer that he made forty years ago. A pretty but sad faced daughter-in-law told us how unhappy she was over her husband's drinking. Then we went up Sassafras Branch to see a five days' old baby, whose mother had just come in from working in the garden, and was knitting woolen socks. We stopped at the post office to wait for the afternoon mail, which had been waterbound for several days. The postmaster's wife "put her foot to it" and crossed the creek to get us some beautiful red apples. Sitting on a log by the side of the river, barefoot, was Granville Stacy, son of the postmaster, who is out on bond for robbing the post office. They say he is "bound for the Pen." His wife, who looked twenty years older, had just come in from working in the fields. On the way home "our Mary" told me in a very quaint and original way of her engagement and marriage. For a long time there had been "hard feeling" between the Cornets and Stacys, the two old families who had been living there for one hundred years. So when young Simon Stacy, in spite of much opposition, married Mary Cornet and took her to his father's house, she had a "mighty sorry time" until they made a home for themselves. When we reached the creek, as we were already wet and bedraggled, we decided just to walk across it, shoes and all.

The Reverend Mr. Rainey has come from Hindman to stay all night and help us to organize the Sabbath School tomorrow.

July 7.   Sleep was interrupted many times last night by the fleas. The candle was lighted and the process of "fleaing" gone through with. Mrs. Stacy said she "flead" three times and caught one hundred forty-eight fleas. It seemed that many were after us. The important question at breakfast was how to cross the creeks to go to our

Sunday School at Sassafras. Carr was impossible and so was Montgomery we thought but Jasper came to help us. He threw a flimsy rail across the first deep place in Montgomery, we handed him the umbrellas, song books and other supplies, while we managed to cross to the large rocks. Then Jasper moved the rail over another deep place where the water was so swift it made us dizzy and we had to slide over the rail side wise to keep it from turning with us. Then the walk around the cliff. The recent rains have washed down the path in some places and it was very slippery all along but we clambered up, stumbling over rocks and fallen trees. The path zigzags up to a huge over-hanging cliff, over which the water was dripping. The path here is very narrow and in one place we had to slide down about three feet to get a footing. When we had time to look away from our feet, we had a beautiful view of the winding creek. There were trailing vines and ferns growing in the crevices of the rocks, towering up on one side and on the other the hill covered with laurel and rhododendron. After climbing over more rocks and trees, we reached the creek where we sank to our ankles in soft mud and climbed a fence to escape deeper mud. Here is Jasper's home with Uncle John and Aunt Mary, his grandparents. Aunt Mary was a picture, with her sun browned face and white hair, smoking her pipe, with a large Bible in her lap. Behind her was a spinning wheel, making a suitable background. Between the puffs of smoke, she said many original things, being just brimful of fun. She is the "Charm Doctor" of the neighborhood. But we were not half way to the Sunday School yet. Jasper pulled us in his boat up to the mouth of "Yaller Creek." The high tide and going against the current made this a hard task. The water was rushing down, making a great sound. The trees were leaning out over the creek, so that we had to duck our heads. It took some "powerful polling" to land us. Jasper called out "Jump and hold the boat." Miss McNab jumped out and grasped the boat until we got out. Then he dragged it to a landing place, while she kept it in the stream with the long pole. To cross Yellow Creek we jumped from rock to rock part of the way and waded the rest, landing in some wet sand in which we sank to our shoe tops. After this the road was pretty good until we reached a sand bar, through which it was very difficult to walk. Turning a sharp curve we came upon the little log school house nestled in the hollow at the foot of two hills. A tall bell pole in front and an old fashioned boxed well between the house and the road. We were encouraged by the attendance and interest in the Sunday School. There were fifty present. Mr. Manton Cornet (our Mary's brother) said he had heard of Sunday Schools and had always wanted to go but had never had a chance before. He is forty-eight years old and brought his large family of children.

Several people stopped with the Stacy's for dinner. At two o'clock we started three miles up Montgomery for the afternoon Sabbath School. This is the roughest branch I know but very picturesque. More than half of the way the path is in the bed of the creek and we had to jump from one large rock to another. Soon we came to an old mill which is almost hidden from sight by the trees, vines and rocks. On one side of it is a waterfall. Looking up the creek there is a curve and the shadows of the trees and rocks falling on the water make it a scene of beauty indeed. On one side of this fall the path leads up a very steep and rocky hill to a level stretch where there are fallen trees to rest on in the shade. Then down again right into the creek to scramble over more rocks and here was perhaps the most beautiful spot of all. There were cascades running swiftly down on either side over ledges of rock, which in some places were covered with mosses, vines and ferns. We next passed a grove of beech trees where the sunlight, touching the top branches, lighted the whole grove, changing the color of the leaves to a pale, shimmering green. We reached the big, bare log school house after four and found forty people waiting for us. Someone said there were "a million" fleas in the school house, so we took the few crude benches out under the trees. Here is a wide valley, where the three streams unite to form Montgomery. There were some earnest people and they seemed pleased to have a

Sunday School. They were divided into four classes with Miss McCartney as leader. A storm was threatening so we hurried on, but it caught us just half way home. It was a picture I am sure to see us jumping from rock to rock, sometimes climbing great boulders or over fallen trees with thunder and lightning overhead and the rain coming down in torrents. There was not a dry thread on us when we reached home. Mrs. Cora Johnson from London, who is visiting her husband's people at the mouth of Breeding's Creek, seven miles away, came with some friends to see us this afternoon. She knew of me through the Circulating Libraries and came to ask us to locate a permanent school at the mouth of Breeding's Creek, where her daughter owned a farm, and offered to donate the land for it. Then she wanted us to go there next Sunday to hold a temperance meeting. She offered to come to the Sassafras school house immediately after the Sunday School for us and the organ and send us back the same night. We consented to go, although it means much extra work for us.

July 8.   We have a new department to our work, a Day Nursery, and I seem to be at the head of it. It came about in this way. Ida Francis, a sixteen year old mother, walked a mile and a half this afternoon around the slippery cliff with Sabrina May (named for Miss Stone), a seven months baby in her arms, to join the sewing class. I took charge of Sabrina May while the mother went to sew, regardless of her cries. I kept her until nearly six. I took her to the house and put her to sleep and then had to keep the flies from her. She was dreadfully broken out, so I bathed her and put talcum powder on. It was pathetic to see them start home, the mother with a smile, saying she would come to the sewing class all the time. Two young men "from over on Ball" spent the afternoon with us. One of them, a nice looking young fellow, could not read at all. Miss McCartney taught him a while and gave him a copy to practice writing and urged him to try to learn to read. Five men and boys who live ten miles away on the Kentucky River came. We showed them shells, games and pictures, but, like everyone else, they liked the organ and singing best and kept asking for more music. Miss McNab had a very encouraging beginning with the kindergarten. Eleven children came, were much interested and took hold of the songs readily. There were only three for the sewing class; one was Jasper, a grown boy with a mustache. His grandmother came and told Miss Stone if he "wouldn't behave himself and larn to sew well, jist to get a hickory stick and make him." Mrs. Godsey and her boy came early and had dinner with us. She seemed keen to know what we could teach her. Said she "wuz a sight glad that you uns who know has come to show us as don't know how." Her daughter wants "to go off with us" when we go home, so she can get to a good school. She came in while we were dressing and seemed pleased to see the way I buttoned my skirts to the waist; said she had always thought that women ought to dress "more healthy, but never knew how."

Jasper helped put up the swings and hammocks under the large trees in the little island in Montgomery, just in front of the house. This is a lovely spot with rippling water on each side. We enjoy it at twilight, when there is such a breeze that wraps are necessary. We call it Comfort Nook.

July 9.   A colored woman came early to do the washing under Miss McCartney's directions and it was a picturesque scene by the creek between the house and Comfort Nook. There was a great fire under the kettle heating the water and the merry sound of the battling of the clothes echoed from mountain to mountain. Mrs. Green and two girls came and wanted to learn to make light bread, but it was so late that we taught them how to make good soda biscuit instead. As we planned to make visits this afternoon we asked Mrs. Stacy to have early dinner. We were busy at the tent, when exactly at ten o'clock the bell rang and the surprising part of it was that we were hungry enough to enjoy the dinner. Miss McCartney attended to the washing, Miss McNab entertained visitors at the tent, while Mrs. Stacy,

Miss Stone and I went two miles up Red Oak Branch, climbing over large trees upturned by the storm, to see Mrs. Enoch Combs. It was a quaint thrifty place. Two queer old women, who work like slaves, live with them and they carry on a regular factory. The corn cribs were full–there seems to be a dearth of corn everywhere else–the porches hung with home made baskets filled with country products, the room upstairs containing beds and shelves with beautiful home-spun blankets, coverlids, linsey and jeans, all ready to be made up. She said she would make a black homespun dress for me and a red one for Miss Humphrey at fifty cents a yard. We asked her to try to get flax to weave us a linen dress. She went with us up the creek to her daughter's, where the boy is very ill with flux.[4] A crowd was around the bed and they were trying to make him drink black coffee, telling him that he would die if he did not take it. I suggested that the coffee was bad for him and they said that it was a sight to hear him pray, he was "so skeered he was going to die." Poor fellow, there hardly seemed to be a chance for him under so many difficulties. The father sat by the window with a big Bible, looking very serious. The baby, who had been sick, was much better and Mrs. Cody said that she felt that they owed its life to Miss McCartney who had told them how to care for it. We made several visits on the way home and waited at the post office for the mail. Jasper met us at the mouth of Yellow Creek with a boat and gave us a beautiful ride down in the twilight. We stopped to see Nanny Stacy, who is quite sick with flux. They sent to us for light bread for her. "Big Granny," Simon's grand-mother, who is eighty-nine years old, is hale and hearty and spends most of the time sitting on the front porch in a straight chair, fanning with a turkey wing. While we were at supper Jasper came with Sam Combs and said they were "plumb bound to have some music." So they went to the tent for the organ and joined in the singing. Miss McCartney was at the organ, Miss McNab holding the smoking lamp without the chimney and leaning over singing with all her soul. We had prayers in the twilight and when the clock struck eight they knew it was our bed time and left.

July 10.   Miss McNab and I had another struggle last night with fleas. This is an all absorbing subject now. I asked a woman what to do to get rid of fleas, she said, "jist keep from swearing, if you can." I spent part of the morning out on the loom house step writing and showing the colored woman how to do the ironing. Miss McNab was ironing at another table, Mr. and Mrs. Stacy stringing beans, while Miss Stone read a belated newspaper to us. It is cheering to see Mr. Stacy in so many ways help his wife. It is beautiful to see them together. After dinner the children and grown people began to come; eight in the sewing class and eight in the kindergarten. Jasper said, "I tell you what. I'm doin' splendid well for one who never did any sewing before." A mother came from the head of Montgomery to bring her children and "learn all she could." She was so interested in seeing the things and was delighted when I told her that she could choose some pictures to take home with her. The lame mother brought the baby and I took charge of her. She slept most of the time in the hammock, so there was no chance for the use of the castile soap which I had ready. The children are learning the songs so well and one little fellow sang one alone. Both classes were taught Bible verses and Miss McCartney had a class in music. While I was sitting out on the Montgomery rocks writing, Fernando Combs came by on a mule. He seemed delighted to see an old friend and told me with great pride that he had just stood the examination for a State certificate,[5] and told me of his year at the State college, of his struggle to make his way and how he would like to go through college if possible. While the others listened to the reading of *Black Rock* in the twilight, I have been writing this account of the day.

July 11.   I was out on the boulders in Montgomery by six this morning to get the temperance talk ready for the service Sunday. Worked on it until the dinner bell rang at ten-thirty. After dinner we wrote letters over at Comfort Nook–which we have very little time for these days–until visitors began to arrive, which is always soon after twelve. A fisherman, who is the disreputable "banjo picker" of the community, stopped by. They asked for the organ, went down to the tent for it and brought it over to Comfort Nook. Many others came, so that we had a large singing class. After that I took them to the tent, showed them "the sights" and let each of them choose a picture, which was a great delight to them. The stereoscope pictures are quite the most wonderful things many of them have seen and it is hard to convince them that such beautiful things are in the world. One woman told me the sad story of her husband's drunkenness, how she had talked with him but it had done no good. He is a bright handsome young fellow. I gave her a Bible, for she said that she had never had one nor her mother and father before her. William Cornet, a bright fourteen year old boy, told me that he often drank. I tried to get him to promise to give it up, but he did not seem to think that he could do it.

Miss McCartney made bread this morning and showed the wash woman how to make it. She gave her the first lesson in reading and also gave Mattie Combs a lesson on the organ. Judge Combs brought her down and said that she would like to go to Harlan again to school. He is so interested in education in the mountains and anxious to have his girls keep on at school and not "settle down at the head of the hollow with some man and go to hoeing corn and building fences." He talked very frankly about his only boy, who is sixteen years old, said he was on the road to ruin as fast as he could go, and that he would give all he possessed to get him away from here and in a school, where he could learn to work. I shall write to the Boy's Farm School at Asheville to see if he can get in. Judge Combs said that Ida had a good school but did not know anything of primary work and asked if some of us could go to her school and help her to get started. Miss McCartney and Miss McNab said that they would gladly help her. Ida will come down to the kindergarten class, help Miss McNab and thereby receive suggestions. Mattie and Ida Combs are the girls that the Lexington Women's Club sent to Harlan school last year, and we are so encouraged by the improvement in them and their home. Jasper seemed disappointed that this was not "sew day," said he "he didn't want to miss nary a time" and told everybody that came "how splendid well he was larning to sew." But he contented himself with nursing the babies. Miss Stone and Miss McNab went to see Nannie Stacy, who is better, then on up Stacy Branch a mile to see a family with five children. They found the mother very interesting. She said she had "heard tell of you uns, and had been aiming to come down with the young uns, but they had to hoe corn." She was having a gnat smoke[6] which is a very important proceeding in the mountains. She had heard of the organ and had told John that she wanted him to come down and hear "hit play." When asked how old a dirty but bright looking baby was, she said, "Waal people I don't know how old hit is." Miss Stone rode Simon's mule up to the post office and on up to Uncle Rob's to get little Florence Cornet and we are so glad to have a child in the house. Simon put half soles on my shoes today, so I think they will be able to stand the rocks.

July 12.   We had our room and tents in order and were out on the rocks by six o'clock to learn the temperance speech and Sunday School lesson. Pretty soon the mill whistle sounded up the creek and there came the men, women and children with turns of corn[7] on their nags. One boy called out as he passed. "We uns is all a comin' down after twelve to larn of you uns, now the crap is laid by." Such a forlorn looking figure came done the road by herself. She proved to be Armilda Brown, Judge Combs' married daughter, who had sent for me to come up today "after twelve" and when she heard that I could not go, she hurried down to see us. She said that she had "such a sorry time fixin'" up for us as she wanted to be clean when we came. She has had a very sick baby and said, "hit has been trying to die for a month and hit peared like hit was goin' to leave me. I've been all destroyed up in my mind, since I was eight years old, when I had brain trouble from over study. We married relations we did, we wuz one another's first cousins but 'taint right to do that way so scripture says." She took dinner with us, and when I took her to the tent her face lighted up as she said, "hit seems the brightest time in my life." There were fifty people here this afternoon, eighteen for sewing, eighteen for kindergarten, some for a singing class and the rest were visitors and fathers who seemed so pleased to see what their children were doing. One man asked for some kind of a history to read to his boys. Many of the books have been taken out and some returned with a request for more already. The men seemed to enjoy the singing and finally joined in. Miss McNab had the long kindergarten table moved down under the cliff by the creek and sand bank. It was much more successful there and the children did good work. The members of the sewing class are learning the Lord's Prayer and Jasper has been telling everybody that he has "quit cussing." Some of the trustees were here and we had talked with them about having the classes at the school after school begins, which they think will be well. The Day Nursery department was quite in evidence today. Sabrina May was the only baby but I had pan, warm water, castile soap, talcum powder and soft clothes and while the mother was busy sewing I undertook to give her a bath, but found I could not manage it alone, so had to call Miss McCartney from her singing class to assist me. We gave her a beautiful bath and to all appearances she had never had such a thorough one before. How she laughed and enjoyed it!

July 13.   Jasper came "by peep of day" to help us move the things out of the supply tent and dig a ditch around it. We had never had a chance before to get the grounds about the camp in order. He cut the tall weeds and we picked them up without a rake, moved the stones and had Jasper dig out steps out of the steep bank and roll a log in front of the fence to make it easier to climb. Four young boys stopped in the road just in front of the camp and passed a bottle around. While we were placing stepping stones and making an easier climb to Comfort Nook we had the primitive picture of Rhoda washing the wool in a basket in the middle of the creek. She held up her dress showing her red linsey skirt, while she pressed the wool in the basket with her feet. She and Mrs. Stacy sheared this wool from the sheep that had been out in the mountains since last fall and could not be found at the regular sheep shearing time. Rhoda Combs, a fourteen year old girl, is a very important member of this household. She has just lived from "here to yander" until a year and a half ago when she came to Mr. and Mrs. Stacy and said she wanted to live with them, because she heard that they would be good to her. They were glad to take her and treat her as they would a daughter. She has proved invaluable to them, working in the fields and helping in every way. She is bright and attractive, has Titian hair and sings many of the old ballads. We could not do without Rhoda. By three o'clock Jasper was back, ready to carry the organ to the school house on George's branch where we were to have the Saturday afternoon Sabbath School. The trustees do not believe in Sunday Schools[8] and let us know early in the week that the house would not be open to us. But we decided to have it anyway under the Sycamore trees. It was only a mile and a half to this place but a very rough way to get there. First we had to be "sot across Carr on a nag," then an easy walk on the road winding under an overhanging cliff through tall weeds, then across the creek again, this time on an insecure fence rail from the bank to the root of a great upturned tree and down another rail over swiftly flowing water to a rock bar and then a jump over rocks to the other side. Jasper with the organ on his shoulders did not have as hard a time crossing as we did. We found forty-five people waiting for us under the trees. Miss McCartney took charge and divided the Sunday School into four classes, as at the other schools. The organ was a great help, they so enjoyed the music, but were slow to join in the singing, as their way is so different from ours. Most of them were absolutely ignorant of the Bible, many families had never had one. Everything was new to them and they were so intensely interested. One ten year old boy in Miss McNab's class wore only one garment, a very short shirt, and it was torn and greasy. He was not at all conscious of being different from the others and children often go to school dressed in that way. Another of her boys had a huge twist of tobacco in his pocket. This class, when asked about Jesus, did not know who he was, had never heard the story or the name except in a profane way. I had a class of girls, one of them, Louisa Sumner, not yet sixteen, had been married and parted from her husband a long time, she told me. A rain came up but we kept the organ dry with umbrellas. Mrs. Mullins, who objects to Sunday Schools, sent word to know if we would stop with the organ on our way home and sing some for her. Then we went to visit the objecting trustee who was very cordial but said nothing about Sunday Schools. Two boys helped Jasper carry the organ home, one they called "Jess' Bill." He is the terror of the neighborhood and shows in his face what a bad boy he is, not yet twenty but he has been married and "parted from his wife." Every Saturday night all the "bad uns" around here "hev a gathering" where they pick the banjo, dance, drink moonshine, swear and fight. They stay all night and go home Sunday morning drunk and shooting down the road. We reached home at twilight with our arms full of rhodo-dendron and laurel.

July 14.   We were up early this morning and out on the rocks to study the Sabbath School lesson. It was diverting to see Rhoda and Mrs. Stacy get ready for Sunday School. They came to us often to help them tie the ribbons about their hair and neck and see if they were all right. When we were ready they mounted the mules to ride, while we walked, for they wore their good store shoes and walking on the rocks would ruin them. Jasper came for the organ. Quite a number of boys were in hand when we reached the school house, we began promptly at nine and before we were through the house was filled. I had a class of very responsive boys on the steep hill side under the trees. After the close we waited for the wagon to take us to the temperance meeting at the mouth of Breeding's Creek. But as it did not come the people waited and we sang until eleven o'clock, when Jasper brought us down Carr in a boat.

Soon after dinner visitors began to come notwithstanding we had requested them not to come on Sunday. They begged for music, but we had to start up Montgomery for the afternoon Sunday School. Judge Combs left one of his horses, which Miss McCartney and Miss McNab rode. We had a beautiful little service under the trees and the people seemed loath to leave. They wanted to talk to us but we had to hurry home, for it is all we can do to get home before dark. They told us that the young people had spent the day picking the banjo and dancing in the school house. Miss Stone has a pedometer so we know every night just how far we have walked. On Sundays it registers ten to twelve miles.

July 15.   We spent the morning rearranging the books, periodicals and pictures at the tent. Uncle Rob Cornet and some of his sons came and seemed so pleased to see the shells, pictures, etc. Mr. Manton Cornet met Mr. Stacy on the road and told him that he was going to see "them women" but did not have any excuse. He said his great grandfather came to this country from Virginia on horseback with his young wife. They had a bundle of jeans and when the Indians got after them, as they were crossing Big Black Mountain, they let the jeans fall and could hear it roll until it got to the bottom. His wife sat there with his head in her lap all night and the next morning he traced the jeans by the path it made through the underbrush until he found it. He told us how he secured his first school. When he went to the County Superintendant for his certificate, he told him to go on and get a school and he would come around to examine him. He came one day after school began, called him out and said, "Can you read?" "Yes, sir." "Can you write?" "Yes, sir." "Here is your certificate."

Chloe Combs, a nice looking fourteen year old girl, came with her little niece to spend the day. They were delighted with everything we showed them. Finally she said, "Come all you uns and go down to Jasper Mullins with me." "What are you going there for?" "To get Sal some bacco," was the reply. "Who is Sal?" "She is my Mammy." I took charge of the tent in the afternoon. Among the visitors was Tucker Roark, a boy twenty years old, who has been married "and parted from his woman." He is studying law now and has a great ambition to be a fine lawyer. When Miss McCartney came home we had a singing class. Miss Stone and Miss McNab walked up to the Sassafras school house in the hot sun for the sewing and kindergarten classes. School began there today with fourteen pupils, but more came for their classes. Robert Kelly, the young teacher, joined the sewing class. Miss Stone read from *The Story of the Bible* while they were sewing. It was a picture to delight the heart of the kindergartner to see the children seated in a circle on the hillside working away so industriously, talking most of the time in an excited whisper about their work. Some large boys said they could make chains all day. They seemed timid until they began to play, when their faces would light up and the laughter ring out. The play life of the child is cramped. They go early into the corn field and from there to the school room about the middle of July. These children are as bright and intelligent as any we have ever seen and all they need is a chance.

July 16.   We were up by daylight, all of us hurrying to get off for a day's tramp up Montgomery. We walked fifteen miles and made eleven visits and this has been the hottest day we have had this season. At each home there were many children and Miss McNab made pin wheels, sang and told them stories. At Jordan Smith's the children had on short shirts and that was all. A ten year old boy was all eagerness to make the bright colored wheel and fairly danced up and down in his delight. One mother asked for paper to make one to put on the gate, so that the people would have something to look at. In one cabin we found some very primitive home-made furniture, a three legged table, the top of it a large stone hollowed out for a wash pan, and the cradle was a rough box nailed to the rockers. Dr. Roark and his wife had asked us to come for dinner and pick blackberries. After some visits and long steep climb up the mountain, in the neighborhood of a moonshine still, we reached there just at eleven, the usual hour for dinner up here. We found the doctor, whom one would naturally expect to have clean and wholesome surroundings, living in the midst of as much dirt as the average mountaineer. The patient, stupid looking wife had a very greasy dinner for us, while the eight children stood around to watch us eat it. Dr. Roark has become a very familiar figure to us as he journeys down Montgomery on his way to see the sick folk on his nag, dressed in a black Prince Albert coat and a high silk hat. After dinner, sitting by a large table covered with medical books, he talked in a very learned way of the vast medical knowledge he had received in Louisville, and seemed eager to discuss the ways of the outside world with us. All the time we could not help wondering why he did not take the little paper labels from his spectacles. They all gathered about us while we sang for them and then we climbed another hill to a fine blackberry patch where Miss McCartney and Miss McNab for the first time picked from the bushes. We filled two buckets to bring home with us.

On the way home we stopped to see Armilda Brown, who lives in the windowless one room log cabin. The two children were sick in bed and she was cooking supper on a big stove in the room. Mr. Brown's grown brother and sister were there and Nan Adams stopped to stay all night, so that made seven in that room with the sick children, cooking stove and no windows. The paper flowers and the way she had arranged the pictures we gave her showed some artistic taste. In this same room is the post office called Kodak, but we could see no place where mail was kept. Mr. Brown walks and carries the mail twice a week up Montgomery in a bag over his shoulders. Many were the stories we heard of the condition of things up that branch, how the boys would insult the girls, of the fighting between wives and husbands, and oh, it was fearful all that we heard.

July 17.   By seven o'clock Miss McCartney was at the Sassa-fras school house to teach singing and to show the teacher how to conduct devotional exercises. By eight the tent was full of men, women and children. Miss McNab had five women learning to weave picture frames out of raffia. They were intensely interested and one woman said, "If I had time I would make lots of this truck." When the frames were finished they put in pictures of George Washington and they went home very proud of their morning's work. They are quick to learn, nimble with their fingers and glad of any suggestion to improve their homes. I cared for the babies while the mothers worked. There were some to sew this morning. Nan Adams was here most of the morning. We are trying to get a hold on her. No one has a good word for her, but we feel there is something in her. While she was here the man and his wife who had had a fight over her Sunday came. We thought there would be a scene but they all worked quietly. Mrs. Johnson and Miss Hilton came from the mouth of Breeding's Creek to explain why she did not send for us on Sunday. Her nephew (who was to bring the wagon) simply failed to come without any reason, which she said was the usual way these people did things. As she went home I rode behind her on the mule to the post office and then walked back to the school, and it was a pretty sight to see the young people sewing on the steep hillside back of the log school house. Miss Stone and Miss McNab had started early in the afternoon. When they reached the boat Jasper was not in sight, but after a loud call he appeared and they were glad to have the boat ride instead of the trudge through the hot sand. There were twenty five in the classes. Ben Feltner, a grown boy, said to be crazy and very rude, said he didn't need to sew as he aimed to have a woman to sew for him. But later he was persuaded to work. Jasper has gotten to be the assistant teacher. It was diverting to watch him and Ailsie (the girl he is in love with) helping each other. A frog was hopping about and Robert Kelley said, "You had better get away froggie, or Miss Stone will have you sewing, too, everybody here must work." It is always hard to get them started home. Robert Stacy, a grown boy, said that he could not go until he had finished his row.

July 18.   Della Roark came about seven this A.M. to spend her eleventh birthday with us. She said, "when I came across the dark hollow mountain I seed the little yaller birds a skipping and a hopping." She is quick and alert and wore her hair in a tight knot on her head and wore a pink calico shirt waist and a long black skirt touching the ground. She told us that she cooked, washed, milked, hoed corn, and "holp maw sew," that she could rein a nag as well as any man and beat the boys up her creek hoeing corn. In an innocent way she told us much of the immorality of the people up Montgomery, that the girls and boys at her school were so bad that she "never goes with ems." It is sad to think how much of the evil in the world these children hear and know. We had many visitors all day and gave out a great number of pictures and books. Mrs. Tom Gent from the head of George's Branch said that she heard that we had a piece with seven patches on it and you couldn't tell it. Tucker Roark told us that the Sheriff had been after Nan Adams all night and that she, Peggy McIntire and Louisa Sumner, had threatened to kill a man, that they had knife and were after him. Louise Sumner is in my Sunday School class. Ever since we heard of the "gatherins" at Al Sumner's on Saturday nights, we have been wondering what we can do to show them how the young people can meet in a social way and have a good time, without doing the dreadful things they do. So we told Jasper that we would give him a social this evening at the Camp. He sent many of his invitations by Nan Adams but as she had to "hide out" all night in the woods she did not get to deliver them. Fifteen came, however; we played games and sang until nine o'clock. They entered heartily into the spirit of the games and as they seemed to be willing to play on all night, which is the custom here, we had prayers and bade them good night.

July 19.   Friday is mill day and we have more visitors than usual from far and near. They began to come this morning before six. Mrs. Godsey, over seventy, brought her turn of corn to the mill and then came here to learn to make bread. Said she never got too old to learn. Miss McCartney also helped Mrs. Brashears to make a dress, for everybody has been "fixin' for meetin'" all week, such dressing, scrubbing and baking pies. We are in a great state of excitement, too, for it is to be a funeral occasion. Ben Feltner, one of the desperate boys, had a fainting spell here today. Miss McCartney took charge of him, put him to bed and gave him medicine. Many new boys came and some picked the banjo for Miss McNab. One man asked for pictures to take to his daughter in Virginia.

About eight o'clock Armilda Combs came in great haste for Mrs. Stacy to "come go up on Yaller Creek to strip little Corie Combs" who died this morning of the flux. She said that it was impossible for her to go and as everybody else was afraid to go and they wanted to "put the child away today or she would mortify" Miss Stone and I offered to go. We asked what we would have to do and she said make the clothes, line and cover the coffin, strip and wash the child and put her in it. We took thread, needles and thimbles and started out walking. Uncle Jim Stacy let us have a big, sharp-backed, stubborn mule, which we had some difficulty to mount, but he told us to "brusk hit up a bit and hit would go." When we reached Mrs. Anderson Combs' she told us that the aunt of the child had been to the store to get goods for the burial clothes but could not get anything white and that she had gone to another store way yon side the mountain, so Miss Stone went back on the mule to the Camp for some white muslin, while I walked on up to Mr. Fielding Combs' the home of the child. It was at the head of a very deep, narrow and lonely hollow, parts of which it is impossible for the sun to reach. I found the little two roomed cabin in dirt and disorder. The child was lying on the bed just as she had died. The family were so grieved. I talked with them a while and read from the Bible. As they had no Bible I gave it to the father and he promised to read it to his family every day. The mother gave careful directions as to how to make the burial clothes. The dress must come to the shoe tops, the underskirt must have pretty hamburg[9] on it and come an inch below the dress. She was sorry the shoes that had been sent did not fit and said when they got across the mountain to the store, that she would buy some and put them on her "cause she was a mighty hand for shoes when she could git 'em 'cause she loved 'em so." I went back to Mrs. Anderson Combs' to meet Miss Stone and help make the clothes. On the way I met Mrs. Ritchie, the aunt who had been to the store for the things. She looked tired and forlorn, her heavy suit of hair hanging down her back un- combed. She had "had a mighty sorry time a getting the burying clothes." They did not have anything but the cheap ugly black and white lawn, but they did not want to let her have that because she did not have the money, but a man told the store keeper that "the law was fer letting a body her burying clothes" and so she got them. She went back with me and while waiting for Miss Stone, we began on the underclothes. She asked me to notch the skirt[10] instead of hemming it, and when I told her I did not know how, she said, "Why I lowed you 'uns would be mighty powerful hands for notchin'." But I was glad to learn, for it seemed an easy way. Miss Stone came with material and made the dress and cap: She wanted a mother hubbard[11] "fer we don't like none of them long waists." We persuaded her not to have any cheap lace on it. She was very careful to have two ruffles of lace on the cap and two strings to tie in a bow. When the men came with the coffin for us to line, they said it would push them to get the burying over before night, so we suggested that they line it. They covered the plain wooden box with cheap black cambric and lined it with "bleach"[12] and put cotton lace around the edge of it. We had to make and fill a pillow. Mrs. Ritchie then brought out some deep purple and bright watermelon pink ribbon and asked me to make six "mighty pretty bows" for the coffin lid. All this shows that our mountain friends are just as careful about the conventionalities of life as we are. When all was ready the men shouldered the coffin and we all started to the sad little home. I never in my life shrank so much from doing anything and all the way up, I kept wishing and wondering how we could escape the ordeal. Nothing had been done, the child was lying on the bed just as she had died. The mother asked at once to see the clothes, showed them to the father and they thought them very fine, but she began to cry because she knew the cap would be too small. She then asked us to "strip" little Corie and fix her nice, said please to be easy and comb her hair many times with a fine tooth comb, gently as possible. She gave us a little black tucking comb to do her hair up with and said that she didn't want the hair to hang around the ears because Corie never liked it that way. We took clothes and soap with us, and they gave us the dish pan, which was the only pan they had, filled with warm water. Then it took all the courage we had to lift the sheet and there lay a sweet looking fair haired child. She had been sick for a week and had on the same little dirty dress she wore when she went to bed. We got it off, washed her, combed her hair and when she was dressed in the white she looked very pretty. When she was ready to put in the coffin, the mother and father came, they thought she was so beautiful and ex-pressed much pleasure and gratitude. She had us to put cotton in the bottom of the coffin to make it soft and they collected an old pewter spoon "which hit loved so" and a picture card to put in the coffin. The aunt pinned fancy brass breast pins all over the front of her dress. All this time the aunt was spread out on the floor with her hair streaming over her face and shouting at the top of her voice. The grandmother, Suze, broke forth in the most terrible shouts and with much loud crying and shrill voices, it was something terrific. She asked us to sing a song and then they all started out walking, a most pathetic little procession, the mother carrying a heavy baby. Just as she left she went to the cupboard, took down the old quart whiskey bottle which had two sticks of candy in it and said that she was going to keep it always because "Corie loved it so." She said once more that she was going to buy a pair of shoes and put them in the coffin when they got across the mountain because "they would still be shoes here after they were all dead and gone." We left them as they started across the mountain. They urged us to go with them but we had to hurry on down to the Sassafras school house where we found Miss McNab and the children waiting for us. I read to them while they were sewing and then walked up for the mail. This has certainly been a trying day and we are both unnerved and more tired than we have ever been.

July 20.   Some of our nights are as full of incident as the days, but last night was unusually so. After a good fleaing, we went to bed as usual at eight o'clock, and as usual the fleas troubled us all during the night. The flea powder and carbolic acid water having no effect before two o'clock, Miss McNab in sheer desperation decided to use pure carbolic acid, but it was not long before she had to call for help. And we got up immediately, trying to relive her badly burned neck and chest. While we were using various remedies the clock struck half past two, and seeing a light outside we looked out the window and there sat Mrs. Stacy and Rhoda peeling apples for breakfast. She had "meeting' in her bones" and said she just couldn't sleep, so she not only got up herself but awakened Rhoda and made her get up to keep her company.

This is the first meeting day since last summer and people from many miles around began to come early and most of them stopped by to see us. The tent was full of new people who were much entertained with the pictures, shells and books, and listening to Miss McNab sing. All of them took literature with them. At twelve we went over to the preaching, which was in Uncle Jim Stacy's orchard, where rough plank seats had been arranged under the trees. Uncle Ira Combs, the most noted preacher in "these parts," was on hand and preached at great length. During the very long prayer, Mrs. Stacy kept nudging me to look at the "widder." "The widder" was Bill Stacy, whose wife died just a year ago and it was her "funeral occasion." He married four months later and the wife came to comfort him. At the close of the service, those who lived near got up and said "Ever body that will go and stay all night with me will be welcome." The people who came from a distance gladly accepted these generous invitations. At four o'clock we went to George's Branch school house for Sunday School and Jasper carried the organ on horse back. One day this week Mr. Grace, one of the trustees, brought us a most remarkable looking "flower pot"–it was a long blooming hollyhock stalk, with various other blossoms tied on to it with strings. We thought that meant the school house would be open to us, so we were not surprised today when they came with the keys and invited us in. It was so much pleasanter under the trees, and we are so used to the out of door life, that we said we would stay out unless it rained, then we would be glad for the use of the school house. Those who are here for the meeting came to Sunday School and some of the girls from one of Mr. Rainey's Sunday Schools helped very much with the singing. It meant much to us for the people here to see that some of the mountain people sing our way. One of these visitors, an old man from "over on Betty's Troublesome" asked for a Bible with large print as he had trouble with his eyes, and we were fortunate to be able to give him just what he wanted, for a friend had sent one and asked us to give it to someone who needed the large print. While we were teaching the classes, Nan Green, fifteen years old, with her satchel, and Spencer Combs, one of the County teachers, with a long shotgun over his shoulder, passed by. Polly Ann, a twelve year old girl, said in a loud whisper, "Do you know that she follows that all the time?" "Follows what?" "Follows the road all the time and lays out nights. I would take an axe and chop my head off before I would do anything like that." The walk home on the bank of the Carr in the twilight was lovely. Floyd and Dishman Combs, half grown boys from the mouth of Carr, came with us to spend the night. Dishman's father has just died and left him in charge of his mother and eight younger children. This woman is thirty-two years old and the mother of nine children. Think of it! Dishman says he "aims" to be a teacher soon, and he told me of his desire to help his mother in every way.

July 21. We have walked twelve miles today, which is just what we do every Sunday. Going to Sassafras Sunday School we met crowds of people on foot, horseback and in wagons hurrying down to Uncle Jim Stacy's orchard to meeting. Some of them stopped with us for Sunday School and then we all went down to the meeting. On the seats under the trees were gathered perhaps a hundred people. Others were grouped around trees near by, the men talking politics or "horse-swapping," the girls and boys sauntering around and the boy with his saddle pockets of moonshine trying to sell it. These funeral occasions are not so depressing as one would naturally expect. They are really the only time the people have for general meeting and diversion and they are looked forward to from year to year. The funeral of all who die during the year in one neighborhood are preached at one big meeting in the summer. And we have attended funerals of those who have been dead ten years. There is not a "church house" within ten miles of here and this is the first religious meeting held here for a year. Many of the people never heard a sermon except by these uneducated mountain preachers. And up in Montgomery there has been no religious service for three years, and some of the people of our Sunday School there told us that they had not heard a sermon for five years. Today in the front row near the preacher, sat the "Bereaved widder" and his wife, both under one torn umbrella, which she held while she fanned him with his hat. Part of the time he sat with his elbows on this knees and his head in his hands and then rested his head on her shoulder, while they both wept. She wore a heavy red and green woolen dress, trimmed in various colored velvet, ribbon and silk, a heavy blue felt hat and a long green calico apron.

Extracts from Uncle Ira's sermon:

My neighbors and my neighbors' children, we have met upon a funeral occasion. May our meeting be done in decency and good order and now let us draw in the wandering and scattering parts of our minds. Let us be unstripped of self and carnality, people under the shadow of my voice. Friend Stacy is not the only widder that's been left, many is a mourning over thar companions. (Loud weeping). I've got my third companion, I've suffered with him and sympathize with him and can't help it. I want to say to Brother Stacy, no friend Stacy, that Sister Liz lies out yander on dry pint and her soul is lingering around the altar. Is she visible in Heaven? She is invisible in carnal shape. She's gone whar no more consumption never comes and Jesus with the handkerchief of his love will wipe all eyes. I believe there is a crown fur Sister Liz and she is wearing hit today. Friend Stacy, if you never find God and he snatches life from you today, you'll never meet Liz in the upper world. Let me ask a question of the friends and relatives of Sister Liz, how many feel to meet her? I don't say as I would meet her but I am proud to be with those who have hope to meet her. Here will come the body of Sister Liz when Gabriel sounds the alarm, not a <u>natural</u> and carnal body but a spiritual body. We'll meet Sister Liz thar. Whar air ye goin' sinner man and sinner woman? Some may say, You've got another woman and Friend Stacy has got another woman, what will you do in Heaven, but thar is no marriage nor giving in marriage thar. I don't know whether your companion ever saw mine but they are acquainted now.

Unless I have another mind, I won't talk to you long. I've just got to follow my mind on a funeral occasion. (He talked just an hour and a half longer.)

Satan tempted the woman for she was then as now the weaker vessel. The Lord asked Eve why she et the forbidden fruit and she said–just like you, my good sister– (pointing at one) that the devil made her do it, and the Lord punished her by making her bring forth children all the days of her life. (In the midst of rhythmic monotone in a high key, he took off his coat saying): I've allus heard it was bad manners to take off your coat at meeting, but I'm going to take mine off, and I'm not mad either. (After a time, in another rhapsody, he searched his trousers' pockets, then picked up his coat and got out a black silk handkerchief to mop his face and said) Let me try to control myself. God is a sperit and religion is a sperital thing and only changes the sperital part of man. It has no effect on the nateral and carnal. We all know the soul inside of us is sanctified but these people that talk about the nateral and carnal body being sanctified has the wrong idee. Now brethern go slow in bad places, for them that do not believe shall be damned. (One time, he quoted Scripture wrong and said) Now brethern, wait until I get that right, I'm might awkerd. Now while that's on my mind I'll say something about it, (and then did not mention it.) I believe religion can be tasted and can be felt. When the golden bowl overflowed, it emptied into the golden candlestick through the golden pipe and did not rust. May God dig about our hearts with the maddock [mattock][13] of his love and break up the fiery grounds to take root downwards and bring forth fruit upwards. (Looking toward us) If these strange preachers come around with their strange doctrine with a gold watch in their pocket and a white shirt so slick that a fly would slip up and bust his brains out, don't have anything to do with 'em. (No one smiled) but if any man comes to your door, poor, even if you don't know who he is, take him and keep him. I think thar's been fourteen children born at my house and they never wanted for bread. I have little ones, too, for I've had the luck to get married three times. When I come to die, if I thought you, brother Mullins, would let 'em go hungry, I'd die mighty dissatisfied. (No enthusiastic response from brother Mullins). I feel now to give away and let brother Felix preach to the people. I've said all I want to and I'll stop. I lied to you before when I said I'd stop, but I won't lie again. Now, brother Felix you git up to speak and when you haven't got no more to say, set down.

Extracts from Prayer:

If hit is Thy will, let a smile from between the Cherubim rest upon us. May thy love be in motion, as I fore remarked. We've been called out on a sad occasion to say comfortable words to her companion, who has asked me and other to come and speak about her. Comfort him with the down pouring of Thy spirit and may this be a mighty day with him. Show him the line that is drawn between him and her that is gone, if he has not the hope to believe. May her dying words be preaching to him.

At the close of the sermons (for they were many) there was shrill singing and much shouting. Then funeral occasions were "denounced"[14] in other neighborhoods up until November and the people were asked to "norate" them about. The eighteen year old boy who had been selling moonshine came forward and "denounced" that his wife's funeral would be "tended" to in two weeks. Uncle Ira closed the funeral service by saying: "Prudence would say come to a dismission. If all hearts are clear, we'll call on God to be dismissed."

After all this, we should have liked a quiet dinner and time to rest before the start up Montgomery, but among others, a terrible looking old woman, with a pretty, bright girl, came "just to see you uns." She told us that the Kuklux had whipped her and her husband in May, that Leslie Whittiker (the eighteen year old "widder" who sold the moonshine at the funeral occasions) was at the head of the band, that her two boys had secured a shotgun and pistol and were ready to waylay him and kill him. She was in great trouble, as she had just heard that the Kuklux band were forming and getting ready for a fight.

We had a good Sunday School up Montgomery, the boys knew the Lord's Prayer and had studied their lessons. We look forward all the week to the walk down Montgomery in the twilight. Nothing could be more charming. On the way home we ate blackberries from the bushes and stopped to see Aunt Peggy Combs, the grandmother of Montgomery. She gave us a bit of her varied life, how no one had ever lived up Montgomery until sixty years ago, when she and her husband settled there at the beginning of their married life. Miss McNab sang for her. We reached home just at dark, found Jasper waiting for music and tired as Miss McNab was she sang for him a long time. We were so grieved to hear that our Jasper had gotten into trouble at a gathering last night. We were told that he had behaved so badly the old folks put him out and told him never to come there again. When he came to bring the organ home this evening we told him how badly we felt over it and he said, "he never did nothing but dance, after the old folks had begged him to, but they jist made him hit the rock-bar any way, so he don't aim to go back on George's Branch to no more parties." So we told him to come here on Saturday evenings to sing.

July 22.   The picture in the front yard presents a busy scene now at four o'clock in the afternoon. Mr. and Mrs. Stacy are spooling cotton thread to make the chain for weaving. Miss Stone has a yard full of visitors learning to patch. When a woman or girl comes to stay very long and won't talk we put her to sewing and she usually wants to come back after the first lesson. This morning we moved everything out of the bedroom and had the floor scrubbed. At seven Miss McCartney was at the Sassafras school for singing and the Bible, and shortly after eight, she called to me from across the creek and we went to visit up George's Branch. The Greens live so far from the road we had to go up a dark ravine, across a hill, through a valley and around a mountain, following a path that was not very plain at times. At the head of a beautiful cove, we found a miserable little cabin. On the broken planks that were laid loosely across to form the porch was an old cooking stove and in front of it on a plank sat three dirty rag dolls. Mrs. Green was in this wretched little dark room making up bread and the old man was standing by. The two children were ill. They urged us to come in, but I did not think we could possibly stand it, so suggested that we have chairs out in the tobacco patch which came right up to the door. This could have been such an attractive place, with the cool breezes, but the smells were such that we could not stay long. Mr. Green, over eighty, gave a very sad account of his life. He also told us the pleasure that the books from our Circulating Library had been to him. His wife–the third one–an indolent dirty woman, while leaning up against the fence with a pipe in her mouth, told of her ailments and of her grief because her daughter was going to ruin. She was then off singing with Louisa Sumner. One of the visits that was of interest was with the grandmother of "Jess' Bill," an old woman who many years ago had a startling dream which stopped her from cussing and made a change in her life. She said, "Wimmen, I jist want to know, what air ye all in these hyar parts fer, hev ye any business, did ye jist come up to look around fer a spell and then go away and never come back? What is you uns here fer any way?" I replied, simply here to spend the summer to learn all we can and teach all we can. And she said "Waal now, hit sounds reasonable."

At the school house we received a very cordial greeting from Mr. Bob Combs, the teacher, who had met me several years ago at Hazard. He urged us to come down to teach and show him all the things that we could, saying, "My time is your time, and I want to learn all I can." He sent word for Miss Stone and Miss McNab to come today at one o'clock and have the entire afternoon. When we reached home, the thermometer stood at one hundred in the shade and we were completely exhausted after a six miles tramp in the sun. Miss McNab had been entertaining visitors at the tent all morning and just in front of it we found some of the Montgomery boys, Cisco Summer, my Sunday School pupil, was picking the banjo. After a few words we went on to the house and the boys started up Montgomery. Soon four men came rushing through the back gate and said they had a warrant to arrest Cisco. Mr. Bob Combs, the teacher, is also deputy sheriff, so he has dismissed his school for the rest of this week, and is ready to go to Virginia, if necessary, to arrest a number of girls and boys for whom he has gone bond. They took Mr. Stacy's shotgun and started running up the branch in pursuit of the boys. They especially wanted to find Nan Adams but she, being warned, had slipped to the woods and hidden. These coves and rocks furnish fine places for hiding.

July 23.   Mr. H. Brashears brought us a chicken and said "the old woman sent hit." She also sent Miss McCartney a beautiful pair of white woolen mitts. It was very warm and we were glad to have the ride with Jasper in the boat, but the walk through the sand bar burned our feet. While Miss Stone and Miss McNab had the classes, I went on to the head of the branch where the colored people live and visited them all. I found five cases of flux and the condition of the homes was wretched. It was late when I reached the school house, and while the class was still sewing Leslie Whittaker and Robert Stacy helped us put pictures and flags on the walls and hang colored paper chains, which the children had made. The teacher was so pleased with the appearance that he swept the room himself while we were there. How we did enjoy the ride home in the boat at twilight, reading our mail. Just a year ago Miss Stone and I spent our first night here, and out on the rocks in Montgomery we planned to spend this summer with Mrs. Stacy.

July 24.   I saw visitors, gave out Bibles, pictures, and periodicals all day. Miss McCartney was at the school house early as usual. Miss Stone and Miss McNab walked through the hot sand to their classes. Mr. and Mrs. Stacy "spooled" all day. Very hot, but we need blankets every night.

July 25.   We left early to spend the day upon Sassafras branch. Mrs. Stacy and Miss McNab rode John, the mule, and Miss Stone and I walked thirteen and one-half miles and made seven visits. The Cornets are all clean and thrifty. We had been invited to take dinner with Mrs. Manton Cornet. They had a good dinner, beautiful honey and whole wheat biscuit from the wheat they had raised themselves. He is the most intelligent and best read man, besides being the best farmer in "these parts." There were other visitors and they gave us a full history of the post office robbery. One man said, "I wouldn' hev thought that Granville would hev done the like of that, he has taught school and he has got a good head piece." Mrs. Jasper Cornet had a house full of very bright, attractive children. The father is an invalid and the burden of the family falls on Ailsie, the eighteen year old daughter, who does the plowing and clearing away of new land. Now that their crop is laid by she is hired out. Mrs. Cornet gave us a beautiful homespun tow linen towel. Mrs. Madden and Mrs. Owens gave us two homemade brooms and Mr. Owens a drinking gourd. At the head of the branch, we found Mrs. Kelly with six girls under ten years of age and three of them were idiots. We tried to persuade the mother to send them to Frankfort to the Feeble Minded Institute, but she said "hit peared like she jist couldn't give 'em up." Mrs. Riley Combs, who has three such nice boys, said: "I jist can't git 'em away from you uns, when ye have any doin's going on." We reached home just at dark and found that Miss McCartney's day had been just as full. After her early morning class at the school house, she went to show Mrs. Watson Combs how to make light bread, then up the branch to see the sick folks, and entertained a tent full of company all afternoon.

July 26.   Mill day again, which always means many visitors. Early in the morning, two women came to learn to make light bread. Miss McCartney and Miss McNab went up to the Montgomery school for classes this afternoon, found many of the mothers there to join them. On the way home they picked blackberries and brought enough for breakfast and supper. We have just heard that the doctor says the child at Judge Combs' has either smallpox or scarlet fever. The people are going there in great crowds, so that every chance is given to spread the disease. Many visitors in the afternoon, whom I had to entertain. Jasper has been trying to get four mules to take us to Hindman to-morrow and says we "must get the nags all mustered up tonight."

July 27.   Hindman. We were up by day break to start to Hindman for the Institute. Of the four mules we had engaged, only two were on hand, and after waiting quite a while for the two that Mr. Brashears promised to have there by daylight, Miss McCartney and Miss McNab mounted John and went ahead to see old Mrs. Kelly who is ill. Miss Stone and I took the other and started to see what had become of Jasper. We found him sitting on a log wondering why the nags did not come. We suggested to him to take one mule and go see. We sat on the road side more than an hour waiting for him, while many people came by on horseback going to meeting on the head of Carr. Among them was Mason Combs and his mother. He is now a fine manly looking young fellow of eighteen, has a first class certificate, a good school and is "aiming" to go to Louisville to study medicine in January. When Jasper did appear he had only one mule, said that Mr. Brashears was working with the other one, regardless of the promise to let us have it. We were sorry that we had not taken Jasper's advice and "mustered in the nags" last night. We started on, two of us on the same mule, whose back was so sharp that I preferred walking. We tried to hire a nag at every house we passed, and after going six miles to the mouth of Irishman, secured one. We reached

Hindman in time for dinner, and while we were to our room, there was a timid knock at the door and Mabel Smith, who has scarlet fever, walked in. Many of the children here have it and are going about the streets peeling off. We went down Troublesome to see our old friend, Mrs. Sturdivant, who told us that she loved us most as much as she loved her tobacco. We had hoped to meet Mr. and Mrs. Williams from Boston, but they did not come. After supper we waited for the mail and our friends came to see us.

July 28.   Hindman. We went to Sunday School, had our old classes and it was a pleasure to see that they kept up their interest, and Miss Stone's girls told her that they read the Bibles she gave them and prayed every day now. There is no regular preacher here. But today Mr. Rainey preached at the Court House. This afternoon Miss McNab went on horseback with Miss Granger to the country Sunday School. While we were sitting under the trees at Mrs. Kilgore's, a wagon came over the bridge and at last Uncle Noah had arrived with Mr. and Mrs. Williams, who have come from Boston simply to meet and know our mountain friends, and we are so glad to have the privilege of introducing them. We took them to call on Mrs. Maggard, whose daughter, Mrs. Cody, (the mother of little Curry) was buried yesterday. She was so glad to see us and told us all about her trouble. Her daughter was ill only a few days. All the family were at her bedside except one brother. She begged her husband to quit drinking and he promised to do so. She fell into a deep sleep and on waking said she had died already, had been to the beautiful City above, where everything was bright and shiny and the trimmings were of gold; she hated to die again but had come back to say good bye to Joe, who came in while she slept, and she made him promise to stop drinking. She sang and shouted at the last. While she was telling all this Mr. Maggard would "argufy religion" with Mr. Williams; spent an hour with the Dukes and Richard entertained us by imitating one of Uncle Ira Combs' sermons.

July 29.   Hindman.   Very early we secured a number of boys and girls to help us decorate the college chapel with bunting, flags, pictures and ferns. On a long table we arranged periodicals, pictures and flags to give the teachers for their schools. All was ready by nine o'clock, when the Institute began. The teachers made us feel very welcome and crowded about us to tell of the periodicals they had received, and how they still had the pictures and flags we gave them last year. Those who had received libraries took special pains to tell us how they liked them, how they had used the books in their schools and the benefit they had been to the community. Some told how disappointed they had been not to receive libraries and are still hoping to get them. Others said they had never received any periodicals through the mail although they had been sent to all of them. They said the postmasters were very careless and in many places it was absolutely impossible to get a newspaper after they had "signed for hit." The postmaster here is drinking now and we are having trouble with our mail. It is not unusual to meet someone on the street or at the table who tells us there is something in the post office for us, that they had seen it as they were looking over the mail. It seems that anyone is privileged to go in and go through the mail and it would be no trouble to take any of it away.

Among the new teachers is an eighteen year old boy, Dillard Ritchie, who has taught just one week, and came to us as soon as he reached town and asked for a temperance pledge to sign, said not a drop of liquor had touched his lips for a year and that he tried to get other boys to stop drinking, but they only laughed at him. We wrote the pledge in a Bible and he seemed relieved when he had put his name to it. When I asked him why he had stopped drinking, he said, "Well, Kelly Day was my teacher and he don't drink and I aim to be like him." He seemed very poor and I have just heard that his father is a Baptist preacher "who goes around where he can get plenty to eat and leaves his family to starve." He has only been to school three five months' terms and last winter, Kelly Day paid his way at school here. Now he has a second class certificate and says he "aims to save his money to go to State College."

As soon as we reached here Profesor Clark and some of the lawyers asked if we would not have a public meeting in the interest of a better school at Hindman. They are very anxious for us to establish a good school here–so this afternoon they called a meeting in Mr. Phillips' office to discuss the needs and plans for the school. Professor and Mrs. Williams were there, asked many questions and offered valuable suggestions. Professor Clark gave an account of his early experience here when, thirteen years ago, he and others had to sit up all night to protect the school property with Winchesters. The rest of the day was spent in giving Mr. and Mrs. Williams a true idea of the conditions here. We took Mr. Williams to see Uncle Solomon Everidge a quaint old man eighty years old, who always goes barefoot and never wears a hat. We found him sitting on the bed by a four months old baby, whose mother had just died and left it to their care, fanning it with a white turkey wing. He said "times is growing wus and wus, when I wuz a boy I wuz purty bad, the next giniration wuz wuser and my grand-children are terrible bad," and then pointing to the baby, he said, "and what will this giniration be." To Mr. Williams' question "Why do you think people are worse," he answered, "I think people is wus on account of the meanness of their manouvres." We went to the sewing room where the young people were rehearsing for an entertainment. Our friends thought that they had never seen any more attractive young people. They sang some of the old time meeting house songs and the ones we taught them last summer. Then we were all asked to Mrs. Sturgill's for a social where there was music by the Maggard band. Mr. and Mrs. Williams were so pleased and affected by the warm-hearted greeting they received and said that it would be hard for them to leave.

July 30. To our great disappointment, as Mrs. Williams was not well, they decided that they must start home today. We have planned so much for them at Sassafras, there is so much for them to see and do. We went to the Institute early. Mrs. Williams presented an Audubon bird chart from the Massachusetts Audubon Society, to the county, for use in the schools, left seven hundred educational Perry Pictures[15] for them and promised to send four Circulating Libraries. She offered to secure a scholarship at the Oread Institute of Domestic Science for a Kentucky girl and a scholarship in Sloyd in Boston for a Kentucky boy or girl. The teachers gathered about them to say good bye and in their quiet way showed their appreciation of what they had done for them. We feel that their visit, although so short, will be productive of good to the mountain people. When they started, I went part of the way with them. A rain storm came and we stopped with Mrs. Collins, where Mrs. Williams made a water color sketch of the fire burning in the old fire place. Mrs. Collins said that she always kept a fire, so when she got ready to cook she did not have to strike a match. At Mrs. Greer's, Mrs. Williams purchased some baskets and I engaged some and made an appointment to take Miss McNab to learn how to make the willow baskets so that she could teach the women at Sassafras. Professor Clark asked Miss McNab to help him get up an entertainment for this evening. She decided to have some games and give the teachers a talk on the importance of playing with and directing the play of their pupils. Late in the afternoon Professor Clark told her that he was leaving the entire evening to her, much to her chagrin, as she was only prepared for part of it. But that is the way they do things up here. Miss McNab was equal to the occasion, however, and after a short talk on the psychological value of play and the dangers of neglecting children at play time, she played kindergarten games with the teachers. At first she had some trouble to get them to take a hold, but they soon responded when called upon to play and it seemed odd to them to see her run about so fast. They said that was what they needed, some games to teach their pupils.

July 31.   Hindman. Spent the day at the Institute and from the discussions of the teachers got a good insight into the methods of teaching up here. In the afternoon Miss McNab and I went to Mrs. Greer's to learn to make willow baskets. Met a girl from Whitesburg who said the people had been so anxious to have us go there this summer. Arminta Stamper, the girl who helped us last summer, came in from the country and was brimful of news. Her Uncle's "widder" had run off with another woman's husband and left her five small children. Mrs. Stamper had taken three of them although she had eleven of her own. This family of sixteen besides ten boarders (log men) lived in a house consisting of a kitchen and two bedrooms. One of the children is named Sarah but everybody calls her "Poppet" because she is so little and looks like a "poppy doll." We have been trying for years to find out why the children call the dolls "poppy dolls" and at Sassafras, where the conditions are even more primitive than any place we have been, they do not say dolls but simply "puppets" which is the old English word meaning small image. To those who are tracing the ancestry of the mountain people this is significant.

August 1.   Hindman. Last night Professor Shipp, the conductor of the Institute, gave an excellent temperance lecture, so convincing and practical. He never loses a chance to give the teachers good advice on bodily religion, which is sadly needed, as some of the teachers are spending these nights of the Institute in drinking and gambling. Today Professor Shipp urged the teachers to put pictures on their walls and try to have more attractive school rooms. I told them if any of the teachers would like to have a roll of pictures for their schools to give me their names and addresses and I should try to have some sent to them. Thirty-two responded and seemed so grateful for this opportunity.

August 2.   Hindman. The last day of the Institute. Very kind and appreciative were the last words of the teachers for all that we had done. They asked two of us to be on the Resolutions Committee, but we declined. We were gratified to hear the following resolutions read:

> Resolved that we appreciate the interest in our welfare manifested by Misses Pettit, Stone and McNab, and that we, the teachers of this County, pledge ourselves to cooperate with them in their efforts to better the children in these adjoining Counties.
> Resolved, that we, as teachers of Knott County, will endeavor to carry out that provision of the law which requires the evil effects of all kinds of narcotics to be taught.

Professor Shipp gave a very earnest talk on the importance of teaching physiology and the evil effects of cigarettes. He spoke of a leaflet on our literature table on "Legislation for the boys" and urged the teachers to take one. Many came for them and for the Humane Leaflets that Mrs. Williams had left for them. When the teachers met to arrange for the various associations this fall, we were asked to meet with the one from our district and to help arrange the program. They asked me to have a temperance speech and Minta Perkins, one of the new teachers, asked us to write something for her to learn to say. We saw many of the teachers mount their horses and start off to go miles away over hill and dale to their schools, loaded down with the periodicals we gave them. We visited around to say good-bye to the friends and went to the old camp ground for quiet and to see the moon rise over the hill once more. The three small Smith children came straight up the hill after us so we had to play games with them. They were just getting over the scarlet fever and peeling off. We had a dear little farewell visit with the Dukes and then on to Miss Granger's Bible class where all the young people seemed to take part.

August 3.　Sassafras. How good to be home again! The country is much more desirable than town even in the mountains. We were awakened several times in the night and could always see a light in Mr. Shade Comb's store and that is the time he disposes of some of the liquor he makes in the government still. We were up by daylight to get an early start home after a week's stay in Hindman. Our old boys, Roy and Dewitt, brought us in a jolt wagon with two very "sorry" mules. This was our fifth trip over Irishman Mountain and as usual we had to walk across it. Just on top of the mountain, where it seemed very lonely, a young looking man was cutting a slab from a solid rock with an axe, which he told us was to be a tombstone for his wife who had died and left him five little children to care for. Passed the little two room cabin on the hillside where Sam Day lives. His brothers, Kelly and Watson Day, live with him. Kelly Day is the new County Superintendant of Schools and we think quite the most ambitious and remarkable boy in the mountains, as he has overcome so many difficulties, to secure an education. When we passed Uncle Jim Stacy's there was a large crowd for another funeral occasion. We had heard Uncle Ira Combs' voice for some time before we came in sight. Miss McCartney who has been keeping Camp and attending to the classes during our absence, had everything in beautiful order and was much disappointed that Mr. and Mrs. Williams did not come. She had not received my card mailed Tuesday telling her that they could not come. Such is the uncertainty of the mail here. Many visitors came by after meeting for periodicals, but by three o'clock we were on the way to George's branch for Sunday School. The neighbors brought their visitors which made very full classes for four teachers. We were tired enough for bed by the time supper was over, but two boys came for music, so an hour or more had to be devoted to them.

August 4. Sunday, our busy day, and there is not time for an extra morning nap. Mrs. Stacy and Rhoda have been in a great state of excitement because this was meeting day and they had us up before daylight. Just as soon as we could, we started for the Sassafras Sunday School, for the people begin coming so early and if we are not there, they go away, saying there will be no Sunday School. We met crowds of people going to meeting, but many of them stopped with us. The funeral occasion was about the same as last time, only the "widder" had not found a new companion and he had another boy with the saddle pockets selling the liquor. Around the well and under the trees were groups of people, who did not hear any of the sermons. We sat near and the expression on the faces of the men in the circle around the preacher was one of blind idolatry. He told the "widder, friend Leslie Whittaker" that he must stop his wicked ways. On account of illness in the family, only the husband, a brother and sister were there, so Uncle Ira suggested that they have another funeral when they all can come.

Extracts from his sermon.

Hit's a hard thing to funeralize, but I'll name hit, if God puts hit on my mind. He hain't got a piece of a Saviour, we've got a whole Saviour. He spore the sinners. The power of God arrested 'em in their wild cayrares (career). I'm a man with a failable recollection. I've viewed my unworthiness and viewed my inabilities. I don't believe hit will leave a spot on the soul. Friend Whittaker, if ye go on yer evil ways, you'll so clap out Jesus. Don't fool yourself and believe what these Predestinarians say, that you can jist go on and shoot down a man and keep on in your wicked ways and then go to Heaven, when you dies. Don't listen to no such doctrine. May the Spirit come a-leaping and skipping over the dead faculties of our souls.

On the way up to Montgomery Sunday School this afternoon, we stopped to see Aunt Peggy, whose days are very lonely now after an active life. She said:

Wimmin air so no-count now, they can't stand nothin' like they used to when I was young. Then they could live on fat meat and corn bread and work out doors all the time. I niver seed any coffee till I was growed and it's a bad thing a body ever seed hit. Hit pears like people didn't use to die like they do now, before I was married, I never seed but one dead person and hit was a baby. I've had sixteen children, twelve still livin', one died last year, but he warn't right, he was the likeliest child I had, when he war a baby, till he took to havin' fits. Hit was a sight in this world how I uster spin and weave, but I never made no colored blankets, I like white uns best 'cause you can see the fleas on 'em.

She and her son D. told us in a graphic way how courting is done up here. In a very innocent way they told us of these things which we think pretty bad. D., who is a widower, said as his mother was too old to do the work, he'd been thinking of marrying again, but he "had looked about and couldn't find a woman here except a right young un or a widder with a family." So he had gotten a matrimonial paper, "Cupid's Columns," and entered into correspondence with several women. He showed us one letter from a Missouri woman, who seems willing to marry him, and asked our advice. He also asked if we could introduce him to a nice "widder woman" where we lived. As he said he knew how to cook and could get along very well, if he had somebody to milk for him, we mildly suggested that he learn to milk himself, which would solve the problem. The children joined us along the way, and walking up the creek with them, listening to their quaint expressions, as they tell us all they do is one of the delights of these days. Diana and Walter are especially refreshing. There were not seats in the school house for all who came, the boys who had been in jail at Hazard, having been released on bond, were all there and seemed very responsive. They are bright, seem eager for the Bibles, and readily learn all the things we give them. As we passed Mr. Green Combs, Betty ran after us with pieces of watermelon, which refreshed us. While we ate it, he came down to the fence to tell us his religious experiences and the hard time he had to bring up his nine children without a mother. He was eloquent in his farewell to Miss McCartney, and said that her influence would long be felt here.

August 5. Up earlier than usual this morning to make beaten biscuit for Miss McCartney's luncheon and get her off by six o'clock. She went on a mule with the mail boy to Hindman, and will go with the various mail boys by way of Prestonburg and by boat to the Cheasapeake and Ohio Railroad. It began to rain early and has poured in torrents all day. We had visions of an entire day without visitors and settled down for a beautiful rest and time to write. But in a little while, men, women and children began to come and there were more than forty here, which goes to prove that settlement workers should not indulge in visions of ease. Two weeks ago we had planned for this evening a social as a farewell to Miss McCartney and a welcome to Mr. and Mrs. Williams, but we never dreamed that anyone could come in this rain. At four o'clock they began to arrive and were here until nine. Among them were an old woman and Aunt Kathrine Grace, an old woman who smokes all the time, and lives far away on the top of a mountain at the head of a very lonely and rough hollow. They entered into the spirit of the games as heartily as any of the young people. These great shy mountain boys unbent and took an active part in all we were trying to do to entertain them. As this was a George's Branch crowd, who usually spend entire nights at their gatherings, and they seemed to have no idea of leaving at nine o'clock, we suggested it by having our usual evening prayers and saying good-bye. When we saw them starting home in the pitch dark, down the way which seems almost impossible to us in the bright sunshine, we decided that it was not best to have any more evening socials.

August 6. It poured rain but we had visitors all day. Leslie Whittaker brought some girls to take dinner with us, and they asked

Mrs. Stacy privately if we ate so much all the time. Miss Stone started alone to George's Branch for the sewing class, found the creek too high to cross, so followed a narrow path under a cliff on this side. When Jasper came and found she had gone alone, he was afraid that something would happen to her and hurried to overtake her, by the time she slide down several banks, climbed over great fallen trees and through underbrush, she was relieved when he came and took possession of her heavy bag. The teacher, Mr. Bob Combs, the father of a grown son, asked to join the sewing class to learn to make a patch, so that he could take it home to show his wife. On the way home, as they wound slowly and carefully around the cliff, someone called to him to come over and fish. Jasper said, "No, come go round up," "No, go by," and Jasper said again, "Guess I'll have to go on up." This kind of conversation takes place every time we meet anybody or pass a mountain home.

August 7.   Jasper took us up to "Yaller" Creek in the boat and before we landed it hung on a log and turned about many times, much to the amusement of the passers by. At Sassafras we had large classes. When one girl brought her sewing for Miss Stone's approval, she noticed that her hands were in a bad condition, and on asking what was the matter, she replied, "I've got the itch, and have had it ever since last winter, and nothin' won't cure it." Tilford got his sewing into quite a tangle and when a boy asked if he hadn't hurt it, he said, "No, hit haint hurt for hit haint got no feelings." When possible, Miss McNab, uses the material at hand in the kindergarten work, the long bull rushes prove a good substitute for raffia, out of which they make picture frames in which they put cards containing the Lord's Prayer, and she teaches them practical lessons in local geography with the sand on the bank, heaping it up for mountains and tracing out the streams. The constructive occupations give especial delight to the children, boys and girls twelve and thirteen making chairs, wagons, cradles and other things out of cardboard. One boy said, "I never seed so much truck made of paper." Some of the girls who had never had a doll, showed unbounded delight when put to work cutting out garments to dress paper dolls. One eleven year old boy asked if he might dress a doll, and his older sister found scraps of cardboard and asked if she might take them home to make a toy chair. Cutting out colored pictures delights the children, chiefly because they can use the little scissors. They call the paste "paint, starch and that truck." We stopped on the way home to see Shade, one of our boys who is very sick as the result of eating a poke of green peaches.

August 8. As Miss Pettit has sprained her wrist, I shall have to take up the daily chronicle for a while. Mrs. and Mr. Stacy and Rhoda went with us to the trial on George's Branch this morning. There were many gathered in groups under the trees waiting for the prisoners to be found, for they had escaped to the woods. Louisa Sumner raised some white ducks which got into Shade Dean's garden and he got rid of them with a shotgun, the usual way of settling such difficulties. The Sumners all got mad and at the next Saturday night "gathering" at their house, Al Sumner, the father of the girl who raised the ducks, suggested that all the company "confederate" to go up early Sunday morning to "wipe out all the Doans." The boys went with shotguns and the girls with knives (most of them our Sunday School pupils). No one was killed, but the Doans were mad this time and had warrants issued against those who had "confederated" against them. After waiting a long time for the Sheriff to find those who had escaped to the woods, across the creek we saw Shade Doan and Al Sumner coming arm in arm. The long bearded Magistrate was sitting by a table with his big law book spread out before him, and the two lawyers who had come fifteen miles from Hazard were impatiently waiting for the trial to begin. The Squire called the cases, but as neither prisoners nor witnesses appeared, one of the lawyers said, "Hit is hard to defend a prisoner who has no defense or one who will not come to trial, but I guess them that had to fix up things has told them hit would be better for them to stay away." The Squire said there seemed to be nothing else to do but dismiss all the warrants. We met a young mother at the trial with a ten months old baby that had a sore head, which she said was itch. We suggested that washing it in soap and warm water would help it, but she was afraid it would "kill hit." We asked if washing its head had ever hurt it and she said she had never tried it. All during the conversation she was chewing tobacco and spitting.

We were glad to be at the school house for the play hour, and at the teacher's request, we taught them some new games, he joining in, for he is one of the few teachers who wants to be with his pupils at play time and make them feel that he is their friend. After Court was over, all returned home except Miss Pettit and me. Under the wide spreading branches of an oak by the side of Carr we ate the luncheon we brought with us and stopped long enough to read the Commencement address that Dr. Abbott made at Wellesley. We have been carrying this about all summer hoping for a chance to read it. We made visits down Carr and all up Scuddy Branch. Mr. Brashears was getting ready to dig a well, the box was to be a hollow tree trunk with a sweep, he is using sycamore, but says that "chestnut is the lastiest." We asked how they happened to name the little girl Narral and they said the father just dreamed it. Old Mr. Godsey has lived at the same place for sixty years and he told us much of interest of the early settlements here. He thought it very unfortunate that we were not married and said anybody with such pretty teeth and so fair ought to get married.

Scuddy is even more narrow, rough and rocky than most of the branches (if possible). We saw some women and girls "sanging" on the hill side, they had been out all day, each had a hoe and a little poke of sang and yellow root. At one unusually thrifty place there was a home-made wooden wheel which ran a turning lathe, in the house were beds with posts made this way and chair rounds on a shelf over the fireplace to season. It was getting late, but as there is simply no chance to go to these out of the way places the second time, we could not turn back without going to see Mr. and Mrs. Grace, who have been so kind to us. Mrs. Wells told us to strike up the hill, that there was no path and it looked as if nobody ever went that way, but if we would just keep on going we would find the house. She was right, there was no path, and it did look as if no one had ever been that way before, but on and up we went around great boulders as big as the house, a steep lonely way, where one would expect to meet only rattle snakes. We kept watching the sun and before it sank behind the hill, we came suddenly upon a waving field of corn, and nestled right at the edge of it was the little one room gray cabin, brightened by the many blooming flowers about it, but we wondered and wondered how anyone could live so far away from every where. Mrs. Grace, with her crippled hands, was peeling potatoes for supper, while Mr. Grace sat by looking on. They were thrifty, he had fine corn, all kinds of fruit, buckwheat, gourds, a good garden and it seemed to us that they could get along very well without going away for anything. They have not had a cow for ten years because his wife has not been able to milk since she had rheumatism in her hands. I suppose it never occurred to him that he could learn to milk. When he moved there he carried everything on his back, he had eighty bushels of corn and carried two bushels at a time. He showed us a "nigher way" home, but it seemed even more unfrequented than the other way. Going down a steep slippery, damp mountain side, Miss Pettit fell and sprained her wrist. We met Mary Grace, the sixteen year old daughter of the house, going home from school and we wondered how many of our city girls would make such an effort to get to school. She told us that she sat up late every night reading the papers we gave her. Polly Ann, a graceful half grown girl poled us across the creek in a little shaky log canoe. It was dark when we reached home.

August 9. Sarah Lizabeth, a sixteen year old negro girl, came to wash for us. Miss Pettit stayed by her all day teaching her to wash by kitchen garden rules. This is mill day and we have had the usual number of visitors. One woman, just thirty-two years old and the mother of nine children, came to mill riding on her turn of corn and a pair of saddle bags, carrying a sick baby in her arms and holding an umbrella over it. The nag frightened and "Flung 'em all off, but they were not much hurt." She said that her boy begged her to come to see us and said "They haint fine ladies and haint proud." Miss McNab and I had to leave visitors to go up Montgomery for our classes. I had several married women and three grown boys, the Sumners, who had figured in the recent trials. They were learning to patch, to work button holes and to sew on buttons. When they finished sewing on a button, they pulled hard at it and were so pleased that they had learned to sew on a button to stay.

In the Kindergarten Class they constructed wagons of pasteboard. Delight shone in their eyes and it was pathetic to see the great boys of thirteen and fourteen trailing the small wagons after them and calling out, "Gee up." But when we stop to think of the cheerless homes from which these boys come, whole families huddled in one room, the dearth of enjoyment, no play things, knowing very few games, we do not feel like smiling at the simple enjoyment of such a little thing. Before we left we had them help us sweep the room, brush down the cob webs and put pictures, flags and kindergarten chains on the walls.

August 10.   Miss McNab spent most of the day directing the ironing. It rained but people came just the same. They do enjoy the pictures and shells. Mr. and Mrs. Kelly were here. They have been married twelve years, have seven children, four of them feeble minded. Judge Combs and Professor Burke of Newport, who had been conducting the Institute at Hazard, walked from Hazard today and stopped by to see us. We had a good Sunday School at George's Branch and stopped by Mrs. Mullins' to see the wool the girls have dyed for our blankets.

August 11.   Sunday School at Sassafras, Mr. Manton Cornet was there with paper knives and napkin rings that he had made for us out of laurel roots. We went to see two of our boys who were quite sick. A man, his wife and five children went in just as we did, saying they thought they ought to come and spend the day with the sick boys. We felt like suggesting that the sick boys needed to be quiet and the mother to be saved the extra work of getting their dinner.

There was great excitement when we reached Montgomery this afternoon. Girls and boys had been coming since seven o'clock this morning and had spent the day picking the banjo, dancing, singing, drinking, quarreling and shouting. The leaders were two grown boys that have always seemed so good. They once told me that they had always had to work so hard that they had never had a chance to learn to read and write. Judge Combs had just stopped the fighting and gotten the room in order when we reached there. He said there was no use for us to try to do anything with these people for they were heathen any way. We called the Sunday School together just as if nothing had happened and they all came in quietly and these boys were our most attentive pupils. Fernando Combs sent us word that he was sorry he could not come to Sunday School, for he wanted to help us, and told his sister, "They's the best of folks where they come from."

It was pouring rain when we started home, several asked us to stop by for the night and thought us very foolish to go on because it would ruin our shoes and clothes, but we came on, wading most of the way. Mr. Stacy said he knew we would never get home in such a rain, but Mrs. Stacy knew us better and had hot cocoa for us.

August 12.   Rain and more rain. "They's a tide coming," so our friends tell us. The tent pegs are almost out of the ground and the poles slanting so that we feared they would fall down. We drove in the pegs as well as we could in the drenching rain, and as soon as the rain slackened, we got Mr. Stacy to tighten things up for us. The view from the tent of the winding Carr with the branches of the trees almost touching the water, is always beautiful, but today is the very first time we have had time to really enjoy it. The mist hovering over the valley and covering the hill tops was beautiful. When it disappeared we could see undulating hills covered with waving corn and forest trees. As it was impossible to cross the creeks, we could not go to Sassafras, which is the first time we have missed the classes. It is what we have longed for, a quiet day without company and a chance to answer business letters. Jasper and his sister Mary came to sew and Mrs. Stacy and Rhoda joined us at the tent. They are so busy all the time carding, spinning, and weaving, aside from the regular house and farm work they have to do, and our time is so full, we really do not have the time to enjoy them as we would like. For they are both just as interesting and entertaining as they can be. We told them about Christmas trees and they asked us to come back and have one for them Christmas, and Mrs. Stacy said, "If you'uns wuz to come and have a Christmas tree, I'd be so proud I'd jist jump right straight up and down and clap my hands." We told them that we could not come back, but if she and Jasper would take charge of it, we would send the things for all of our Sunday School children. They are keen to do it.[16] We told her where to get the carbolic acid and castile soap to give to any mother who came for them when we were away, for we had told those whose children had sore heads and the itch that these things would help them. But she knew a better cure than that for the itch–"Take dock weed, mix hit with lard; put hit in a can, bury hit under the ground for forty-eight hours, grease the body all over with hit and keep on the same clothes fur three weeks, they's no other sure cure."

August 13.   Judge Combs passed by this morning taking Ida to her school, which began yesterday, but as it rained she did not go. Such is the importance the teachers place on being at their work! We had a nice morning writing at the tent, for it was raining too hard for anyone to come, this afternoon we had to go around the cliff to George's Branch; this is never an easy trip, but it was worse today. First we jump over several little rivulets before we reach the path, sit down there and rest a while, the view is so beautiful, but time being short and the path only a foot wide, and made up of crumbling rock, we have to be going and that carefully, till we come to a narrow passage between two rocks leading to a higher wall, one side of which is green with mosses and overhauling vines and water trickling down, and the other side a very steep precipice, which we are likely to slip over any time. Then we come to the top of the mountain and a walk through a grove of beech and oak trees, across cascades rushing down every little ravine, then an immense fallen tree raised about a foot from the ground, under which we have to crawl. Then more jumping and climbing and another fallen tree, this time we have to climb over and as the ground slopes off on the lower side, this is a difficult task. Finally we get to the shore of the creek, walking through high weeds and brushwood, and after climbing another cliff, a fence and walking through a garden, we have half a mile of wagon road before we come to George's Branch School House. In spite of the tide, there were as many as we could attend to. The children made chains and imagination was at play while they did this, one boy calling the chain a rattle snake and one who only had a few links said he just got the rattles made. Teaching them the kindergarten songs is a delight to Miss McNab, they are so alert and they try with all their might to sing. They really know no songs and have to be drilled over and over on the same ones. The order at all the schools is very good. This was the first chance to put up pictures and flags in the school house. The first time we came we saw a picture of George Washington on the wall which we gave to the former teacher several years ago at Hazard. This was the only picture they had ever had and it was in good condition. This is a good house and when we had finished, it looked quite as well as some at home. As the teacher walked down the branch with us, a six year old boy, who once told us his name was

"John Nothing," said to him, "Come, Bob, let's go up," and the teacher responded, "No I can't go now." "Waal, come when you have time." Everybody calls everybody else by their first name, and it seems odd to us to have little children speak to very old people in the same familiar way as they do to their playmates.

August 14. Early after breakfast while we were getting the tent in order, D. came down Montgomery in the pouring rain, dressed in his best black suit, barefoot and carrying a new pair of shoes in his hands. He asked if he could sit in the tent and wait for a wagon that he was going to Jackson in. We were glad of this opportunity to send some letters by a responsible person to the railroad for we had some written that we were afraid to risk through the Sassafras post office. At dinner Mrs. Stacy said that she and Simon had talked it all over, and D. had no business in Jackson–no, she just believed he was going to meet that woman from Missouri that he'd been writing to all winter. He certainly seemed to be very mysterious.

Granville Stacy told us he had a fine library of nearly one hundred volumes. Some years ago, when he was teaching school, a man came and organized a Sunday School, which was named for the son of the woman who gave the library for the use of the school and the neighborhood. When he finished teaching, he took possession of the books and kept them for his own use, and in telling about it, it seemed never to have occurred to him that the books belonged to the school and not to him.

Robert Stacy, son of the postmaster, was here when I was fixing to send a library key by mail and wondering the best way to do it, as I feared the curiosity of the Postmaster's family would not let it pass through unmolested, so he suggested putting it in a letter–"Anybody can tell by feeling hit, hit is a key and will not bother hit."

The rain and high waters kept us from going to the classes at Sassafras. Jasper came to bring our mail, the first since Sunday, it was his twentieth birthday and he celebrated it by making a beautiful patch for me and helping us to beat biscuit for supper.

MRS. STACY'S DESCRIPTION OF STEPS IN WEAVING

This is the Cotton Warp.

I first buy some bale cotton thread and boil it good and take it out of the kettle and put clean water in, and then dye and color it and take it out and dry it; then make a thick starch out of cornmeal and size it in that; then take it out and dry it; then spool it and warp it; then beam it and pint it through the gears and then through the slade; then tie it in and I am ready to go to weaving.[17]

How I do the Wool.

This is how I call my sheep, "Sheep Cunanna, Sheep!" Here is some salt in a gourd for them. Then I catch them and tie the feet together and then the heads down and then lay them on a big box turned upside down, then I shear them and let them go; then I wash the wool with my feet in a basket in the branch and put it out to dry on top of the coal shed and then bring it in the house and pick it, and then grease it with lard; then card and spin and reel it. Now it is yarn. Now I must wash it in good warm soap suds, and then color it and hang it out to dry, and then I must quill it and weave it. Now it is cloth and I must wet it thoroughly and dry it and then sprinkle it with water and iron it with a hot iron.

Mary B. Stacy

August 15. Another rainy day, spent in the tent writing and sewing. No one came to stay but Mary Mullins, who finished her patch and began a necktie. She had to wade knee deep to cross Montgomery and sat all day in her wet dress, regardless of having a bad cold;

we talked to her of the importance of keeping well and strong. She is fifteen years old, pretty, tall and graceful. It is a picture to see her poling the boat across the river. She is a very intense nature and sticks to her work steadily. Dr. Roark passed by on his nag wearing two hats, he stopped at the fence to talk about the schools and said, "The teacher don't know nothing, there's some boys he can't teach any, the trustees is the block-headedest fools I ever saw. I am going to send Della down to spend another day with you. She will learn more from you uns than she does at school."

Miss McNab showed Mrs. Stacy how to fry apples for supper.

August 16.   There seems to be some excitement up Montgomery over D.'s sudden departure. He didn't tell his mother where he was going and she thinks he has run away with Becky Brown, who, Mrs. Stacy says, "pears to be a nice, seeming, smart, pretty woman, but lives no where and is no body." Owing to big waters, very few could get to mill today, but we got the benefit of those that did come. One man sat quietly in the corner and spent an hour looking at the stereoscopic pictures for the second time. He said the rain would not stop until the first quarter of the moon, which will be August 22nd. Tucker brought me a Louisville paper about two weeks old saying, "Half of Louisville is burned up and people dead; you don't get no news except from a regular subscription paper." The creek was too high for us to walk to Montgomery, so Miss McNab and I rode John, the mule. We got there at three-quarters of an hour before school closed, and as there were no seats, we sat in the doorway waiting. This is a large, bare, log house, the only furniture is a stove in the center, four rough benches and a long high work bench. About twenty-five children were crowded into these seats. In this short time, he called five classes. "Second Spelling Class come forward." Four little boys stood up. "Spell the-zis–(theory)–the-or-ry, gid-di-ness." These boys spelled very well. "Come forward class number three, primary reading." About five little ones with their books; spelled the words, each child one word and the teacher pronounced it quickly after them as he stood behind each one who read. The children never pronounced a word themselves. "Advanced Geography class." Two grown boys with moustaches arose. "Bound North America." No response. Teacher read answer out of the book and boys joined in on the last few words. "What does it mean to bound a country?" No answer. Many questions, but the boys did not answer one; just stood dumb. "Second Geography class." Five girls. "What is a monarchy?" No reply. "How many kinds of monarchies are there?" He went through the entire list of questions but the girls were absolutely silent, no attempt to answer at all. Then he said, "You can set down and git that there one and this here one for the next lesson." "Advanced Spelling class." A great crowd, about ten at the blackboard and some writing on slates. Each one had his own board space and the teacher gave out ten words for them to write. "Circus." Each one looked to the right and left to see what the others wrote. Not one spelled it correctly. Most of them, of course, had no idea what the words meant. When the ten words were written the teacher took a book in his hand and said, "Now grade yourselves." He spelled the words correctly and each one wrote ten after his word. He called the names and asked for the grades and almost everyone called out "One hundred," when probably not one had more than three or four words right. The teacher did not look at the words nor question the children's One hundred, but just wrote down in his book. Then he said, "I won't keep you any longer today, these ladies have some kind of exercises for you, when they get through with you, go straight home. Your parents will have use for you when you get there and all of you come back Monday morning." Then we took charge and had a very trying time, because there were so many grown boys and men, standing around giggling and distracting the attention of the children. One woman asked me please to show her next time how to crochet yarn lace for a linsey skirt. The women were all glad to learn to stay button holes to make them strong. As we were leaving, a grown boy grabbed Chloe (only fourteen years old, but seems quite grown up), jerked the hair pins out of her hair, pulled back her head against him and kissed her, regardless of spectators. We came home in the pouring rain, loaded down with plums and apples they had given us. We found Dilce waiting to know if [we] would not give him a social tomorrow evening; he said he would tell everybody down the creek to come and not do like Jasper, stay away from his own social. We enjoyed the good supper that Mrs. Stacy had for us. Rhoda took charge of the evening worship and they have promised to have prayers every evening after we leave.

August 17.   Another rainy day. Jasper came for Miss Pettit to go out on the cliff for laurel and rhododendron roots to make paper knives. Diana Combs came for us to make her a white sun bonnet. I had never made one before, but Mrs. Stacy quilted the "head piece" and I managed to get through the rest of it. We told Mrs. Stacy yesterday that she ought to have another cupboard with shelves in it for the clothes, and today the cupboard is made, filled, in its place, with curtains in front of it. She has been wanting a cot like ours and we told her we knew Simon could make one. He took a camp stool for a model and did make a good one. We covered it with one of her beautiful blue and white coverlids, some pretty sofa pillows and a bright striped blanket folded across the foot.

We all went around the cliff this afternoon to George's Branch Sunday School. The attendance was smaller than usual, probably owing to the rain and bad roads. Sally Mullins had finished the purple and white blanket which we liked so much. Two old women were fishing and when we asked why they did not come to Sunday School, one said, "Jist pure triflingness." Some of our Montgomery boys came to Sunday School and as they offered to set us across the creek on the mule, we did not have the rough climb home around the cliff. The ford was very deep and Tucker's mule was small, but we managed to get our feet out of the water and get over safely. I rode on behind him to the next ford and Mr. Godsey said he wondered if Tucker could keep from swearing so long. Then he "sot" us all across again. We found Cisco Sumner and Mary Mullins waiting for us. They, with these two Montgomery boys and Jasper, made up the social. Dilce did not appear. They thawed out considerably and played the new games with zest. We had to tell them when it was time for them to go home. Jasper made a pine torch to light him around the cliff, and the other three boys mounted the little mule, which could find the way up the stony creek without a light. Miss McNab is still nervous from stepping over a large snake this afternoon, which Polly Ann said, "in any amount of reason" was a copperhead.

August 18.   We had to go by way of the cliff to the Sassafras Sunday School this morning. The door was locked, as Robert Kelly had gone to meeting with the keys in his pocket, we had the classes by the roadside, and had a song service. Met Aunt Peggy on horseback going up to the mouth of Irishman to the burying of her grandchild. Aunt Mary was sitting out on her porch reading her Bible and would have us to "stop by." She said, "You know my grandson John S., you've been in his company, haint you, he's a rambling nater,[18] his paw was such a pretty man, his maw died of the breast complaint, some calls it consumpt, but we jist say breast complaint. I've got more than forty grandchildren but seems like Jasper seems the nighest to us." Uncle John came in with a measure of meal saying he had lost his sack, she said, "Didn't I tell you not to let that sack out of your hands, hit had the two letters of his name on hit, fer I sot em there." Jasper told us of a ballad that Basil Beverley had written about Granville Stacy robbing the post office and said he would get the "receipt" for us. Squire Gent and Dilce came for dinner. Dilce said he "had a lawful excuse for not coming to his social, his maw was sick and his paw was not at home." Squire Gent came to bring us some rattle snake skins and had a thrilling story to tell of how he went upon a mountain to put out some bee bait and found a den of snakes. With a stout chestnut pole he killed eleven rattle snakes and a copperhead. After dinner we stole away for a quiet rest before starting up Montgomery, but visitors aroused Miss McNab from the hammock to play and sing for them. Squire Gent and Jasper went with us and on the way pointed out the rock where Judge Combs' nephew once hid and shot him as he passed by. We passed a group of grown boys playing marbles while the men stood around and took the keenest interest in the game. We said, "Boys, come go up to Sunday School," and they followed. As they were walking along with us all (Judge Combs and Squire Gent the County Superintendant and Magistrate), one of the boys fired off his pistol right behind Miss McNab. These boys never miss Sunday School and are our most attentive pupils. Mr. Banks and his two daughters from Bull Creek were there to know if we would not come to their school to teach them some of the things we are teaching over here. We regretted to have to say that we would not have the time. In going down the creek the boys teased Jack Sumner for having given us peaches and Jasper for carrying the organ. Jasper told one of them to behave and he said he was not at home "when have came around." Tucker was pretty drunk and he said he had to take his father and two other men home, as they were too drunk to go alone. We asked him if he did not feel sad to see his father drink, he said, "No, he thought it was funny." Jack said he didn't aim to drink nor use tobacco any more. Spencer Combs and Nannie Green walked along hand in hand. The story about D. grows more mysterious. Betty says he may not be back for weeks. As we passed there, Walter came across to bring us a bucket of large apples and asked us to bring him some peaches the next time we came by. We got home just at dark, found Mr. and Mrs. Stacy waiting for us at the fence and though she said this morning she was too ill natured to go to Sunday School, her face was beaming. Dilce and Rhoda had stood around in the yard and talked all afternoon and Mrs. Stacy told us before her, that she and Simon had "plumb cleaned" Rhoda out about it.

August 19.   Mr. Grace came all the way from his home on the mountain, several miles up Scuddy Branch, just to bring a basket of grapes because, "you girls are so far away from home, that I want you to feel like you have got some friends up here to bring you things. Now, girls, I am going to require of you the same I did of Miss McCartney. I want you all to write to me when you go home and you'll hear from me." He told us that Mary was still sitting up late at night reading the books from the Circulating Library. Then he had to walk all the way back home to get his axe to help at Kenton Cornet's log hewing. Simon went to this hewing, too, and came very near being killed by an axe that flew out of a man's hand and struck the tree and cut a great gash in it. Judge Combs stopped by to say that he could use two Circulating Libraries at Hazard. Miss McNab went up the creek and gathered willows, which we skinned to make baskets. We went to Sassafras for the classes, the trip around the cliff was rough and slippery. Jasper "sot" us across in the boat, but could not take us up, as he was helping Uncle Jim in the hay harvest. Robert Kelly began to hemstitch a handkerchief. All the time we were there we could hear the great crash of the trees falling on the mountain nearby, where men were getting out poplar timber. Miss Pettit went to the post office and on to see Louisa about sending us a wash woman. On her way up the branch she met a small funeral procession. Down the narrow, rough branch came first a colored man carrying on his shoulder the little coffin made of rough plank covered with brown calico, with little ribbon bows all on the top of it. Next to him came two colored girls, one behind the other, dressed in their best, one carrying a tin can of bright marigolds. Then the mother, a young white woman (the father of the dead child was a negro man) walking alone very weak and trembling, for she was sick herself. It was after four o'clock and they had to walk three miles each way to bury the child. Martha Stacy was behind on a mule. She said she knew people talked about that poor white girl and it was wrong for her to do that way, "but she had just been raised from here to yander and lived any where since she was a chunk of a chap, and if she ever had any father and mother, nobody knew where they were, so she just felt sorry for her and went up there to help her." We stopped to see Sam Combs, who is ill, and they have sent for the doctor three times, but he is too drunk to come. The other boys, who are just getting well, looked like the famine starved children of India. Willie had crumbs on his mouth and said he had eaten all the crackers he could get at the store and they had both been begging their mother to send to "them wimmin" to cook them something they could eat, some good hard bread. We promised to send them some beaten biscuit and go Wednesday to show the mother how to make them. Jasper met us at Yellow Creek and brought us to the cliff in the boat. Miss Pettit worked the butter and I made cocoa for supper, while Miss McNab played and sang for Jasper and Simon.

August 20. "Miss Eliza" came early to wash and while she was making the fire under the kettle by the side of the branch, Miss Pettit and Miss McNab made the beaten biscuit for the sick boys. Then Miss McNab worked on the material for the basket weaving class. The washing was a success in spite of frequent showers, when the clothes had to be gathered in and then hung out again when the sun reappeared. Leslie Whittaker came to say goodbye and says he is going to Texas "to see the world and take up there if he likes it." Others tell us he is going to try to avoid being tried for selling moonshine and leading in the Kuklux Band. We gave him a Testament which he promised to keep and read. A woman from Acup Branch told us that her husband had been at Frankfort Penitentiary for a year and a half and was soon coming home. She had a baby a year old and he sent word to name it James Still. When she left, Aunt Peggy, who was here, said "her man wuz jist one of them outsiders." Miss McNab and I had an exciting walk around the cliff to George's Branch where we had more than forty in the class, besides several visitors. One of my boys had sprained his wrist and I bandaged it and told him what to do for it. Mr. Bob Combs had a pension check stolen from him when he was twenty miles away on Leatherwood last week and to-day one of the girls found it in her book. On the back of it was written, "Give this to R.W. Combs, his check."

After supper, Jasper brought a friend to hear some music.

August 21.   Mrs. Stacy had us up before four o'clock, because she wanted to pickle some beans for next winter. A hard struggle with "Miss Eliza," the rain and the ironing. Mr. Green Combs stopped by to say, "I'm afraid I'll be losing my baby-girl, she's so took up with you uns, she wants to be a comin' down all the time." Minta and Martha Banks from five miles away on Bull Creek came on a mule, riding on a big poke of wool which they exchanged at the store for new hats to wear to meeting Friday. They were twelve and thirteen years old, but looked and dressed as if they were eighteen. They exclaimed with delight over the shells and the pictures and said they did not know there were so many "fine things" in the world. As they said when they could get anything to read, they would sit up at night to read it, we gave them enough papers and magazines to fill their bag and while they were putting them in, they would stop to look through and read them. A woman came from White Oak Branch, with a sore-headed boy to get the castile soap we had promised her. She seemed so pleased to get the soap and borax and said she would use them right away and bring the baby back for us to see. She could not read, but wanted some papers to "line her house." As so many people want them to read, we told her we could not give them to use in that way. Mrs. Green asked us to give Nan and Candesta some clothes to wear to school (begging is unusual here). She wanted to borrow some money to buy herself some shoes to "keep her feet off the ground," and she and Nan would wash to pay for it. Uncle Jake Fields, whom we have known for years, stopped by to see us. He was on his way to Whitesburg with horses for three preachers to go to Hazard and Big Creek. He told us of two Sunday School workers, who are boarding at his house this summer "teaching singing and catechism of the Bible." Miss McNab went to Sassafras school this afternoon. Ida Francis (the sixteen year old lame mother) walked down with a pint of flour to learn to make beaten biscuit for her sick brothers. They had eaten all we had sent them and had just begged her to come and make more, and although she had been washing all day, said she had washed every "bed kiver" they had, she cheerfully did it. I made apple-tapioca pudding and gave her some of the tapioca to take to them. At the same time in the rain "Miss Eliza" and Alice were ironing and moving from place to place two small tables, put together and covered with one blanket. They were finally settled under the oil cloth, while I cooked the pudding and Ida watched the biscuit bake. She told us that she would not be able to come to the sewing class any more, because her husband was so mean to her and said she must stay at home and "do up the things." She said until she saw us she did not know there was anything else for a girl of her age to do but marry and now she wished she was not married and could go home with us to learn how to do things.

A party of sangers with hoes over their shoulders stopped by. Aunt Peggy sent Suze down to tell Simon to get his white hog out of their orchard before D. comes home or he will shoot it, and peaceful Simon went to moulding bullets and said he would be ready for him. After a hard day all around we are preparing for bed before seven o'clock.

August 22. Miss McNab spent the morning getting ready for a mother's meeting. Old Mrs. Godsey stopped on her way up to the mouth of Irishman, seven miles, to buy a turn of corn and said she would as soon be caught stealing corn as having to buy it. Although she is seventy-five years old, she did not mind starting on a trip that would take her all day. Mr. Godsey says there is plenty of corn in this country, but, while people are starving for a meal, Uncle Enoch Combs is selling his on Macey's Creek to make liquor. D. has come home, walked from Jackson and said he had had a time of it. He went to Rowan and Montgomery Counties, said his mother ought to have known he would be gone a long time and didn't we tell her where he went (he had not told us any more than he did Aunt Peggy). Miss Pettit went to make beaten biscuit for the sick boys while they all looked on asked if it was worth while to go to so much trouble. The mother said they just stood around the cupboard all the time hunting something to eat, and yesterday Shade confessed he had eaten twelve apples, which caused his backset. They had read the books we sent them and asked for more. After dinner Mrs. Stacy and Rhoda left the weaving long enough to mount John and go to the corn field on top of the mountain to get beans to dry. Then Mrs. Stacy and Miss McNab went to Uncle Rob's where they were spinning, and Miss McNab tried to learn. Late in the afternoon Uncle Jake stopped by with Dr. McElroy of Lexington, Dr. Brown of Cincinnati, and Mr. Barret of Anchorage, who have been preaching over in Letcher. It was pouring rain and they were due in Hazard tonight. Some of them asked if we had any cold beans, we understood and hastened to get out all the cold things Mrs. Stacy had in the cellar, so when she got home there was nothing to eat on the place. Two boys came just to see "them strange men," who had passed the school house singing.

August 23. Dr. Roark and Tucker passed early and left us some apples and plums. The doctor spoke of that "fool Tom Martin, whose child has diptheria and he won't come after any medicine. You can't do nothing with these people, but I'll pay em back and jist let em tough hit out and I won't go to see em if they die dead." Tucker asked for a social so we told him he might have it on next Friday afternoon. A children's missionary band at Lexington has asked us to select a girl for them to educate at the Harlan School. We very quickly decided to give this chance to Diana Combs, so on the way up Montgomery this afternoon, we called her brother Fernando out to tell him about it. We knew he would understand what a privilege this was, for he has been to the State College and is very ambitious for a good education and we did not know how the father would feel about it. Fernando was so pleased and said he would talk it over with his father and let us know as soon as we came back. So on the way home, they both came down to the fence in the rain, and the father said:

> When Nando called me I was out in the field setting a trap for squirrels and I jist knowed, the thought flashed through my mind, that you girls wanted to take Diana off to school, and I asked myself what I should do, but it did not take me two minutes to decide to let her go. So when I got down to the house I said to Nando, "do them girls want to take my little girl off to school?" He laughed and said, 'Paw, how did you know?' Then he told me of your offer, so just now when Diana came home and I told her about it, she was keen to go. I took her in my lap and asked her which my baby loved the best, me or you girls and she said very solemnly, she jist didn't know.

He said he was glad for Diana to get away from home, because the conditions are so bad here. There is no social life of the right kind and the people on Montgomery are so bad he counsels his children not to go with them or to their gatherings, and they don't go often, but one of his boys said, "Paw, I know hits wrong, but I jist have to go somewhere sometimes." Judge Combs said that this chance for Diana was worth a thousand dollars to her.

We had unusually good classes this afternoon. Mr. Brown gave the school over to us as soon as we got there. Mrs. Taylor Combs tried to learn to crochet, but "one of her eyes hurt her so bad and she was so trimblish," she could not do much good. She told us with delight that she had received some papers and a letter from a lady in Boston wanting her to answer it and she aimed to try, but she had never written a letter in her life. She said her baby, a year old, had been "sawing" since he heard the children last week sing the Carpenter's Song. Nan Adams was in the class for the first time, and she worked good button holes. While she is considered such a bad character, there is something sweet about her and we feel there is something good in her and she could be different if she only had a chance. Della Roark brought us a basket of plums.

August 24. By seven o'clock the mothers began to come in answer to Miss McNab's invitation to meet and weave willow baskets. Thirteen came and most of them brought willows with them. While they were working, they talked about their children and each mother agreed hers were the worst in the world. She told them of the various occupations that children could learn to keep them out of mischief. Some boys, large and small, played with kindergarten materials. They stayed until three o'clock, many of them said they were sure they could make baskets by themselves if they could just get away from this crowd. We had not expected that they would stay so long, so had nothing for them to eat. But they seemed satisfied with fruit we passed. Miss Pettit made beaten biscuit at the tent to show them how and as she had been entertaining the babies, when left to themselves, they sat on the floor and cried. After the basket weaving was over Miss McNab sang kindergarten songs, explaining the meaning, while some of the mothers sat on the outside and smoked their pipes. Most of them have learned not to spit on the floor. Mrs. Brashears, who is very lame, came on a mule with her baby. When she was ready to go and found her mule had slipped the bridle, a neighbor offered to carry the baby for her, so she started home walking.

The Doane boy came to the George's Branch Sunday School in his one garment. Right in the midst of a class a little boy fell backwards off the log and his brother-in-law who was spitting (towards us) all the time, yelled out, "You'd better behave yourself or I'll brush you with a limb."

August 25. Miss McNab had Sassafras Sunday School, thirty-eight, all by herself. Rhoda led the singing, Jasper and Mrs. Stacy helping. Nannie and William Stacy were there for the first time. When it was time for the lesson, Jasper and William started to leave, and when she asked them where they were going, they said to the post office. "Oh, just sit down, we should like to have you here this morning to help," they smiled and sat down. The children answered intelligently and were not ashamed before the grown people. Miss McNab rode home on a mule behind Martha Stacy. Jack Sumner came to take the organ up Montgomery on his nag. The boys laughed at him saying, "Is he another Jasper?"

Harry Eversole and Mason Combs, two of our old boys from Hazard, were there and helped with the singing. Aunt Peggy came for the first time, walking over a mile, barefoot, up the creek. During the service, in came a mother holding in her arms a five weeks old baby in a long black calico dress. She stopped just in front of me as I was teaching and made a very low bow (I managed to go on without smiling).

Judge Combs said that Mattie had had a very liberal offer, better than the chance to go to Harlan, it was to cook for a woman in Hazard and thus pay her way at school. He wanted her nearer home if she got sick.

Fernando had two large watermelons cooling in a shady spot in the creek, so we sat on the rocks in the twilight to eat them, knowing all the time it would be pitch dark when we got home. Aunt Peggy thought we ought to stay all night, said she did not know what we could do all the time to keep so busy, and by the time we told her of a few of the things we do, she said, "Wall, I jist wouldn't be so confined." Jack brought the organ home and offered to come for it any time. Jasper and Robert Stacy were here for supper and waited around for Miss McNab to play and sing, but she was too tired and had to go to bed early.

August 26.   Another new wash woman. So we do not lack for a chance to carry out the settlement idea of teaching as many people as many things as possible.

Mr. Combs brought us some gourds. We went up Yellow Creek to make visits before time for the classes at Sassafras. When we saw Ida's home (the little lame mother), we did not wonder that her husband thought she ought to stay at home "to do up the things," for they certainly needed doing up. The cooking stove, beds and all of their possessions were in one little windowless log room, which looked as though it had never been swept and put in order. Then a mile on further up to Mrs. Anderson Combs', climbing fences and walking through corn fields to get there. On the way we met Tilford Beverley who was suffering so from rheumatism that his teacher had sent him home. It was so pathetic to see this brave little fellow with his joints all twisted and to hear him tell how he had suffered this way for years. The path to Tilford's home led up a ravine and through a corn field; in fact all the hillsides around were covered with waving corn. Suddenly at the head of a cove, we came upon a tiny log house, where all around the door and lining the path were masses of flowers, and gourd vines running up the side of the cabin. Mrs. Beverley told us that Tilford crawled around on his hands and knees to plant them, for he said he couldn't live any place without "blossoms." The cabin was quaint and picturesque on the outside, but what a difference when we entered, such filth and misery! The mother, a small wizened woman with bent back and wrinkled face, had on a dirty, greasy dress. She has eight children, but has been an invalid all her life. All of these children, with the mother and father, sleep in this one room about 14 x 16 feet. There was but one bed with just a heap of ragged quilts on it, a little stove in one corner, two chairs, two barrels, and a small table were the remaining pieces of furniture. Tilford sat on the churn and sang a mournful ballad, which his mother said was her favorite, because it "hurt her feelings so." Apples were drying on a dirty quilt on the floor, some of the children walked over them, but that was not noticed. Beans and cornbread were cooking for dinner and Mrs. Beverley invited us to stay.

August 27.   This morning Miss McNab showed Mary Ann about
the ironing, while we saw visitors at the tent. "Old" Simon Stacy
(the postmaster) came for the first time. He told us how they carried
the mail, the letters in saddle bags with locks and papers and pack-
ages in a bag fastened with a draw string, so that anyone can get into
it, and that oftentimes when the mail bags were heavy, the mail boys
would throw the papers aside and that was one reason why people
did not get their papers. He said that he would rather be poor than
dishonest. This afternoon was Miss McNab's last kindergarten class
at George's Branch and she had thirty-nine, they made baskets, chairs
and dolls. Boys from thirteen to sixteen were eager to make them.
The girls dressed the paper dolls and four girls of the sewing class
stayed after school and asked her to cut these doll patterns for them.
We had some physical exercises, suggested by the stooped shoulders
and listless figures of the children. After singing the kindergarten
songs, the teacher said he had a few words to say, which proved to be
a farewell speech to Miss McNab. He was very much affected and
spoke earnestly, "children, if you feel as I do, and I know you do, it
will appear like the going down of the sun when this lady leaves us.
If I'd had the chance you children are having and have had for these
past weeks, I could have been anything I wanted to be." He thanked
us for our endeavors and said he could never forget us. Miss McNab
responded by telling them the value of obeying and loving their
mother, teacher and Jesus, and after singing a good-bye song, she shook
hands with each of them as they passed out of the door. Jasper came and
begged for a few tunes on the "little new cupboard" before bedtime.

August 28.   Writing, entertaining visitors and getting ready for class
work all morning. Basil Beverley, who is twenty-one years old, spent
most of the morning and is one of the most appreciative of visitors.
He said:

I love to read awful well, but I haven't got nothin' at home to read. I never went to but one school, just learned to read and write at home. I'd go to school now if I didn't have to work for maw and the little children. We haven't got no Bible. We had an old one, but hit was all faded and worn out so I couldn't read hit to do no good, and I love to read the Bible awful well. I'm short winded in my breast and I'm got heart trouble. Did you uns hear tell of the ballad I wrote about Granville Stacy's robbing the post office? Hit wasn't much long, jist twenty-four verses. I follow writing ballads. I am to write one about you uns and the tent.

Mr. Green Combs came down and thanked us for giving Diana the chance to go away to school and to ask what clothes she would need, as all she had was a gray calico dress and a pair of shoes. After dinner, we went up Red Oak to see Mrs. Enoch Combs, who carries on a regular factory on the front porch. She was walking back and forth spinning yarn at the big wheel. In the kitchen two very old women were carding wool, both had gray hair and were thin and bony; they were dressed only in their chemise and an old dress skirt. They were sitting side by side on low chairs, each with a basket of wool and a chair for her rolls, after it was carded. Near the house was one of these three old maid sisters in a short faded cotton dress, a red rag on her head, smoking a pipe, washing clothes in a trough, hollowed out of a log, and battling them on the end of it. Mrs. Combs showed us for the second time all of her pretty coverlids, blankets, quilts and linsey for dresses and underskirts, and gave us samples of linsey and homespun tow linen towels. She told us that she would try to have our linsey dresses ready by the first of October. Miss McNab and I went on back to Sassafras for the classes, while Miss Pettit went up to the head of Red Oak to see Mrs. Combs' daughter, Mrs. Cody, and thus describes her visit:

I found Mrs. Cody "mighty nigh stripped" and three little girls in their shirts, "hit was so warm." These shirts were made of yellow "factory" and came just below their waists. She held her nine months old baby in her arms, "hit was powerful puny, only weighed one pound than when hit was bornded." The little girls gathered about me, feeling my hands, face, handkerchief and the book I had. The father then came in and yelled at them in a very rough voice to "get away from that woman." He is known as one of the religious men, who sit in the circle around the preacher on funeral occasions. His children paid absolutely no attention to his fierce suggestion that they leave me, but as both wanted the book at the same time, one pushed the other aside, calling her a "little devil." Then there was quite a commotion, including some mild swearing on the part of the little girls. He tried to stop it, but as he was not successful, he turned to me in a helpless way and asked me what I thought of little girls who talked ugly before company. As he does not believe in Sunday Schools, I could not resist the temptation to say, "If you had been sending them to Sunday School all summer, perhaps Miss McNab would have taught them that it is not right to swear." To quiet them, the mother said if Elsie would come away from me, she could rock and sing to the "puppet," so she unlocked the safe and got out a doll in a blue dress. It was pathetic to see how eagerly Elsie took it, set down to a rocking chair and began to "sing big" one of the old Baptist meeting songs, but as the "puppet" belonged to Millie she soon left me and tried to get it; while Elsie held it tight, sang louder and rocked harder, then there were was more swearing and a fight, the mother and father yelling at the top of their voices, "You air the meanest young uns I ever seed. I'll brush you hard with a limb if you don't stop doing bad before the woman." The uproar increased until finally the mother took the doll by force from Elsie and locked it up. The father appeased her with a peach from his pocket, she soon discovered that he had two, demanded them both and tried to eat both at once, but Millie, who really owned the doll, was not to be quieted in that way. She begged for it just to "rock and sing to hit one time," the mother said that she was afraid that Elsie would not like it, but Millie fell on the floor in a rage, screamed and yelled while Elsie looked on munching the two peaches with a Satanic smile. She told Millie if she would get out on "yon" side of the house with the "puppet" so that Elsie could not see it, that she could have it, but Elsie spied her and rushed after her, so the same scene followed out doors, and they were left to "fight hit out," while the parents told me what mean children they had. I urged the father to purchase another doll (they can well afford it) and told them the care of it would greatly help them to be loving and obedient. The mother told me that Tilda, who is older than these two girls, of five and six, is known all over the community as "the worst child that ever wuz," that she would "slip and put on long dresses and walk around and say that she was somebody else and fool that way all day." I tried to explain to them that this imagination was a good thing if well directed, but she said "hit was pure meanness and she ought to be kilt for hit." So much energy and activity, it seemed sad to see parents who knew so little how to manage it. In all this din, Mr. Cody wanted to talk about the pictures of the Bible primary chart that we had given one of his neighbors and said "hit peared like he would give any amount of money if he could git some to put on his wall, so when he wuz a reflecting on the Bible, he could just lift up his eyes and there would be the picture of maybe the very thing that he wuz reflecting on, and some of the Bible writ out on hit in big letters, that he could just set and reflect without getting up and then if he wanted any more to reflect on, thar wuz the reference whar he could look in the Bible for more." All of which I thought was a very strong argument why he should have Bible pictures, but I could not help thinking that it would help more if he spent a little time on reflecting on how to have obedient girls. As I walked home down Red Oak in the gentle shower with the rainbow in the sky, I had very solemn thoughts of the needs of these people, and of my responsibility to give them the kind of a school that will make wiser parents for the next generation. I had the kodak and a homespun towel filled with apples, but managed to get over the fallen trees and jump from rock to rock in the stream. By the time I reached Carr, it was pouring rain, the boat half full of water, was on my side, but no one in sight, and as I am not an expert at poling, I did not like to undertake it with my lame wrist, so I sat down on a log with an umbrella over me for nearly an hour, reading some of Wordsworth's nature poems (which are realities here). Finally Martha Stacy came along on a bare back mule going for some apples and "sot me across." I went for the mail and it was getting dark when I reached the school where they were still busy at work. As I was already drenched, I let Miss Stone and Miss McNab take the cliff, which was dark and slippery, while I "jist put my foot to hit" and waded Carr. When we reached home, Rhoda and Mrs. Stacy were sitting in the doorway with hymn books, singing Miss McNab's songs "yuourn way–not ourn."

August 29. We were up earlier than usual to get to the log raising up on Scuddy. Rhoda called to two men on the other side of the creek to come "sot them women across" here and at the mouth of Scuddy. Polly Ann poled us across in an old canoe, made out of a log and so shaky we could not stand up in it. After a rough climb up Scuddy, we came to a little bench (a small flat place) on the hillside where eighteen men were gathering around the beginning of the new home for Kenton Cornet and his young wife. Several weeks ago they invited us to this log raising and we were eager to go, for we knew we should see the same primitive conditions under which our ancestors in the Bluegrass made their homes. The neighbors had come to help this young couple start out in life, the women to bring supplies and cook the dinner at a house nearby, while the men "raised the logs." When we told them we thought it good of them to help each other, one of them said, "Waal, we are neighbor boys, you know, and we couldn't afford not to help him out." They had already been working a month to cut the trees, saw the logs, put them on poles, hew, score and haul them to this place. Every man had sharpened his own axe and brought it with him. Mr. Cornet said, "We choosed this place because hit's the only level spot on our farm big enough to put a house on, we haint got no spring, but they's a little hollow coming down over that; these branch farms don't have much garden place, none of this land haint been cultivated lessen the Indians did hit." It was to be a cabin of one room sixteen feet square and twelve logs high. They had laid four logs before we got there, and in the three hours we were there they raised only four logs all around. Two men stood on the top of each corner with axes and plumb lines, some worked in shoes, some in socks and some barefoot and one man had a horse shoe on the heel of his boot. It took four or five men to lift each large poplar, lynn or beech log into place and then the corner men would scribe and fit them, it taking from fifteen to twenty minutes to fit each log. As we watched this interesting process, we sat on the logs talking with the reserve force. This was a gala day, as "a working" in the mountains is a social time for all. Some of the things said:

Come on, you men that's in such a hurry, you'll have to scribe 'em lengthways.

Robert, come take this axe, I haint a good hand, pears like I don't hardly crave up thar (meaning on the corner fitting logs).

Robert, be good to your relative, he's needing your help.
Now men, we must be rushing, if we aim to get these walls up.

Pears like they haint much harm in love songs, but the old folks around here thinks they air bad.

I'm not much of a good songster. I could sing before tunes come in fashion, but not much good since.

We peel the logs, so the borers won't destroy all the timber.

Keep yer buildings kivered and yer all right.

I don't think Basil has enough brains about his skull piece to make that song ballad about Granville.

You never hardly did see a cloudy day but what the sun did shine about twelve, and the sun's not many minutes from this place now.

He's a tolerable sensible chap, peart like and pears like he takes delight in learning.

At twelve the men stopped for dinner, they thought they could get the walls up today, then they would take their time to put on the roof, chink the walls, make the door, window and chimney just when they could. We went prepared to make a plea for windows, but found they "had no notion of not having one." It was encouraging to see them so progressive. At Mrs. Brashears where they were getting the dinner they begged us to stay and seemed to feel hurt when we declined, but we had to hurry home to go up Montgomery, we barely had time for a bite of dinner, and then did not reach the school house until four. A long stretch from the head of Scuddy to the head of Montgomery! There was a large sewing class out under the trees till a rain came pouring down and drove us in. Several of my big girls were so interested in the children's songs that they left me and went to join the kindergarten. Some strange boys passed by and said they would like to join the sewing class if I would show them how to put on buttons, so they would not come off. They learned that and then started on a patch. We started home late and in the pouring rain.

Miss Pettit and I walked in the mud and water, while Miss McNab got a ride. Spencer Combs was waiting for us with watermelon and D. with cantaloupe, which we took in our hands and ate as we hurried on in the rain.

It was after seven and dark when we got home and Miss McNab was just sending the lantern to us by Fernando.

Bud Combs, (twenty years old) came sidling up to us as we left the school house and, as he was riding and we walking in the rain, he shyly offered to carry our basket. Miss McNab thus describes her experiences with this young moonshiner:

> I told him he might carry me too, if he wished (on his spare horse) and he timidly consented. I had heard what a bad boy he was, running a moonshine still, getting drunk, and "other meanesses," so I was glad of this chance to know him better. He told about a man who shot four other men and I asked why he did it, "because he was naterly mean and full of whiskey." I remarked that it was terrible, the harm whiskey did and he said earnestly, "Yes, whiskey is the cause of all the meanness in the country" (this from a moonshiner). He asked me, "did you ever see a drunken man on a horse?" I confessed I hadn't, so he told me they "could ride better when drunk and never hurt themselves when they fell, because they don't try to catch." The catching is evidently what causes the harm. He was such a bright young boy, you never would think he was bad. I asked him to tell me what they did at their parties, but he said he "lowed I wouldn't like to know." I was glad to land safe at home, for I had been scared riding sidewise on a man's saddle down the rough creek.

August 30.   Mrs. Stacy and Rhoda were up by half past three o'clock to string beans and peel apples before breakfast, so that they could "do up the things" early and get ready for the social this afternoon. We spent the morning making beaten biscuit, soda biscuit and four cakes for the Teachers Association tomorrow and candy for the social. Mrs. Enoch Combs and the two little Cody children came for the first time. She found a big black snake in front of the tent and took a rail off the fence and killed it. They began to come for the social before two o'clock and there were about fifty altogether. This was Tucker's social, but he was not here. It was a bright, beautiful day and we played games in the tent and out of doors. Harlan Combs did so enjoy these games that it does seem something good could be made of him if his environment was different. Two old men and Squire Gent were here and entered into the games as eagerly as any and sat on the floor for an hour looking at shells and pictures. The young people were much dressed up. Some of the girls on leaving went to the side of the tent, took off their shoes and stockings and carried them home in their hands. Mrs. Stacy said they were all "well pleased with the candy treat." Simon went to Jackson the first of this week to bring a load of goods for his father's store. We miss his help and "good counsel."

August 31.   We were awakened at three o'clock this morning by a severe rain storm and in a few minutes heard Jasper's voice calling to us, he was much excited, said, "they was a big tide coming, hit was all he could do get across Montgomery wading above his knees" and he was sure we could not get to the Teachers' Association today, as it was impossible for the wagon to come down from Green Combs' or to cross Carr in a wagon or on horseback. As we had promised a month ago to go to this Association, to take the organ and give them talks along our line of work, we were not willing to give up going until every effort was made, so Jasper went to see if he could get two mules from Uncle Jim, saying he would take us across the creek in a boat if he could get them. We put the lunch in the basket and were waiting to start, when a regular cloud burst and wind storm came, blowing down corn, breaking down trees and fences, and the oil cloth that covered the kitchen; a peach tree fell on the stove which was soon full of water. So Mary and Rhoda chopped down the tree and by themselves moved the stove into the dining room, or as Rhoda said, "we jist put her on timbers and scooted her in." By the time Jasper got back, we were compelled to abandon all idea of going, for we could not cross either Carr or Montgomery in any way. We went to the tent to write and watch the waters tearing down, the streams carrying great logs, fence rails and brushwood. Carr had risen eight feet and was inside the fence just in front of the tent. There was not much traveling today, but late this afternoon we looked across Carr and saw John C., Bud and Nannie Combs on two horses wondering how to get over. It never occurred to us there was anything else to do but spend the night on the other side, but they found a way. Bud and Nannie dismounted, carried the two saddles and a large bag up to where they could cross in the boat and walked a mile over the hill to Montgomery, a half mile above the mouth, while John C. drove the horses into Carr and they swam across and on up Montgomery to where they were waiting. After John C. had crossed in the boat and climbed over the hill, they did what seemed to us a very dangerous thing, went right up the surging stream. Bud had gone over thirty miles to bring Nannie from Ned where she was teaching school, because she was so homesick she just couldn't stand it. He had tried so hard to get back in time for the social, told his sister that he had promised to be here and must come, but she was just afraid to travel the washed out roads in the night. We thought he was equally as anxious to be here for the Teachers' Association at the mouth of Irishman to dispose of his moonshine.

September 1.   Mary is anxious about Simon and we are all wondering how the tide has served him. He was due here yesterday, but there are no certainties in this country. We hardly thought it possible to get to Sassafras Sunday School this morning, but Jasper came and did get us across Montgomery. He said the cliff was "slicker and steeper" than ever, but if we would hold on to the laurel, we could get there. The ride in the boat to and from yellow Creek was not the dreamy one we have been having these hot summer afternoons, but was a hard struggle up the stream and an exciting dash down with the tide. After all this effort, when we reached the school house, the door was locked and no one there. We sat down by the roadside and sang until others came with the key. After Sunday School they hung around to talk, as it was the last time Miss McNab would be with them. Elhannon told us that he had not smoked a cigarette since he had promised Miss McCartney to stop, although Robert Kelley, his teacher, tried to get him to smoke with him. But we hear he has a pistol and his sister Alcie told us that when he was riding behind her on the way from the social, he fired it off. We have been asked to select another girl for the Harlan school; we offered the scholarship to Alcie Cornet, who seemed so pleased and eager to go, but was afraid her mother and father would not give her up. When we were telling them what we do at Christmas time, they asked us if it was new Christmas or old Christmas. We asked what they meant by old and new Christmas, and we were told that the old Christmas, January 6th, was Christ's birthday and the old people observed that and the young people had their frolics on new Christmas, December 25th. There is no giving of presents or any religious celebration, but much drinking of moonshine, fighting and general carousing.

This subject of old and new Christmas is new to us and very interesting. We wonder what connection it has with the old English Twelfth Night. We know there was a change of eleven days in the calendar in England and America about one hundred and fifty years ago, but did not know that any people today adhere to the old dates. Another subject for inquiry for those interested in the ancestry of these people!

But a more important subject for us just now is how to get Miss McNab to Jackson, as she must be in Louisville by Wednesday night. For days a wagon has been engaged to start with her in the morning but the tides have made the roads impassable for at least a week and she says she will walk if there is no other way. The only hope was to get Uncle John's boat and two men to take her. We stopped to consult him and when he saw how anxious she was, although his boat was in constant use, he was willing to give it up for three dollars, just what it cost him. Jasper offered to get Sam Mullins, who has logged all his life and knows the river well, and said they could get her there all right. Aunt Mary said Jasper was all the child she had and she wouldn't take six hundred dollars for him, so Miss McNab musn't take him home with her. As usual Aunt Mary was smoking her pipe and said, "I've smoked ever since I wuz a little chunk of a girl. My old granny uster look so purty smoking and I cotch hit from her."

Montgomery was still so high it was impossible to walk, so Miss McNab rode behind Jasper on his grandpap's horse and we rode on Uncle Jim's mule. We started an hour earlier than usual, as D. had been telling us for a week that he would have the biggest watermelon of the season ready for us today. The horses clambered along around the big rocks, splashing the water all over us. Those that rode behind had to hold pretty tight for we never knew when we might come to a deep hole, where the horse might mire in the quicksand or stumble. When we reached D.'s, we called out to Walter to "come go up to Sunday School," D. came out and said the water was too high but not a word about watermelons, so we did not like to stop and went on to Sunday School, where there was a crowd waiting. An old man told us that there had never been such a high tide in Montgomery. The people realized this was probably the last time they would see Miss McNab and seemed very loath to give her up. D. was watching for us as we came home, for he said Miss McNab should not go away without eating a piece of his big watermelon. Maggie Stacy came early in the afternoon and Rhoda persuaded her to stay all night. At nine o'clock we were helping Miss McNab pack, I looked out the window and saw a pine torch coming down the creek, and in a few minutes heard frantic cries for Mary Stacy. It was Maggie's mother, who was so anxious when she did not come home, that she and Martha had walked a mile and a half down the lonely washed out roads to search for her and seemed to [be] relieved to find she was here. Maggie would get out of bed to go home with her, and as she was not well, her mother took her in her arms and waded to her waist across the creek. And now after fixing Miss McNab's lunch basket, we have everything arranged for her to start at daylight tomorrow or as Jasper says, "as soon as we can discover to get into the boat."

September 2.   The first day without Miss McNab, how we miss her! Jasper and Sam had the boat well caulked and in good order, with shelves for the boxes, she had a comfortable seat on her telescope, leaning against the boxes. There was oil cloth enough to cover everything. The water was much lower than yesterday so the men took off their shoes and socks and started off pulling the boat through the shoals while we watched them out of sight. She was brave to start out to go one hundred miles down the river that way, but knowing these two men as we did and the respect all mountaineers have for women, we felt, and she did, that she was just as safe as she would have been with her own brothers. I think we realized this morning how far away we were from everywhere, but the same amount of work must go on, even if there are only two of us left. One taught the "washing lesson" on the side of the creek, while the other had experiences at the tent. One woman came from White Creek and said she wanted "you fellows" (a change from the usual title, "them women") to give her a Bible, some of them big pictures of Christ, some picture cards and enough papers to line her house. We gladly gave her the Bible and a picture, but told her we didn't furnish papers to line houses. She then turned to the postmaster's wife and told her she would be up there Friday to buy some papers to line her house. It was not hard for us to understand that this was one of the reasons the people do not get the papers they subscribe for. We are beginning to realize how hard it is for us to do without Jasper, but Uncle John took his place and "sot us across" on his nag, he said he "missed his boat terrible", as he had to carry all the water on his nag from the well across the creek. Miss Pettit took Miss McNab's place and had the kindergarten children. One boy in the sewing class was discouraged and said he aimed to hire him somebody to "finish his'n." Another replied, "I wouldn't swap myself a sewin' fer nobody." On the way home we met Simon just getting into his pap's with the wagon, we waited for him to set us across on John. He had been away a week and it was charming to see the delight on his and Mary's faces when they met. In his hand he carried a bundle wrapped in a bordered handkerchief, which proved to be white muslin for dresses for Rhoda and Mary. He met Miss McNab in the boat nearly to Hazard and said the tide was taking them down very fast.

September 3. While we were trying to sleep last night, we could hear Simon relating his wonderful experiences to Rhoda and Mary. When he came to explain about the new telephone from Jackson to Hazard, their exclamations of surprise were very amusing. "Now Simon, you know that haint so," "Waal now what about that any-way?" "How big's the wire?" "And one at one end and one at t'other and ye can hear em talk from Hazard to Jackson, forty mile away!" "Waal now don't hit beat all!" "Simon, is that sho nuff?" "How Miss McNab was a-telling me something about that, but I couldn't see how t'wuz." All of which made us feel sorry that we did not have more time to tell them of the outside world. A lesson given in ironing and the usual number at the tent to see to. Nannie Combs was of real interest; she was sent for, for a few months last year, to the Harlan school by the Young Women's Guild of the Warren Memorial Church at Louisville. She talked intelligently about the pictures and the places represented by them. Mrs. Williams had sent us several hundred Perry Pictures for the teachers, which Nannie helped us to sort. She showed good taste in the ones she selected for her school. She is the first one who has cared for black and white pictures on the gray mats, as all of the others want the brightest colored ones. We showed her how to mount magazine pictures on colored paper. She was especially pleased with one with Lincoln in the centre and small pictures of all the presidents around it. She told us how glad she would be to have good reading matter at her school, and wants to get her younger brother to go with her to Berea after Christmas. When her father came for her, he was just from the post office with a letter that they told him was from California and he thought it was from his boy in the Army, but he could not read, and asked her to see what he said. After all the company had gone we went out on the rocks to study our Bible lesson. Mr. Mitchell from Hazard came to spend the night and Mrs. Stacy sent him out there to find us. He has been trying all summer to see us, for as he started us in our first "Camp Industrial" he was anxious to see how the third one was coming on. He said some of the Hazard girls were anxious to have us come back there next year. He was much interested in our work here and our plans for the permanent school. By dinner–at half past ten today–Mrs. Stacy had finished both the white dress skirts and before dark, one of the waists.

September 4.   One of the visitors this morning showed so much pleasure at receiving some colored paper and pictures, she was fairly hungry for color. Said she aimed to make us some brooms. Small classes at Sassafras, some being sick and others busy "pulling fodder."[19] Beginning Monday the schools will stop two weeks for the "foddering season."

September 5.   We started on John, immediately after breakfast, hoping to visit everybody from here to the mouth of Carr today. At Uncle Ira Comb's store down on the river, we found a busy scene, he handles goods with the same enthusiasm he shows in preaching funerals. Old Aunt Peggy Godsey had ridden over five miles to do her trading. She bought a sack of flour, one of bacon, a large bucket of sugar and many other things and when they were loaded on her nag with her on top of them, it was well she did not have to cross a mountain to get home. Along with her were some of her neighbors walking, a man carried their purchases and the mother carried her five weeks old baby six miles each way. We spent an interesting hour with Mrs. Lou Annie Combs, her husband, Uncle Clint Combs, who was ninety-seven years old, died last year and when Uncle Ira preached his funeral this summer he said a good many times in the course of the service that he had known Uncle Clint all of his life and had never known any good of him. While he was saying this about their father, his widow, sons and daughters were kneeling around his grave weeping. Uncle Clint was a famous moonshiner and had spent several terms in the State Prison. This had been his home all his life and in his early days it must have been a pretentious one, as there were two rooms and a "dog run"[20] between. Aunt Lou Annie lives alone now with her youngest boy of eighteen. Although his father and all his brothers drank and used tobacco, this boy, Mason, we hear of wherever we go as the one who has never tasted a drop of liquor in his life and does not use tobacco nor swear. And he is remarkable, a tall, graceful, refined looking boy with a very attractive face. He sold his part of the land for $600.00 to get an education, has gone to school at Hindman one winter and at Hazard three winters. He has now a first class certificate, is teaching school and after Christmas is going to Louisville to a medical college. Aunt Lou Annie told us all this with pride, as she showed us through her house. She had a tall cherry corner cupboard and a cherry sugar chest with glass knobs that was made "nigh a hundred years ago right here." Mrs. Jinnie Combs was expecting us for dinner when we got there. We stopped at Ida Combs' school. She had her face swollen badly and was lame from bruises received when she was thrown from her horse which mired in the quicksand as she was crossing in the tide last Sunday on the way to school. The room looks very pretty with the pictures and flags we had given her tastefully arranged. I showed her how to make pin wheels for the children, while Katherine put the temperance gloves[21] on them and gave them all some Scripture cards. Mrs. Samp Combs was canning peaches and gave us some to eat. She has three idiot children and says she has never known anything but trouble since she married. She is so anxious for Alcie to accept the chance to go to Harlan, says her parents won't let her go for they need her to work, but that Alcie told them she would marry if they did not let her go and she could not bear to think of getting married, for it meant only trouble. As we mounted the mule at one place, we saw two stalwart figures striding up the road and Jasper's rousing voice revealed who they were, so they walked along with us, as we rode home in the twilight and told us of their boat ride to Jackson. They had a fine trip and are ready to start back with us any time. They did not reach Jackson until eleven o'clock at night and Sam Mullins said he felt sorry for her when he had to tell her just at dark that they were several hours out from Jackson, that she said, "What would my mother say if she could see me out here in the river to-night?" And then she wrapped herself in the oil cloth and said, "You both sing, Lead me oh Thou Great Jehova'," and "we sang it, too, all the way to Jackson," he said. They told us that the people here were so bad to talk that they had "studied" it over and decided that it would be well not to tell anybody they got there so late, that they "knowed Miss McNab was an honest little girl and would give no body no reason to say nothing against her credit."

September 6. Remind Combs' oldest "gal" came from the head of Acup to bring us a basket of large peaches. She said she hated to go to mill, but came today just to get to look at us, that she had heard her sister talk so much about us. She said her sisters came from school yesterday and said "two o' the whitest ladies that ever wuz had been there and give them all pretty cards and put some gloves on 'em that wuz jist as good for summer as winter." This girl asked very tenderly for Miss McCartney. While we were at Hindman Miss McCartney was with them when her sister died and helped to prepare her for burial. She wanted the Bible that she had promised them. Mr. Washington Combs and D. came to say they "had a little writin' they wanted us to fix up." I have never seen anything more pathetic than this poor, ignorant old father in trouble over his son. The boy, so weak minded, joined the Army, was sent to the Philippines, discharged and is over in California without any money to get home. He can neither read nor write, so a man wrote for him to ask his father to send him money to pay his way home. From the tone of the letter we think the man may be an imposter, so advised the father not to send money. We wrote to the postmaster of the town to look into the matter and let us know the best way to help the boy. The father wanted to pay for the writing, said he "didn't have much, but it peared like he would give us anything for helping him out of trouble." D. asked us to stop this afternoon, as he had a good watermelon and cantaloupe ready. We started early and did stop for them and he had fine apples ready for us to bring home with us. The classes were larger than usual and it was more than we could do to attend to them all. A teacher from over on the river said he could sew buttons on one way, but he thought my way would save sewing them on to many times, so he sewed all afternoon and asked us to come to his school to teach them sewing and kindergarten. The little children have learned the rainbow colors by stringing the second gift beads. On the way home, loaded down with apples, we were stopped at Green Combs and did our part toward eating a thirty-pound watermelon, consequently it was dark when we reached home After supper and prayers we have had to get together clothes, pictures and flags for a visit on the river and the Teachers' Association.

September 7.   As soon as breakfast was over, we started walking to meeting over on the river; there was a heavy mist, the grass was very wet and we were loaded down with luggage. To avoid crossing the creek, we walked around the cliffs, climbed fences, went through meadows, fields, high weeds and sand for over three miles. Then we had to cross the creek and to do this walked one half mile out of the way to find a boat. Opposite Mr. Burke Combs' there was a log canoe on our side, but we were afraid to cross by ourselves, so we called out to the old man to tell us how to get across, but he said "it depended on what notion took him" and immediately called out, "If that woman don't step faster she'll mire in the quicksand," and then by his directions we managed to pole the boat over. Now we had to cross a steep, rough mountain, where we were joined by others on their way to meeting. The climb took our breath and made us very warm before we reached the top. When we got to the foot of the mountain, nearly to the meeting place, the girls sat down and put on their shoes and stockings. At Uncle Rob Brashears' a crowd was assembled for the funeral occasion. We were so bedraggled, that we had to change shoes and skirts. They gave us the dish pan to wash in. The place of meeting was a beautiful spot under great trees on a steep mountain side overlooking the river. The houses over the graves were new and freshly painted, there were several preachers and services lasted several hours, with the usual walking about, drinking water and talking by the congregation. There was a platform with chairs on it for the preachers; on a pillow at their feet lay a little girl sick with scarlet fever, her throat badly swollen and she was moaning most of the time, and asking for water, while the mother and father fanned her. They had come to have the funeral of two of their children preached and did not seem to realize the danger to their sick child or the danger to all the other children there. In fact no one seemed alarmed.

After meeting was over, without adjournment, a Teachers' Association was held. When Uncle Ira gave the chair to Judge Combs, he said to the five other preachers, "Wall, let's get back and take our seats and listen to them talk and believe just what we want." As Miss Pettit passed him, she said, "just as we do with what you say, but I want you to tell me when I get through, if you believe what I say." There were earnest talks by some of the teachers, which showed they were thinking, and then Judge Combs said, "Now, Miss Pettit, you come entertain us a while." While she was speaking of the evils of whiskey and tobacco, there was strict attention, and some of the boys in the outskirts were heard to say, "that's a lie, taint so, etc." Uncle Ira, who gets drunk himself said, "I believe every word you spoke," and some old mothers told her, "hit was mighty good counsel fer the young." Judge Combs gave a fine talk on the importance of training the children to be good citizens and the influences of the home, the Sunday School and society (he was brave to praise Sunday Schools to that audience). He said the mountain people used to be a strong stalwart race, but for lack of proper physical training, they are fast degenerating into a race of pigmies. The teachers seemed to appreciate the pictures and flags we gave them for their school houses. We were urged to take dinner and spend the night at Uncle Rob Brashears', but as there were thirty to stay there and Mrs. Singleton was looking for us, we declined. Fernando Combs, with Diana behind him on a mule, came eight miles out of his way to see us, as they started to Harlan to school. Diana was bright and did not seem to mind leaving home for so long, she had on a new dark blue dress, yarn stockings, winter shoes and the white sun bonnet we had made. She carried nothing with her except the gray calico dress on which she rode. John C. Combs says she is the brightest child he ever taught and we have made no mistake to choose her. We walked three miles further to Mrs. Singleton's at the mouth of Macey's Creek, where we found the most complete home we have seen in the mountains, a two story house with six rooms and a nice cellar, everything clean and attractive, on the side porch a large bath tub, and tooth brushes. Mr. Singleton has a bicycle and everything shows them to be intelligent and progressive. We were specially anxious to know Mrs. Singleton, because she always has a Christmas tree for the children on Macey's Creek. There are about twenty of us here to spend the night, and at twilight as we were sitting on the front porch, a man rode up and when he lifted his hat, we had quite a sensation, for we knew it was someone from the outside world. When he spoke, we recognized Judge Moss, who is on his way to Circuit Court at Hazard. We certainly were glad when supper was ready, for we had had nothing to eat since breakfast at daylight, had walked eleven miles and spent four hours at meeting, and it was the best cooked meal we have ever eaten in the mountains, and she has never been to the railroad. All evening they have kept us busy at the organ, the entire company joining in the singing.

September 8.   Clarissa Singleton and Lizzie Hall, two pretty bright half grown girls, slept on the floor in the room with us, none of us got much sleep for they talked most of the night in an excited whisper about the "meetin' and the fellows." Mrs. Singleton, who weighs over three hundred pounds, walked to meeting with us. It took two boats to take us all across the river, which seemed very wide and deep by the side of our Carr. The girls made fans out of the large magnolia leaves from the roadside. There was a much larger crowd today than yesterday. They opened by singing in a shrill, high voice, twelve verses of the hymn beginning–

A twelvemonth more has rolled around,
Since we attended on this ground,
Ten thousand scenes have marked the year
Since we met last to worship here.

Full many a friend and many a foe
Have left this weeping world below,
And many a homeless Wanderer's tear
Has fallen since we worshiped here.
Full many a father's lost his son,
And many a mother's daughter gone;
The orphan's cry and widow's tear
Have mingled since we worshiped here.

Uncle Ira began by saying he would not preach long, as he was hoarse; but he did speak long and loud. The funerals of seven persons were "attended to," Jim Brashears' wife, who died last Christmas day in Texas, or as the preacher said, "in a far away and absent country," and six of Uncle Rob's grandchildren. At the close there was much shouting, especially by the mother of the sick child which excited her so that she was much worse.

Without any dinner, we started on the seven-miles journey home with all the rest who lived "yon side" of the mountain. Old Mrs. Godsey showed us the place where the horse slipped over the bank with her this morning. She was picked up unconscious, but soon recovered enough to walk on over the mountain to meeting in spite of seventy-five years, several cuts on her head and a badly bruised back. She said she was not going to tell her husband, because he would not "favor her going to no more meetins'." At Mrs. Bob Combs' we were asked to stop by and eat cantaloupe, our first refreshment since breakfast except two or three "sorry" little apples given us by "Jess' Bills father" and some cake from somebody's lunch basket at the meeting. Everybody was full of the trouble they had at the meeting. Bridles had been cut, rocks put under saddles, blankets stolen and horses turned loose, which made us feel thankful that we had no "nags to be pestered." Mary and Rhoda wore their new white dresses, the first time they have ever had a white dress and they were the admiration of all the maidens at the meeting.

September 9.   Many visitors all day. Old Mrs. Wash Combs stopped on her way home from meeting. She was riding a man's saddle and saddle bags. She rarely gets away from home, as she is "fitified." We were glad that we were able to give her so much pleasure as she found in the pretty tent and our "show things." She was so grateful when we helped her on her horse to start home with a bag full of papers and pictures. Two little girls came from Acup with a basket of peaches for us.

During "foddering season" we are to have the classes at the tent and there were thirty children here this afternoon, the rest were at work in the field. While we were busy with the classes, the visitors were entertaining themselves and we overheard the following conversation:

> Hev ye he'rd tell that Green Combs has let his little Diana go off to school for four years? You'uns know he's crazy or he wouldn't ha' done it. D. says hits the wust pass Green ever done to let her go. Them wimmin sent her off and they are trying to get all the girls off. They say they's a school off there, but who knows? They couldn't git one o' mine. I wonder what they want 'em to go off fer anyway.

We gave away a large number of periodicals. Maggie Stacy came to invite us to a "workin'" there Wednesday, said the men would pull fodder while the women would quilt and the young people come for a candy pulling, if we would make the candy. Mrs. Owens told us how Alcie and Elhannon got to go to meeting. Their father said they shouldn't go, they had to pull fodder, but Alcie went to Mr. Owens, fell at his feet, put her arms around his knees and begged him to pull fodder in her place, so he left his field and went to theirs, so they could go off.

Simon went to Hazard to Court today and brought Mary and Rhoda each a long string of beads, Rhoda put her arms around him and jumped up and down, she was so pleased.

September 10. We had the weekly "washing lesson" and the tent of visitors to attend to all morning. Fernando came to tell us of his trip to Harlan with Diana, said she got "some tired," riding the forty miles behind him on the sharp backed mule, that she thought Pine Mountain was the biggest thing she "ever seed" and when they came to town asked "what ailed them houses, they's so nigh together." That was the first time she had ever seen a town. He was much pleased with the school and thought Diana would do well. He said that five or six years ago he heard so much about the train and had such a desire to see it, that he walked the sixty-five miles to Jackson just for that purpose, secured work at the mill and stayed there a week so that he could see the train every day. He was so pleased when we gave him his choice of some books and he selected Shakespeare, Ruskin and *David Copperfield*, said he had never read a novel in his life, nor his father before him, and thought it wrong for him to read *Black Rock* when I sent it up to him. Old Mrs. Cornet gave the directions for old fashioned vegetable dyes, the way her mother had showed her.

September 11. When we went down to the tent this morning, old Mr. Godsey was sitting in one of the steamer chairs, he had removed his hat and when I asked him not to get up to speak to us, he said, "I must get up to shake hands with such nice ladies." After a bit he apologized for having to put on his hat, as he was afraid of taking cold, and never takes it off except to eat or sleep. When he looked at the stereoscopic views, he talked very intelligently about Washington City, the different presidents and the Virginia Natural Bridge. He brought back a book we had loaned him, *The Son of Man*, by Alexander,[22] said he had read it twice and liked it better than anything he ever read, so we gave it to him to keep. He quoted a long historical rhyme by Peter Parley, which he said he learned more than seventy years ago. I asked if he had better schools where he came from in Virginia than they have here, but he said, "no," his teacher "was nobody from nowhere and never knowed nothin when he got thar." He asked for two more large Sunday School pictures. On the way to the "workin" we stopped to see if "little Granny Stacy" would sell us some of her pretty blankets, but could not persuade her to part with them. The visit to Aunt Mary was full of interest as always. As she is a "charm-doctor," Katherine asked her to charm away the sprained wrist. Aunt Mary said she would do her best and if she didn't do her any good, she wouldn't do her any harm. She explained that an old man had taught her the charm many years ago, but if she revealed the secret to us, she would lose her power, because a woman could tell it to three men and a man to three women. She must know the full name of the person, the "nater" of the trouble and between sunset and dark she goes out to look at a green apple tree and says a "few words of ceremony" (which is the secret). She says she can cure cancer and most anything and has cured thousands. We went on up Red Oak to see if Mrs. Enoch Combs could not make a gray mixed linsey instead of all black, found her in despair about ever making any linsey, as all the old maids are in the fields pulling fodder and Mary so "bad off" that she has to stay by her. She gave us a beautiful old indigo blue and madder red coverlid. We went for the mail and got the first paper for days.

September 12.   A rainy morning in the tent trying to write and seeing visitors. Clarinda Combs, an eighteen year old girl, who lives alone with her father, wanted pretty things for her house, and said the pictures and colored paper we gave her were the "beautifulest things" she ever saw, that she kept a little table with pictures and things to read on it, but that her father had not "larnin'." She said, "You'uns is so nice, you look so pleased and is always friendly and glad to see folks, hit makes 'em feel better." She walked home, three miles through the mud carrying a load of pictures, paper and the Bible we gave her, for she said they had none.

Late this afternoon, when we were sitting out on the rocks writing, Chloe stopped with us. She had been to buy a calico dress to wear to meetin' over on the Rock house, but as there was no calico to be had, she "couldn't get to go to meetin'." I went back to the tent to get her books to read and when I gave her colored paper to make pretty things of, she said she could make blossoms and wheels but didn't know how to make pretty things. When she went to put the things in the saddle bags, she found the green coffee had spilled out and picked it up off the road, digging it out of the dirt, where the horse had tramped it and put it in loose with the chewing and smoking tobacco. While we were picking up the coffee, she told me if I would give her a Bible, she would try to be a good girl. Her two brothers passed by walking home from Hazard, looking as nice as if they were walking down the streets of a city, instead of jumping the rocks in Montgomery. They have been teaching in the County for several years and studying law and today they passed an examination and secured a law license. This shows what persistent effort will do, for they have had a hard struggle to get an education. Their mother and father cannot read nor write. Chloe had to hurry home to get supper, for her mother had had a fit the night before and could not do anything. This frail girl of fourteen has all the care of the home, as the mother is hardly ever able to do anything.

Just as we had finished supper and begun to write up the day's happenings, Tucker Roark rushed in on his way from the Law examination. He said he:

> didn't miss but one question, but they wouldn't pass him on account of his handwrite, and one of them Combs boys told 'em he wasn't old enough and didn't have enough education, and he wouldn't swear he was twenty-one, cause he wasn't, the failure was worth fifty dollars to him for now he would go to a law school and study hard till he got his diploma.

September 13.   At twelve last night we were awakened by a severe rain storm, and the water was running down the back of my neck and standing in pools on my top cover, the room seemed to be leaking generally and a dry place large enough for the cot could not be found, so I had to move it into Mrs. Stacy's room.

Mill day and all of it spent with visitors. Spencer Combs came for some books to take away to his school on Macey's Creek. He says he loves to read, especially poetry; he is twenty years old and has never been to school except to the country school here and one month at Hazard, but he has a second class certificate and will begin his school Monday. He said there was no good tobacco and he never used it and even if he had gotten drunk a few times, he was going to teach his pupils that it was wrong. He didn't believe in whipping except as a last resort. He continued, "I aim to teach this school, then go two months to the winter school here, if they's one, help paw put in his crap, teach another fall school, and help with another crap, save all my money and then go somewhar off to school for a whole year."

Enoch Polly brought a little boy from "way over yon side of the mountain to git some books," said everybody over there that "seed" his wanted some. A girl from Irishman said she loved to read better that anything and as she had been "kinder puny all her life and could not work in the fields, they let her go to school a big grain." Mrs. Smith sang "Barbara Allen" for us and said her daughter wanted to come down to sing ballads with us. She told us her sister on Smith's Branch had some beautiful blankets for sale, so we are going to see them. After dinner we found Rhoda at the well, scrubbing her teeth with scourine and when I told her it was bad for them, she said that it got the table white and she thought it would make her teeth white. Mrs. Stacy and Rhoda never saw a tooth brush until we gave them these and now they use them regularly and she says "hit pears like I jist don't feel right if I don't brush my teeth." Like Booker Washington, we believe in the Gospel of the tooth brush and have given many away and really they take more readily to this than to most of our customs. One woman to who we had given one, came back miles to say that her brother from over on Lot' s Creek wanted us to send him one. John C., Rankin and Fernando Combs spent the entire afternoon and these wise young lawyers told many things of the "ways of the people of this country." Rankin is anxious for us to get a scholarship some place for one of his pupils, a man twenty-six years old, who had his arm shot off in a drunken fight last Christmas and now thinks there is no other way for him to make a living except by teaching and as he has no money, would be glad of help to get an education. I promised to write to Berea about him. Rankin says he notices that we do not understand some of their expressions, which mean just the opposite to the way we use them, for instance, when Katherine asked him if he wanted some flags and pictures for his school, he replied, "I don't care to," and he saw we thought he meant he did not want them, but he meant he would really be glad to have them. Mrs. Stacy asked me to go with her over on Lot's Creek to see her sister, Mrs. Young, who was very ill. She rode behind me on John but we had to walk and lead him across the rough mountain. The family and neighbors had come and were standing about with no idea what to do for a sick person. It is pathetic to see the hard lives of the women and their absolute ignorance of how to take proper care of themselves and their families. Mrs. Young had been married sixteen years and had eleven children.

September 14.   Up by daylight and just as soon as breakfast was over, we started on John for an all day trip up George's Branch. We went up the three forks and made eleven visits. At Al Sumner's where they have the Saturday night "gatherings," and where they "confederated" against the Shade Doans' for killing the ducks, everything was very clean and orderly. Mrs. Sumner was a tall, gaunt woman dressed in a narrow, one pieced dress, very short, showing her feet and ankles, she stood with her hands on her hips, while she talked to us, and her husband, who sat in the kitchen, where we could not see him, joined in the conversation. Neither of them nor their grown children can read or write. One little boy had been to school and told us how he liked to read the book we had loaned him, and wanted another. His mother went to get it, where it was carefully put away in a trunk, "fer lowed you'uns would come fer hit," but we told her he could have it. Everywhere we go we find the people take excellent care of the books we loan them, even when they do not take care of their own things. No one was at home at Mrs. Gent's, they were still over at Uncle Rob's, where their little sick girl had died. As we had some papers and pictures to leave, we untied the latch string and went into one of the cleanest homes we have seen this summer. Sitting in a row in the corner were several little rag dolls and on the shelf above were seven paper dolls like Miss McNab had taught them to make, on the walls were paper chains, pictures and papers we had given them. Little Ellie Sumner, eleven years old, one of the brightest girls in the sewing class, had the entire care of a family of nine with a sick mother and young baby. The mother said as she was sickly most of the time, Ellie had all the cooking, washing and milking to do, besides helping in the fields, said she cried because she couldn't go to sew every time, and her pale face and shrunken shoulders showed just how hard her young life was. Oh, these hard worked little girls, how one would like to give them a free, joyous child's life with dolls to nurse and love instead of so much of the real burden of life! The oldest daughter, fourteen, had married the Squire's son who makes moonshine whiskey, which they both drink. Ellie said she "tried to shame her not to marry but she couldn't." Mrs. Shade Doan was making lye out of doors, in a dress up to her knees, while the two boys who come to Sunday School in their shirts, were in the same undress condition, and all the other children were as dirty and ragged; she asked us into the house first, but the smells were too much for us, so we went out to watch her make the lye. We left the mule at the head of the branch in care of Sewall Smith, while we walked over the mountain and down Big Branch to see if Mrs. Eli Brashears had any flax and blankets to sell. Although she had nothing for sale, she took pleasure in showing us the beautiful converlids she had been making all her life. When they were taking them out of the box, we saw some books we had given Enoch Polly, who had gone to meeting and asked Sarah to take care of them, and she had been reading some of them. Mrs. Brashears said that this neat, bright looking girl was her granddaughter, Sarah Watts, or rather Sarah Tucker, as she had married Roark's boy, but Sarah protested, said she had left him and did not want to be called by his name. This twenty-year-old Tucker had married this girl, who was much older, after knowing her just two weeks. After the climb up the mountain we were ready for the luncheon we had with us and ate it under a great tree just on top, where we had a view of the valley on both sides. It was superb. It seemed very lonely up there, as if few ever came that way, but going down we met Mr. Jim Brashears, who had just been helping the Gent's home. Mrs. Gent rode and carried the baby, he brought two on his horse, two little girls walked and Mr. Gent walked and drove the cow, which they had to take over for the little sick child. When we got on John after the long tramp, in the heat, we congratulated ourselves that we had a nag that two could ride on so comfortably. But we had not gone far, when this same comfortable nag gave us a shock, for we were going slowly up a steep bank when he whirled around very suddenly and "flung" us both off backwards from the top of the high mule down the bank, into the branch. I fell flat on a big rock, Katherine right on my chest, we were both under John's feet but he kindly moved out of the way and stood waiting for us. We were both badly shaken up and bruised and felt faint for an instant, but when we discovered that all our hairpins were broken and our side combs floating down the stream, we quickly recovered and rushed after them (for we remembered that they cannot be purchased in "in this country.") Some of the Shade Doans' saw the plight we were in and came to us, but they were so afraid of the mule they were not much help. So notwithstanding the bruises and a sprained wrist, we straightened the saddle, mounted and went on to Sunday School, stopping first at Mrs. Mullins to get brushed up. We had a larger attendance than usual, really more than two can manage, and when we got home we were stiff enough to go to bed.

September 15.   Another high tide in Montgomery and Carr. My chest hurt so I could not get up, and as it was so rainy, we knew there would not be many at Sunday School, so Katherine started by herself. Mr. Stacy took her behind him on the same John as far as Yellow Creek and she walked from there in the rain, wading through mud, sand and water. The school house was locked and no none there, so she went on (in some places knee deep in the mud) to the post office for the key, but it was not there, so she hurried home. Opposite the tent, on the other side of Carr she stood, wondering how to cross, when Mr. Stacy came with John. The water was then up to the mule's body and in a little while she would have been compelled to stay on the other side, so we were waterbound for the rest of the day, no one came but Jasper and we had the Bible lesson and as Rhoda and Mrs. Stacy have learned to play some hymns on the organ, they sang most of the day. Uncle Jim Stacy sent us word that our ribs may be broken, but that we would know for sure in eight days.

September 16.   Water going down some, but still very high, we managed to get down to the tent, Jack Sumner, Mose and Nannie Adams waded down Montgomery to stay all day and finish their patches and Nannie her necktie. These two are grown boys and one of them has been married and separated from his wife and is now going to school for the first time, learning to read and write. We gave them pocket needle books, each containing a temperance pledge, asked them to study about it and when they were willing to sign it, to write and tell us. D. Combs and his sister, Mrs. Whittaker, from the Rock House came. She was sad and broken hearted over her boy, Leslie; asked if we knew where he had gone, said she knew he had not gone so far as Texas, because he didn't have any money. Her face lighted up as she took the papers and pictures and she said her daughter aimed to come and see us. There were fifteen children here for sewing and kindergarten, some of them walking three and four miles down branches and around cliffs and we wondered how they got here, for a tide makes traveling almost impossible. Mr. Wells, one of the fathers, helped with the kindergarten class and thought what they were learning was "good fer 'em."

September 17.   Another high tide and a cold wave! We were not out of the house all day, not even at the tent, but sat by the fire and wrote and mended, while Mrs. Stacy and Rhoda sang old ballads, while they carded and spun. No one came but Jasper going squirrel hunting and John White Sumner on his way to Hazard, stopped to take our mail, but Carr was too high to cross and he had to go back.

September 18.   Cold and clear! Soon after breakfast a man stopped to tell us that Sally Mullins wanted us to come down to see about dyeing the wool for our blanket, so we started at once, a new way over the hill to George's Branch. We climbed over many fallen trees, and crossed some beautiful little cascades, pouring down over the rocks, we had a fine view of the winding stream and distant hills. Sally and Tilda were washing and not expecting us until after twelve, but they hurried to get the clothes out, rinsing them right in the branch, and we began coloring the wool, which was not altogether a success. As it would not be dry enough to quill and weave for several hours, we went on to make some visits up Water Branch. At Mrs. Godsey's, shelled corn and strings of beans were spread out on a dirty quilt in front of the fire to dry. There was a pretty old indigo blue and madder red coverlid that had been used for a saddle blanket, hanging on the fence, which they said we might have when they saw we liked it. The children told us they had read all the books we had given them. We climbed the mountain side for more than a mile, following this branch before we came to a house. Mrs. Bony Combs and little "John Nothing" were sitting by a low fire, while she picked soft white wool from a home-made basket, he striking her in the back and calling her "Bets." He would have us go out to see his "peets," as he called the chickens. He went to show us how to get up to Aunt

Katherine Grace's and on the way used many oaths. When a hog crossed the path, he called out, "Devil take you, don't raise your bristles at me." We asked him not to swear and he said he would stop if he could, but he "didn't guess he could." He is so bright, but there seems little hope where he is. Aunt Katherine was sitting in the open kitchen, huddled over the stove with a pipe in her mouth, watching a big pot of beans, all she was cooking for dinner for herself and [an] old maid sister, over eighty years old, who was out in the field pulling fodder. She had some pretty homemade baskets that her husband had made years ago and a big "fat gourd" which I longed to have, until I saw a hole in it. She started us off loaded down with apples and Mrs. Combs was waiting at the fence to give us more apples, which were all the dinner we had. Sally Mullins had commenced weaving on the blanket by the time we got back there, and we stayed long enough to see all the colors in. Mrs. Ashley had three tiny little drinking gourds for us which were sent by a little girl ten miles away, who had never seen us. Simon came along at the first ford and offered to take us across, but the water was so deep we preferred to go back over the hill, but let him carry the coverlid, gourds and various things that had been given us on the way. Mrs. Jasper Cornet and Mrs. Smith were waiting at the tent to see us and get reading matter. Jasper came in the evening for "just one tune on the little new cupboard," and although we were still suffering from the fall from the mule, we could not refuse.

September 19. Robert Kelley, the teacher at Sassafras, came and sewed all day to finish hemstitching his handkerchief. Mrs. Enoch Combs came to tell us to come over to Uncle Jim's to take her picture warping the piece for our dresses and said she was willing to sell us five blankets, as she wanted money to buy a sewing machine, for her son-in-law, P. Cody, was mad because Uncle Enoch had willed his property to his children instead of to him and he was going to move away and take his machine. She said it would be a great deal of trouble to make the gray mixed linsey and she did not know whether she could do it, for the old maid sisters were still pulling fodder and could not help, but before she left she had concluded she could do it. Mr. Jesse Combs (the father of Bill) wants to make a boat and take us down the river to Jackson when we go home. We told him that we expect to leave here October 1st at daylight and if he has his boat ready by that time, we shall go with him. We also told him that we could write a book on mountain people making engagements and breaking them, and we hoped that he would not add another chapter to it. He said he would "sure have the boat done" in plenty of time and nothing but sickness would keep him from going and he would be sure to let us know beforehand. He said he was going to hew the gunwales out of a big log up Red Oak, I suggested that he begin on it at once, as I knew it would be a slow process, but he said, "they wuz meetin' Saturday and Sunday" and he would commence as soon as it was over.

September 20. Mill day and lots of visitors! Uncle Jim has lost a mule, all hands are out hunting for it, even Simon has gone, so there was no one to grind corn and all had to leave their turns and come back for them tomorrow. Mrs. Taylor Combs came for another lesson in crocheting. Jack Sumner brought his cousin Peggy McIntire from over on the river. He was riding on two meal sacks and a flour sack. Peggy is another young girl who has been married and separated from her husband a long time, she is notoriously bad, but asked us for a Bible to read and said she wants to be good. She is a strong, bold, hard looking girl. Mr. Taylor Combs sent us word he is making us a little log cabin to take home with us. We have been trying all summer to get flax to weave ourselves and today Mrs. Singleton sent us some from Macey's Creek.

September 21. Ellie Sumner came, saying, she was "just bound to stay with you'uns one more time." She had gotten breakfast, milled and put the dinner on and said she ran most of the way (four miles), and was completely exhausted and out of breath when she got there. Mrs. Manton Cornet, Mary's sister-in-law, who has not been here before for nine years and sometimes does not get off her branch for a year, did enjoy being with us today. Her husband and his two brothers have gone to Frankfort as witnesses against Granville Stacy for robbing the post office. We sized the cotton chain for the piece we are to weave. This means stiffening it in corn meal starch. We walked over the hill again to George's Branch Sunday School, Ellie Sumner carried a heavy bundle of papers and books which we wanted her to leave until someone was passing on a horse, but she was afraid she would never get them. Everett and Avery Mullins, seven and eight years old, came to return books and walked back with us. They found and dug ginseng and gathered "mushrooners and ground shells." They told us with much pride that they had new shirts and new shoes already to wear to the funeral at Bob Combs' in November. Mr. and Mrs. Gent were there with the five little girls, the youngest one sick with scarlet fever and the mother carried her in her arms, said she just would come. She had on white yarn stockings, a white shawl over her head and looked so pretty, one of the girls, three years old, had on a blue and white calico shirt waist, a purple and green calico skirt to her knees, a white ribbon around her neck and waist, white yarn stockings and copper toed shoes. One little girl, almost blind from granulated sore eyes, had walked three miles and had to be led all the way. We put the temperance gloves on the children, they learned them at once and one little girl said she was going to put them on her doll. Our Simon returned with the lost mule after a two days' search in the densely wooded mountains. He stopped at the post office for the mail, but the postmaster had gone to Frankfort to his son's trial, Robert was away with the key to the mail bag and it could not be opened.

September 22. I was scared last night, for I thought Katherine was taking pneumonia and put her to bed early with the hot water bag and mustard plaster, but we are relieved to know that it is only two broken ribs knitting together, as Uncle Jim Stacy told us they would hurt this way in about eight days, if they were really broken. We had known all week that there was some trouble there with both of us, and I have concluded that the pain in my chest comes from a broken rib, too. Notwithstanding all this, we were up early this morning helping Mary and Rhoda for the funeral meeting. They looked so nice in their new white dresses as they rode off on John. We could not leave Sunday School to go to the funeral, but it was of unusual interest, as a man was having his wife's funeral preached and his own at the same time, for he said he did not want anybody to be "a-bothering to preach his funeral when he was dead and gone." At Sassafras the door was locked and Robert Kelley had gone to meeting with the key in his pocket, so had the Sunday School under the trees by the roadside. At Montgomery the house was filled with boys and young men who seemed to be really impressed with the temperance lesson and the talk on the same subject that was given at the close of the lesson. The young moonshiner who is always there, looked very serious and thoughtful and hung around us on leaving as if he wanted to say something.

September 23.　　Gave the last washing lesson this morning (but I suppose this is an important part of Settlement work), and began to spool cotton for our chain. Mrs. Stacy says she knows we shall never learn to weave, for it will take a week to get the piece in and another week to weave it, that it would take a day to learn to tie the weaver's knot. But we learned to tie the weaver's knot without any trouble and are determined to get the piece in the loom and all the flax woven before we leave, if one has to weave all the time, while the other does settlement work, for we have been looking forward for a chance to learn to weave for three years. The last class at Sassafras school house and they were all eager to finish up the work they had on hand

and one boy said he wouldn't take fifty dollars for what we had taught him. Indeed, they all seemed to be grateful for what they had learned and realized that this would probably be the last chance they would ever have for anything of this kind. We went to the post office, but the bag was still unopened as Robert had not come home with the key. I had received notice that there were some registered letters there for me, so one of the children unlocked the door and the postmaster's wife, who could not read, went into the office with us, the registered letters were lying out on the table where anyone could pick them up. Had to look through the drawers to find the receipt to sign before I took the letters. We asked for fifty cents worth of stamps and she gave us the box to help ourselves, saying she thought they were cheaper if we got that many. On the way home we met Basil Beverley waiting to tell us that his "paw aimed to send Tilford off with you'uns to that horsepittal to get cured up, but he was mighty skeared of fires in the City." He was suffering with a very sore hand which was swollen to twice its usual size. He had cut it with an axe clearing away timber and had been "doctoring hit with first one yarb and then another until his was all poisoned up." A little further down sitting on the fence waiting for us was our old friend Mr. Austin Ritchie from Vest, he had brought Mary, his blind girl, for us to take to the school at Louisville. She said she would come and stay awhile and if she liked us, she would go with us. She came behind him on his nag, she was bareheaded, without a wrap and he took some clothes out of the saddle bags saying they "didn't know just what she would need, but they had made some lawns and calicos." This has been a beautiful evening and it was hard to realize that we were not living in the time of our great-grandmothers. By a bright firelight Rhoda carding, Mrs. Stacy spinning at the large wheel, one of us spooling at the little wheel, while the other kept the winding blades straight and tied the broken thread in a weaver's knot. Mary sang an old ballad, while Simon and Mr. Ritchie cut out the drinking gourds and talked about the "craps" and the primitive conditions under which they lived, much as we supposed our great grandparents would have talked.

September 24.   Finished spooling and Mrs. Stacy went with me over to "Simon's Maw's" to show me how to warp our piece. She could not get over the fact that we had spooled it so quickly and that I did learn to warp. While I was warping, Katherine had the tent full of people to look after. They seem sorry that our departure is so near at hand and are coming in crowds these last days. We are giving away the books that we have had for a Circulating Library all summer and it is encouraging to see the selection most of them make, that many of them really have a taste for good reading, and the books that have been in constant use these three months are all in good condition. Judge Combs says that Mattie was not satisfied at Hazard and if the chance is still open to her she would like to go to Harlan. But we could not let him know until we hear from another girl, to whom we have offered the scholarship. We heard that Jess just went up Red Oak today to begin hewing out the gunwales for the boat, everybody tells us that Jess is mighty slow, but Simon says he is the most reliable person we can get when he does move. This is the fourth week there has been no school at George's Branch, so all the children from there came here this afternoon for their last work with us. Blind Mary joined the kindergarten class, stringing the beads and quickly learning the different shapes by touch. I had to manage them all, as Katherine was beginning to put the piece in the loom. Mrs. Stacy still insisting that it will take a week to get the piece in. Mr. Ritchie has been with us all day and says Mary seems satisfied to let him go home in the morning. The rocking chair is what brought about this satisfaction, I think, as she never sat in one before and has rocked hard most of the day. This evening was spent like the last, except we quilled flax to weave instead of spooling the cotton for the chain. If the loom room had not been dark and cold we should have kept on putting in the piece (for warp). We had had prayers and were just starting to bed when we heard loud talking at the gate and Rhoda looked out and said, "They's nags thar and people's gettin' offen 'em." Robert Kelley and Robert Stacy had gathered twelve young people and come for a candy pulling, without any warning. Rhoda was delighted and Simon and Mary were pleased, so we did not say anything about the broken ribs needing rest, but measured out the sugar and got everything ready, while Simon made the fire in the kitchen stove. None of them had ever been to a candy pulling before nor eaten any homemade candy, except what we had at the last social. While the candy was cooking, they sang old ballads in their own peculiar way. Each one took his plate of candy out into the yard to cool and they said they had the "best time ever wuz" while they pulled it in the moonlight. Then we went into the house and had games and more music before they left.

September 25.   Two weeks ago we began planning to spend today upon Smith's Branch, twelve miles up Carr, but I had to stay to finish getting the piece in the loom (for we are on trial before Mrs. Stacy), so Katherine mounted John soon after daylight and took a bag of periodicals and pictures and a large meal sack to hold the five blankets that she hoped to purchase. She was still suffering with the broken ribs and sprained wrist and felt shaky about riding John. In passing she called to Jasper that Miss Stone wanted to see him right away. John wheeled around twice before she got to Grandmother Cornet's, where Ailsie was waiting for her. Mrs. Cornet was wading across the deep creek, driving the cows to milk, but called to her to wait and look at the coverlid and blanket that she wanted to trade for some of "you'uns plunder." They were not the pretty bright colors we wanted, but she insisted on her taking them anyway, said one color would keep her just as warm as another. Katherine wanted to change nags with Ailsie but she said hers was "the wildest beastie that ever wuz," so she was content with John. Our Mrs. Smith met them at the mouth of Smith's Branch to introduce them all the way up. When they came to Barbara Smith's, the deformed woman who had the blankets for sale, her sister had her stand up before them and asked them if "she was not the awfulest sight in this world," and she seemed proud of the fact that there was something unusual about her. There was general excitement on Smith's Branch because there was a "stir off" with grandmother Smith at the head of it. There she sat stirring the great boiling mass of cane juice in a long pan over a log fire made in a deep trench. Nearby a girl was riding a horse round and round the tread mill, crushing the juice out of the cane. When it came time to take it off, they called up and down the creek and men, women and children came running and dipped into the kettle, and there were exclamations of satisfaction as the sticks went back and forth between their mouths and the kettle. Just in the midst of it, a man came with a paper under his arm and said in an exited way, "people, I just want you to listen to what I've got to read to you," and he sat down on a log while they all stopped to listen to the account of the last days and words of President McKinley. Nearly all of the housekeepers on this branch had prepared dinner for them, but they went to the head to take dinner with Hillard Smith's mother and sister, as they stayed at home expecting them. The mother was so pleased that they knew her boy Hillard, a lawyer in Hindman, of whom she is so proud. Katherine bought only one blanket, as all the others she saw had been used and were not bright colored. This was a very pretty striped one and had stripes of natural black sheep's wool. She stopped to see everybody down Carr on the way home. While they sat on the grass eating watermelon at Mr. Spencer Combs', he told them that the people here are just seventy-five years behind those of the Bluegrass. Mrs. Buck Ashley, a woman nearly blind, told them of her sorrow, that her husband was in jail, her six children scattered about and she was trying to get them together and the people wouldn't give them up and kept them to work in the fields.

As soon as Katherine called Jasper this morning, he started post haste to see what I wanted before he had time to get his breath. I said, "Come on, Jasper, let's go to work" and we went to the loom-house and spent most of the day getting the piece in, which was a very tedious process, that only those who know how to weave can understand, but we did get the piece in and I began to weave before dark, much to Mrs. Stacy's surprise. I entertained most of the visitors in the loom-room, but had to go to the tent with some of them. The woman with the sore headed baby came for more castile soap and borax, said she had used what we gave her every day and brought the baby for me to see that its head was nearly well, she wanted some papers to line her house, a pretty for the old grandmother (whom we had never seen) to remember us by and a Bible. She and her husband could not read but her little girls were learning at school. Her four-year-old boy kept crying for a "little red Bible book" and would not be comforted with pictures, just kept saying he wanted a Bible book, but as we had given one to that family and the others were promised, we had to let him go away crying for the "Bible book."

William Riley Gent, one of our nice boys, brought his sister from over on the Rock House, and she said her husband, Bige, wanted a Bible with pretty reading in it, like the one we gave William Riley. I asked her if she thought the Bible had pretty reading in it and she said, "Wall, his'n did." Jasper said he was going up Yellow Creek tomorrow logging and I told him I hoped he would not go back to swearing when he got out with the log men, and he replied, "that he was done with swearing." Mrs. Stacy says if we hadn't done any other good this summer, it was worth our coming to make such a change in Jasper. Mary Ritchie has been happy all day without her father, for when she was not rocking in the chair, she was picking out tunes on the organ. Her father left her in our care, seeming to have perfect confidence in our being able to do everything for her. He gave me twenty dollars and told me to buy her a hat and whatever she needed.

September 26.   Weaving has not stopped us today, first one and then the other at the loom and Mrs. Stacy thinks it a marvel that we have woven a whole yard. Hillard Smith was here most of the day and said he was so proud that we had been to see his mother and sister, who lead such lonely lives at the head of the branch. Some young boys from Virginia have just come here to do surveying and as they have been in the mountains since last March, when they heard there was a bit of the outside world here, they came at once to see us and they were just as eager to get something to read as the mountain folks for they, too, have trouble with the mails. They told us that at one house they saw such a pretty picture on the wall, that they asked where it came from and the man said, "Them strange wimmin follows retchin' 'em out."

Mr. Taylor Combs came walking down Montgomery with a log cabin on his shoulders, as he thought we would need something to remind us of the mountains, when we reached home. It is a typical home made of oak and lynn logs chinked with mud, stick and clay chimney and no windows. I think he felt repaid for giving us this pleasure when he saw our delight and when we told his wife she could have one of the steamer chairs. His brother, the young moonshiner, came with him, stayed around where we were and seemed to want to tell us something, but went away without saying anything.

September 27. Weaving, mill day, visitors. Most of the visitors stood around the loom to "watch at" us weave. They gave very conflicting advice but we adhered strictly to our Mrs. Stacy's rules and are getting on famously, even if the threads will break and "there's striving in the gears" oftentimes. Mrs. Stacy or Rhoda comes when there is any trouble. These are farewell visits we are having now, and the presents they bring, if not altogether useful, show a kindly feeling. Mrs. Wells brought us two red pepper pods, a piece, a pair of ground hog-skin shoe strings, and two little gourds.

We hear on every hand that "Jess will never get that thar boat done by the time you are ready to go off," so as he has not gotten the gunwales out yet, and has not been to see us about it, we have begun to look around for a wagon to take us to the mouth of Carr, for Uncle Ira said anytime we came he would sell us his boat. It was hard for both of us to stop weaving long enough to go up Montgomery for the class work. There were more than usual and they were all hurrying to learn all they could the last time. We have given every grown boy in the sewing class a pocket needle book with the temperance pledge sewed into it. Our friends greeted us with fruit and watermelons along the way home, and Mr. Green Combs was down at the fence to say that every word we said last Sunday about temperance was true and he was so glad that the young people had that kind of counsel. Dicie Francis, one of the prettiest girls we know in the mountains, came tonight. Katherine stopped at her school at Smithsboro the other day, and she had the walls filled with pictures we had given her during the Institute at Hindman and others we had sent to her through the mail. Hillard Smith got his school for himself last spring and Dicie, who is his sweetheart, tried to get one over on Ball, but she failed and he let her have his. The broken ribs are better and while we filled quills this evening, Mrs. Stacy, Rhoda and Mary sang at the organ.

September 28.   Everybody came today, for all summer they have been asking to buy some of our things and we told them we would sell what they wanted at the last. We should rather store these things and keep them here for future use, but they have so few conveniences that we feel we ought not to pack away anything that will add to their comfort. So many of the things were sold. Old Mr. and Mrs. Godsey bought enough to start to housekeeping, said she had never had none of those things and she was going to have them now, if she was old. She said that we had done so much for the children here, that everybody ought to pay us their respects and "I wish you good luck and plenty of it." Mr. Garretson and his family and his father-in-law and his family all came down to see the tent one more time and to bring us another little log cabin, and some of the men who saw the cabins made some furniture for them. We hear that Jess is still up Red Oak hewing on the gunwales and the lumber is not sawed for the rest of the boat. The merry sound of the loom has not stopped from sunrise to sunset, for this is the last day for weaving, we must get the piece out and we must pack Monday, so Katherine stayed to weave and I went to George's Branch Sunday School with Rhoda to lead in the singing. It was a full class of all ages, from one to seventy-five years. When I got back, found Katherine had woven a yard and would have finished but it was too dark. All day there has not been a minute to think or plan for the social and good-bye campfire we were to have tonight. They began to come before I got back from Sunday School or Katherine away from the loom, but Mrs. Stacy and Jasper started them with games at the tent. They came from far and near, from the rivers and creeks beyond the river, more than have been here at any other time. Tucker and Sarah both were here and everybody was on the alert to see if they would notice each other. The boys had gathered up logs and brushwood on the edge of the creek and just at twilight we all went down and started the campfire. Even then they were not tired of games and, encircled about the fire, kept them up until we felt that good-night must be said, so we sang mountain ballads and hymns and spoke a few parting words. Robert Kelley was drunk and so was another teacher from over on the river, all the other young people were so ashamed and said they ought to have known better than to come where we were in this condition. Louisa and Jim Sumner came just as we were leaving the camp fire to ask them all to go to their house for a "gathering" and some of them went for the first time since we began having the socials. Geneva Hall Craft, Mrs. Singleton's niece from Macey's Creek, stayed all night, she is unusually bright and attractive. Five of Mrs. Stacy's relations stayed also, so the house is full. They had heard so much of the last candy pulling that Mrs. Stacy was "keen for us to have one for her folks," and although we had done a good deal more than one day's work, we made the candy and went out into the moonlight, where we had to show each one how to take it and pull it. Alcie told us that we talked so different from the people up there, that our "voices were softer and more lovin'."

September 29.   Visitors even on Sunday morning before we could get off to Sunday School, we just left them at the tent to talk to each other, and help themselves to periodicals. On the way back we stopped to say good-bye to all the friends and it was with real regret we parted with Aunt Mary, who has added so much to our pleasure this summer.

It is hard for us to think that we have taken our last tramp up Montgomery and have had the last lesson with those bright, responsive boys and girls. We started the first Sunday in July with the story of the creation and closed today with the review of this quarter and although at first it seemed hopeless as so few knew anything at all about the Bible, after the review at all the Sunday Schools, we felt repaid for every effort we have made from week to week to get to them and to teach them these Bible stories. It was most gratifying, some of them could begin with the very first lesson and tell the entire story, as we have had it in the classes. The favorite lesson was about Noah, because "that big boat must have looked funny with all those two kinds of animals." One boy said God punished Adam "'cause he eat apples when he should not. He got him outside and put him to work." And one little fellow said he "spected hit wuz hoeing corn." At the close of the lesson, Judge Combs asked if he could say a few words, but he spoke at length thanking us on behalf of the people of this community for coming to help them and ended by saying, "We thank you for the gentle and patient labors among us. People say you come here for various reasons, for curiosity, or a tour of the country, but we know that you wouldn't trudge over these rough roads and the rocks of Montgomery just to see the scenery and us mountain people have not done as much for you as you have done for them." We have tried to leave organized Sunday Schools at these places, but there is no one to take charge at any of them, so we offered to send lesson quarterlies to any families who would promise to keep up the study of the lesson and several have responded.

September 30.   The piece was finished early this morning and is out of the loom in less time than Mrs. Stacy said it would take to put it in. We have been so busy packing all day that there has been scarcely time to speak to all the people who came. Mr. Beverley brought Tilford and said he "aimed to start him off with us to-morrow, but he didn't have no money to give him and he was in rags." We told him we would take him just as he was. Mrs. Enoch Combs brought five blankets and fifteen yards of linsey and said she was in the business now and ready to make all the homespun we want. She gave us a homespun towel. The blankets were beautiful and we are so pleased with our linsey dresses, if we did have to make so many trips up Red Oak to get them. She was rather surprised when we said we are ready to leave early in the morning, said she passed Jess up on Red Oak hewing on the gunwales of the boat, he said he "would have it done the last of the week maybe, and he 'lowed we would wait that long." And all this time he has not been to see us nor sent us any word. We told her to tell him that we are still ready to keep our part of the contract.

Mrs. Eli Brashears from Big Branch gave us a beautiful old indigo blue and white coverlid, she sent it over by her granddaughter. And now everything is ready for an early start tomorrow, and we are out on the rocks in Montgomery thinking of what this summer has brought to us.

October 1.   Breakfast over, lunch baskets and cots packed before daylight, and just before dawn as Simon was helping us roll the cots, a dark figure appeared in the doorway and Harlan Combs said "Fernando and I want you to take us down with you to Berea school." Then came Mr. Beverley with Tilford, a most pathetic little creature, in a new brown derby that was below his ears, a new black coat, a faded checked shirt, very ragged trousers and where there were not holes, there were patches, brand new shoes without any stocking and absolutely no luggage to be bothered with. By five thirty we were sitting on our boxes waiting for the wagon, which Mr. Mullins had promised to have there by that time sure. It was just two hours late, which was more prompt than most mountain people are. Harlan, Fernando and Jasper went on ahead to the mouth of Carr to have the boat cleaned, caulked and in order to start just as soon as we could get there. Many, especially the old women who never saw the river, have been telling us that they are sure there is not enough water to take us down, but we told them there would be plenty of water in the deep places, that we could unload and the boys pull the boat through the shoals, and if necessary we could get a team to help us through. They then said they "reckoned" we would get there. Mary and Rhoda seemed very sad to say good-bye, but they stood on the bank and sang as we started off. Our friends were at the doors to wave good-bye, and as we stopped to speak to the men who were working the road, our young moonshiner came near and whispered, "If you' uns will find out how much it costs to go to Berea and write back to me, I aim to sell my nag and go." So then we knew what he had had on his mind. We were jolting down Carr in the wagon, when the driver suddenly threw down the lines, jumped out and went running ahead, then we saw Mr. Bob Combs, the deputy sheriff and teacher at George's Branch, running around the cliff and keeping behind the underbrush, as if he was trying to catch someone. All our forces joined in the pursuit until they caught Jim Sumner, who was trying to escape to Jackson. This man, although one of the best teachers in the County, does not seem to realize the responsibility of his calling. The schools have to begin in summer and close before cold weather, because the buildings are not warm enough, and the children cannot walk over the mountains and down the swollen streams in winter. For the last four weeks Mr. Combs has had no school, he gave two weeks for foddering and the other time he has been away hunting criminals. So the conditions here are not surprising when one realizes the little chance the young people have.

Aunt Lou Anne Combs let us have the cherry sugar chest over one hundred years old and said there was no other person to whom she would be willing to give it up.

At the river no boat and no boys, we heard the boat had drifted down with the last tide and the boys had gone on to find it. After walking two miles, for there was no room in the wagon after the chest was put in, we found them bailing and caulking a very, dirty boat. The jolting of the wagon over seven miles of rough road had, as Harlan said, "unraveled the knitting of our ribs," and anyway they hurt so much, we were willing to start in any kind of a boat, before we should undertake a two days' trip in the wagon. The teamsters brought the chest down to the river and went on to Jackson with the rest of our luggage. Then we all turned our attention to getting the boat ready, rags were secured from a cabin nearby, the leaks stopped, four sticks nailed to the sides, a canopy made of the little boxes. We had luncheon on the riverside before we "set sail." A unique boat load it was, starting one hundred miles down the North fork of the Kentucky River, a blind girl, a lame boy, "the worst boy in all the mountains, who would be in a penitentiary in a few months if you'uns do not take him off and do something with him" (as his father said to us in his presence this morning), all in the charge of two girls with broken ribs and a sprained wrist. As we pushed out with Jasper in front with a long cucumber pole, and Fernando in the back with a paddle, Jasper called out, "Now we're off; now fer a purty ride," but it was not long before the three boys had their shoes off and waded in to pull the boat through the shoals. Mary and Tilford were delighted, for this was quite the most exciting experience they had ever had. Poor Tilford's feet were blistered by the rubbing of the new shoes without any stockings, so we had to get them off and care for him. It was a beautiful afternoon on the river with trailing crimson vines touching the water in some places and the new autumn tints on the hill tops, even the boys appreciated it, for one of them said, "pon my honor, Miss Pettit, what about that, the sunlight on them red trees is actually purty." Many times they have to be out wading to their waists pulling the boat over the shoals or prizing it off the rocks. "It comes as handy to me as old corn bread to get out," exclaimed Jasper. "Go yon way a little more," and then as the boat mired in the quicksand, "Wall, what about this now, let 'em git behind and prize, a bushel of prizing is worth ten bushels of pulling." "Now pull, Harlan; wiggle Harlan; pull Harlan; hits wiggling that does it; we ought to be way over on yon side; now, what about us," as the boat sank deeper in the quicksand. But wiggling and pushing and prizing brought us to a long stretch of deep water, when Harlan said, "Now is a good time to eat a watermelon." While we floated, Jasper called to Tilford, "here son, come bail out," and then suddenly, "Now Harlan, jump quick and push hard, I know'd we stop; when I get my teeth together I mean business, no Harlan; now Jasper; prize up as I push, whupee!!" As they jumped into the boat, splashing water on us all, and we went rapidly over the shoals now, "We're having a happy ride." In this way, we landed after dark a half mile above Hazard. Judge Combs was waiting to tell us we could go no further, so helped us unload and carry the things to the hotel, where we had a cordial welcome from our old friends, Mr. and Mrs. Dave Combs. We urged the boys to go to bed early so we could start by daylight in the morning.

October 2.   At the mouth of Willard on the North Fork of the Kentucky River. As Mary and Tilford had never been to a town before, there were many things to explain to them. None of us had as much rest as we expected, as there was a wedding in town last night, followed by a long charivari,[23] and when that was over Aunt Sally Davidson began to shout, which drew out the neighbors and kept everybody in that part of town awake. It was hard for Mary and Tilford, who live at the head of a quiet hollow, to understand all this. After a good breakfast, the boys took the boat down to Walker's Mill dam, a mile below town, we walked with Mr. Mitchell, Mr. Logan of Jackson, and Judge Combs, who helped us unload and carry the things around, while the boys jumped out of the boat as it went over the dam. We reloaded and as we started off, the men foreboded all kinds of trouble for us, but we told them we were ready for anything that came. Judge Combs' parting words to his son were, "This is the turning point in your life, but I reckon you'll go to the bad."

The brilliantly colored hills, the water sparkling in the sunlight, the bracing mountain air and the buoyant spirits of the boys have made this a Red-Letter day in our experience.

"Fernando, what do you think of this boat ride?" Just then Fernando fell back into the water. "Don't let her swing, boys, push her back. Every man jump and grab. All pull at once. If you stand and look at hit, we'll never get thar. Keep a shoving, that's the main idie, boys. Let her go slonchways." Just then Fernando broke his pole and we had to go to the shore to cut a new one. We all got out to have luncheon by the riverside. An afternoon of hard work by the boys brought us here to Mr. Pete Stacy's just at dark. As we were cold and wet, a great big log fire in the family room was just what we had been hoping for and following the custom of mountain women, we hastened to the fire to change our shoes and stockings, although the room seemed to be full of men, as well as women and children. There was so much smoke we could hardly see, but when I asked if the house was on fire, a boy answered, "No, jist about two pounds of tobacco burning in our pipes." Although they had a large family, they took us in and at our request gave us a room to ourselves.

October 3. Thirty-one miles from Jackson on the North Fork of the Kentucky River.

Slept some last night, not much. They had breakfast for the men first and then asked Mary and me to the kitchen, but as they were washing the dishes in the wash bowl out of our room, I did not try to eat anything, but talked to the mother and father very earnestly about sending their little blind girl to the school at Louisville. The boys had the boat bailed out, caulked anew and loaded by the time we got there and as there was deep water, we had an easy ride for a mile to the mouth of Forked Branch, where we waited for Miss Pettit, who says:

I started by moonlight this morning to go up Forked Branch to Jeff Fugate's, for I have been promising our deaf friend, Willie, for some years to give his sister a chance to go to school, and when I learned last night that they lived in that neighborhood, I was determined to see her and give her the scholarship we have for the Harlan School. They live at the head of six forks and the directions were very vague and not many stirring on the way to ask, but I followed the lonely log path up the mountain by the moonlight and found the Fugate's living in a one roomed, windowless log house. The mother was very good looking with her seven children around her; the oldest girl was blind, and before I told them my name, they asked if I was not Miss Pettit, Willie's friend. I told them that I had come to see if one of them wanted to go to Harlan to school and suggested sending the thirteen-year-old-girl, but Sally, who is sixteen, put her head on her mother's shoulder and began to cry, saying that Willie had always promised that she should go to school and be like he was and if they didn't let her go now, there would never be another way. So I told her she could go. I had to go on another road to find her father, who said he would be glad for her to go, but he had no nag to take her, but Sally eagerly said, "If you'll just let me go and there's no other way, I'll put my clothes in a meal sack and walk thar, I'd ruther do that than not git to school." She looked so picturesque with a red fascinator[24] over her head as she walked down to the river with me and told in her own language of what a hard time they had getting to do anything, "fer Paw and his kin don't believe in eddication, and Maw and her kin dows, and when Maw just would send Willie away to the deaf school, Paw's kin said she was just sending him whar they'd treat him mean, and they done all they could to keep Paw from letting him go, but now they are mighty proud of him." She said Pete Stacy, where we stayed last night, "is the wickedest man in all the world, he cussed God Almighty hisself when the wind blew his corn down, said thar was not dependence to be put in Him." I felt as if I had been away for days when I saw them in the boat waiting for me at the mouth of Forked Branch, for I had walked seven miles in two hours and forty-five minutes.

It had been cold all day and the boys had to struggle against the wind, for there was much deep water and they could only use the paddles. While we were having lunch on the sand, Harlan, who has proved to be the most valuable man on the boat, and whose judgement we find we can rely on, said if we didn't get another man to help us, he didn't believe we would ever get to Jackson, so we called to a man who was standing in front of a little cabin on the bank "to come help us to Jackson." He replied, "all right, jist as quick as I can git my coat." So he came running down and when he saw the flags, he said, "I like to see them things swinging thar," and saying, "Hold up your end, boys, and don't fling these wimmin out. These boys will all git baptized in the river before we git thar. Now you can let her go. The wind's going to blow us pintedly away. I never went down the river in my life that my head didn't strike the bottom, but I aller like to dry up before laying down time."

As we would exclaim with delight at the beautiful scenery on the way and what a good time we were having, Harlan would sing out, "Hits a mighty happy time fer the ladies, but taint much happy fer the gentlemens." Our new captain was telling us all the afternoon of a fine place to stay all night with his friend Andy Stiddam, but when we got here they were reluctant to take us in, till he said he "didn't aim to go any further tonight," unloaded and brought us in, and the fire is giving us a cheery welcome even if they did not.

October 4.   Jackson–Arlington Hotel. The boys discovered while they were trying to sleep on the floor why the Stiddams did not want to take us in, for they overheard them discussing the flags on the boat, which they thought meant we were Republicans and they "aimed" to tear them down. We hardly understand this, for the son of the house has just returned from the Philippines, where he has been fighting for the flag. It was a miserable night for us all, we slept in a room with a woman, her husband and baby, while all the rest, fifteen, slept in one room, our boys on the floor. They told us of Miss Louise Sanders and her work up here and how everybody loved her.

An early start before six, faster traveling with two in front with poles and two in the back with paddles, deeper water and the captain says we will make the thirty miles to Jackson tonight, in spite of the wind. It was a long steady pull with a few minutes stop on the sand-bar, where we ate everything that was left in the lunch baskets. After dark, still some distance out of Jackson and the boys were cold and tired and hungry. We saw a light in a cabin by the river and suggested that they tie the boat to the shore and go to see if they could get some supper, and ride on the river after night. I don't know what we should have done without the chest to keep the bags and lunch baskets dry, for in spite of the constant bailing of Mary and Tilford and our caulking there has been water in the boat most of the way. We made room for Mary and Tilford in the chest, wrapped them in oil cloth and told them they must not get out till we got to Jackson. Then we wrapped ourselves and sat there alone with solemn thoughts until the boys came back with renewed energy and determination to get us in to Jackson, although the captain at first refused to go any further. The mist settled over and around us until we seemed a very part of it, the boys sang though till we got to where the boom was locked and the river filled with loose logs. There was absolutely no chance to get through, so we pushed back a little and unloaded in the dim starlight on some logs in the river and stepped from floating log to log until we reached the land and then climbed a steep bank through underbrush to the road, and with the lame boy, blind girl, and all the luggage, waded through the mud a mile to Jackson. Here we had as great a sensation when we saw the newly fitted up hotel, with the dressed up ladies and gentlemen walking around on brussels carpets, as they must have had when this muddy, wet, forlorn looking crowd from one hundred miles up the river appeared in the hall and asked for rooms. They sent a hot supper to our room, even at that late hour, and did everything for our comfort. While we were repacking and getting ready for the early start on the train in the morning, we told Mary she must take a bath, but she did not understand what it was. When we explained, she said she had never taken one in her life, but was willing to do as we told her, and this eleven-year-old girl has had her first bath tonight. The boys are eagerly anticipating their year at Berea, Tilford hoping to be made well and straight at the hospital, and Mary already talking about how much she will know when she comes home from school. Jasper has bidden us good-bye, and will start alone tomorrow to walk sixty miles back to Sassafras, "where," he says, "I will likely spend the rest of my days a-fishin' and loggin'" on Carr and the only enjoyment I'll see will be goin' to the post office to see if they's a letter from you'uns."

Well, we look back on the sad and lonely lives of those with whom and for whom we have lived the past months, and feel that the most important question for us, is how to bring the strong, wealthy and learned Kentuckians into healthful touch with the poorest, most ignorant and humblest mountaineer and at the same time make the one appreciate the vitalizing, strengthening influence of the other– How can we make the people of the Bluegrass feel and see the need of the people in the lowliest cabin on the mountain sides!

May Stone
Katherine R. Pettit

Photo Essay;
The Hindman Settlement School: Early Years

When Katherine Pettit and May Stone were first approached by the citizens of Hindman to establish a school in the town, they protested that they had no experience with schools and weren't teachers. But once they agreed to undertake the combined school and social settlement, they went about it with their usual energy. The three summer camps had made clear some pressing needs of the mountaineers: better education of both the academic and vocational variety, better health care and hygiene and better ways for mountaineers to earn a living without leaving their beloved mountains. Applying these lessons, the Hindman Settlement School grew rapidly, fulfilling an obvious need and making a major impact upon the people of the entire Kentucky mountain region. As the Hindman Settlement School moves toward the celebration of its centennial, the struggles and achievements of these early years and of its founders deserve renewed recognition.

The Hindman Settlement School opened its doors on August 5, 1902, with 162 students. Only a few were boarding students since there were no campus facilities yet.

In the early days Katherine Pettit and May Stone supervised the construction of the campus, shown in following three photos. Above, the "first house."

Setting the mill stone.

Building the well.

They actively supervised the construction of the twenty-eight room Log House in 1905 as well. Pictured here, Katherine Pettit in sunbonnet and Francis Beauchamp, President of the WCTU in halo headgear.

The Log House which burned only a few months after completion.

Uncle Solomon Everidge, pictured here, is called the Settlement School's "founding father." William Aspenwall Bradley in "The Women on Troublesome" wrote this description of him. "In appearance he conformed to the old hunter and trapper type even then fast disappearing from the mountains. He wore homespun trousers and a white home-woven shirt of flax and he was both bareheaded and barefooted....For the rest, his aspect was patriarchal and imposing. He was tall, straight, and still strong-looking. He had a massive head, with thick white hair and heavy eyebrows...with an expression of remarkable intelligence and nobility."

The school and the town both grew rapidly. A view of Hindman from the campus in 1905 shows many new buildings.

With its emphasis on vocational training, a wood working shop was one of the first building to go up. The school buildings were filled with the furniture made by students. Here, the interiors of two rooms.

The majority of the campus and its buildings were built on the right side of Troublesome Creek at its forks and were reached by a bridge.

Troublesome Creek was aptly named since it regularly overflowed and cut off the campus from the town. Such minor inconveniences hardly daunted the fotched-on women and some ingenious methods of crossing were devised as this picture illustrates.

May Stone is shown standing at the foot of the bridge leading to the campus at a time when Troublesome Creek was less troublesome than in the earlier scene.

Pictured here are Ann Cobb and Katherine Pettit. Cobb came to the school from Massachusetts in 1905 and remained for more than three decades. A beloved teacher, she also wrote many poems based on her life in the mountains and at the school which were collected in a volume titled, Kinfolks.

Another long-time member of the social settlement family was Lucy Furman, childhood friend of Katherine Pettit who arrived in 1907 intending a short stay for reasons of health. She remained for more than twenty five years serving as house-mother for the boys and super-visor of the farm and outdoor work. She wrote three novels which used the school for their settings.

In 1909, nineteen year old Elizabeth Watts, pictured here, arrived. She would become the assistant director of the school in 1924 and its director upon the death of May Stone in 1946. She actively served the school for forty-seven years, remain-ing on its board until her death at the age of 103 in 1993. She is buried on the campus.

Shown here are teachers unpacking donated clothing and other items upon which the school depended.

A group of teachers are pictured here, seated on the porch of Hillside House. They were celebrating Ann Cobb's birthday. Included are Cobb, second from the right. Behind and to the left is Elizabeth Watts and in the back corner of the porch is May Stone.

Harriet Baker, a nurse, began the social settlement's extensive work in health education and community nursing.

Pictured here, Lucy Furman and some of her "boys." Furman's first novel, Mothering On Perilous, *was a series of stories about her adventures during her first year as housemother to twelve boys. Here is a small sample of the stories: "Last night Taulbee, the eldest, who is very opinionated, took occasion to enter a general protest against innovations such as nightgowns, tooth-brushes, fine-combs and the like, and wound up by arraigning the school's methods of cooking. 'Them little small biscuits you-all have don't make half a good bite,' he declared."*

𝔚𝔞𝔫𝔱𝔢𝔡—𝔄 𝔉𝔞𝔯𝔪.

The W. C. T. U. Settlement School at Hindman, in the Kentucky Mountains has grown so rapidly in the last five years that a farm of our own is an absolute necessity.

1st. To give work and thereby a chance for an education to the many boys whom we are now turning away.

2d. To furnish adequate supplies for our constantly growing household, which now numbers nearly fifty.

3d. To provide a model farm in a large agricultural community.

The right man is here, with enthusiasm and practical knowledge, to carry on the work.

To buy and equip such a farm we need $3,000.

COMMITTEE IN CHARGE ⎰ MISS MAY STONE, 1400 Third Ave., Louisville, Ky.
⎱ MISS KATHERINE R. PETTIT, Lexington, Ky.

Fundraising was constant in the early days when the school and its needs expanded rapidly. Here is an appeal which was sent out to help raise money to purchase a farm.

Albert Stewart was probably the youngest boarding student to come to the settlement in the early days and was known as the "Settlement baby" because of his arrival at the age of five. Lucy Furman became like a mother to him and a great influence in his life. He became a well known poet and founder of the Appalachian Heritage Magazine *and the Appalachian Writer's Conference still held annually at the school.*

Aside from academic work, a regular part of the school curriculum for girls were the sewing classes.

Without modern conveniences, hair washing was done outside on the porch steps under the supervision of the housemother. Personal hygiene was a major virtue the school worked to instill.

Saturday was wash day, a laborious task described by Lucy Furman. She wrote with sympathy about "the duties of the unfortunate wash-boy, who must rise before day on Saturdays to build fires and fill kettles, and then for nine long hours toil wearily, chopping wood, carrying water and otherwise "slaving" for the washgirls". According to her, it was the most hated task among the boys not because it was hard but because it was viewed as "girls' work."

In addition to the wash, on Saturday, all the buildings were cleaned and all the floors scrubbed down. Shown here are the editor's mother and aunt, aged about eight, scrubbing the porch of Orchard House.

The school grew most of its own food and students helped with this and with general outdoor repairs which never ended. Two scenes of such work.

The school was well equipped to teach wood working and made quality furniture which was both used at the school and sold through the Fireside Industries to help support the school. These scenes show a class and a student with his finished product.

Early letters speak of learning to make furniture from the boxes that goods came in. This picture appeared in a fundraising brochure.

Health care and education was a major concern of the school from the outset, both for the students and the community in general. In 1909 this hospital was built on the campus. A larger structure was erected five years later which served the community for several decades.

Drama and theater were a regular feature of school life, often involving the production of Shakespearean plays in an outdoor setting. This may be an example of one such production.

Acting out songs and stories were also popular such as this scene which depicts the song, "Where are you going my pretty maid?"

Sports also became an important element of school life. Here is the 1909 baseball team with Josiah Combs in the front row on the far right. Combs would be one of the school's first two graduates and go on to earn a Ph.D. at the Sorbonne in Paris with a study of mountain folklore.

HINDMAN SETTLEMENT SCHOOL
INCORPORATED
HINDMAN, KENTUCKY

When I was five years old, I walked forty-five miles to the Hindman School.

There was no room for me, so I walked home again.

The next year my brothers tried to get me in.

The next year my father wrote for a place for me.

The next year I walked over there again but the Little Girls' house had burned down and of course there was no room for me.

Now a new Little Girls' House is to be built and I hope I can go. Don't you?

There are over 600 other little and big girls and boys who want to go.

Won't you help us?

Fundraising appeals became increasingly sophisticated over time. This is typical of the kind of appeal made for scholarships so that more students could attend. The girl pictured is Celia Stone from Quicksand.

Christmas at the Hindman Settlement School was very special. When Pettit and Stone arrived in the mountains at the turn of the century, December 25 was not celebrated as Christmas. They did much to popularize it as a holiday. Here is a partial description of the Settlement School Christmas from the 1908 annual letter: "We had all hung our stockings on Christmas Eve–all of us, from Miss Stone and Miss Pettit down to little Goldie, who still believed in Santa Claus...eighty-four stockings were all hung, in a long thin dangly row around the fire place, up into the corner and way across the other side of the room." Shown here, the hanging stockings and Christmas tree with poppet dolls surrounding it.

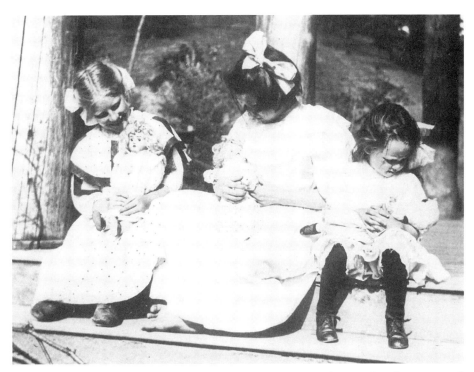

The dolls were very popular with the young girls such as these three shown tending their "poppets."

The school was very anxious to try to preserve the traditional methods of craftsmanship which had been employed such as natural vegetable dyes for the woven goods. Pictured here is a woman preparing vegetable dye.

A Kentucky Mountain Story

MOTHERING ON PERILOUS

——By——
LUCY FURMAN
With Illustrations by
Mary Lane McMillan

Decorated
Cloth
12mo,
$1.50 net
Postpaid,
$1.63

PUBLISHED BY

The MACMILLAN COMPANY
64-66 FIFTH AVENUE   NEW YORK

ON SALE AT ALL BOOK STORES

After Lucy Furman's first book appeared in 1913, the school used its popularity and the interest it generated to appeal for funds. It reproduced the dust cover and some reviews with this appeal.

W.C.T.U. Settlement School
HINDMAN, KNOTT COUNTY :: :: KENTUCKY

WE believe that our friends will be interested in hearing that this school is the scene of a book recently brought out by the Macmillan Company, entitled "MOTHERING ON PERILOUS," by Lucy Furman. The "Perilous Creek" of the story is none other than our own Troublesome, with which the readers of our annual letters are already familiar, and Miss Furman has been a worker in the school for more than six years. Many of the incidents and characters of the book are true, and will give a real insight into the difficulties and joys of our work. Some of this material has already been published in the form of short stories in the *Century Magazine*; but it is now put into one long story, of which a recent editorial in the *Louisville Courier-Journal* speaks as follows :

"'Mothering on Perilous' is a revelation of humor, pathos, sociology and folk-lore that would be hard to match in interest and delight . . . . A distinct achievement for Kentucky literature, and for the understanding of some Kentucky problems . . . . She shows us the heart of the mountain folk as it is. Things not said, but surprisingly inferred, leap out at the reader with even more vividness sometimes than the written records. In the completed portraits of 'Philip,' 'Geordie,' 'Nucky' and 'Killis,' there is a gallery of immortality of boys; and the story of 'Blant' and his tragedy looms over half the book with absorbing portent . . . . It is one of those books that will appeal to the taste of the most jaded reader as well as to that of quiet households where books redolent of their own truth find the widest circles of readers. In that sense it will be a classic."

We trust that this book will bring home to our friends and supporters a vital sense of the personality and value of our mountain children, and increase their interest in the work we are doing.

MAY STONE   } *Committee in*
RUTH HUNTINGTON   } *Charge*

FILLING ORDERS

THE FIRESIDE INDUSTRIES

OF THE

W. C. T. U.
SETTLEMENT SCHOOL

HINDMAN, KNOTT COUNTY,
KENTUCKY

The school encouraged local crafts by marketing them to its wide audience. This is a cover of a typical Fireside Industries brochure with the inside pages illustrating handmade baskets available from the school. Some were produced by local craftsmen and some by the students. Homespun by the yard and blankets and coverlets were also offered for sale.

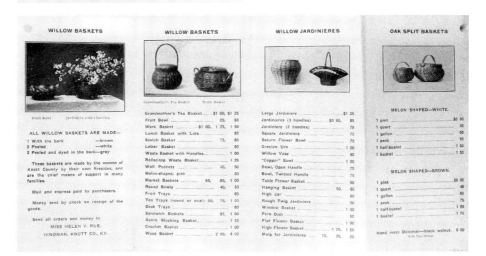

Preservation of the musical heritage of the mountains was another goal of the school. This included both the music and the musical instruments on which it was played. Shown here are Nelson Ritchie, of the famous singing Ritchie family, playing the banjo and Ed Thomas, probably the first dulcimer maker in the region. He sold his dulcimers to the teachers at the school and soon began to receive orders from as far away as New York and New England. He was an equally accomplished musician.

One of the best known contributions of the school to community health was its attack on trachoma, the eye disease which blinded so many. Clinics held at the school led the government to create a number of trachoma hospitals to eradicate the disease. Here are some of the many patients who traveled long distances to be treated. Below, Dr. Stucky of Lexington who headed the work.

Katherine Pettit left to found a school at Pine Mountain eleven years after the Hindman School opened. Here is a rare photo of Pettit from about that date.

After Katherine Pettit left for Pine Mountain, administration of the Hindman Settlement School was largely in the hands of May Stone, Elizabeth Watts and Ruth Huntington who became principal of the high school. Huntington is shown on the left with Watts center and May Stone on the right.

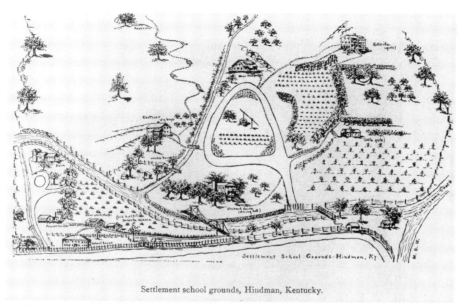

Settlement school grounds, Hindman, Kentucky.

By 1918 the campus was complete with two hundred twenty five acres and twenty buildings. A staff of twenty-nine served more than one hundred boarding students. This sketch comes from William Aspenwall Bradley's article, "The Women on Troublesome," published in that year.

Pettit remained as director of the Pine Mountain school until 1930. Pictured here in later life, she wrote to a friend shortly before her death: "This has been a glorious world to work in. I am eager to see what the next will be."

Katherine Pettit's home at Pine Mountain, named "Big Log."

May Stone remained director of the Hindman Settlement School until her death in 1946. The love her mountain neighbors bore her was apparent in the scores of girls named May in her honor.

May Stone is shown here in one of her favorite places, the porch of Hillside House with its view of the hill where the first tents were pitched in 1900. She remained, to the end, "the Ladyest."

"In time, and the time in some places is at hand, the isolation of the Highlands will be overcome by railroads and good thoroughfares and their wild beauty disfigured by commercial exploitation while the Highlander himself, his individualism and his picturesqueness gone, will become no better, no worse, but quite as uninteresting as other men."– *John C. Campbell,* The Southern Highlander and His Homeland.

Epilogue;
The World We Have Lost

Not all scholars of the region speak positively about the appearance of outsiders in the mountains at the turn of the century. Two images of Appalachia at that time continue to compete in the popular mind and in the debates of those who study the region. One is the image created by more than two hundred literary works written in the nineteenth century–essays, travel accounts and novels. Both Cratis Williams in *The Southern Mountaineer in Fact and Ficition* and Henry Shapiro in his book, *Appalachia On Our Mind*, described the development of a stereotype of the mountain people as "contemporary ancestors" who were primitive, violent and lived in a static culture little changed since colonial days. The debate among modern scholars has extended this image in such important works as Jack Weller's, *Yesterday's People*. When the War On Poverty in the 1960s "discovered" Appalachia again, Weller and others argued that the continuing problems of the region were the consequence of a folk culture resistant to necessary change.[1]

Another image of the region competes with this one. It views mountain culture at the turn of the century as undergoing rapid change, especially economic change, which deeply affected its culture as well. This Appalachia has been most thoroughly documented by Ronald Eller in *Miners, Millhands, and Mountaineers, Industrialization of the Appalachian South, 1880-1930*. Eller chronicled the rapid decline of mountain agriculture and the substitution of non-agricultural employment in mining, logging, mills and other activities as the key environment at the time when Katherine Pettit and May Stone arrived in Eastern Kentucky. The economic consequences of these events meant the end of the area's isolation and its integration into the national economy. The process occurred in such a way, however, that the region's interests and people were subordinated to outsiders.[2] Eller sees modern mountain culture as a reaction to rapid change and the powerlessness produced by the introduction of industrial capitalism. His viewpoint echoes one of the best known works on twentieth century Appalachia, Harry Caudill's, *Night Comes to the Cumberlands*. Caudill described Appalachia as "the last unchallenged stronghold of western colonialism."[3]

How this debate relates to May Stone and Katherine Pettit and the institutions they founded is that the "colonial" or "exploitive" interpretation of the region's experience has come to encompass cultural as well as economic intrusion. One who wrote from this perspective was David Whisnant who published an extensive study of the Hindman Settlement School nearly fifteen years ago. In his essay, "'Hit Sounds Reasonable', Cultural and Social Change at Hindman Settlement School" in *All That Is Native and Fine: The Politics of Culture in an American Region*, he branded Stone and Pettit's work as cultural exploitation. He saw their programs as "romantic and contrived" and "based upon a flawed reading of local culture." While he recognized the superior education created for the region's children, he viewed the women and their institutions as conservative and, at least, inadvertently, working hand in hand with the economic exploiters of the region.[4]

Rhonda England in her study, "Voices From the History of Teaching," discussed Whisnant's argument that both students and adults incurred cultural losses through the process of schooling and intervention which the Settlement School provided. She noted that Whisnant's study showed the teachers only as manipulators acting upon the culture. In his discussion the teachers had no voice; rather, he stereotyped them simply as Bluegrass women with romantic notions about the mountaineers and their region. In contrast, she argued that her study shows ways that the teachers learned from the mountain people and reveals the reciprocity which was part of a dynamic educational and cultural process at Hindman.[5] She recognized that there were cultural losses during this period but views many of them as inevitable whether Pettit and Stone had come or not, given the rapid change overtaking the area. And, in her view, there were real cultural gains as well.

Pettit and Stone, of course, brought cultural biases with them. Their views of religion, of patriarchy and other elements of the contemporary mountain culture were often negative and in keeping with the views of American, urban, middle-class Progressives of the time. But if they were cultural conservatives, they were certainly social activists. Their health care work, emphasis on vocational and practical training, encouragement of improved agricultural techniques, introduction of kindergarten for the very young and the creation of the Fireside Industries to aid a local economy increasingly unable to sustain itself by subsistence farming may not seem radical today. Introduced almost one hundred years ago, these programs were major innovations. The fact that so many of them were taken over by public schools and other public agencies speaks volumes about the success of the social settlement work they conducted.

It is probably correct to observe, as Whisnant did, that one of their important ideals, "to educate people back to their homes not away from them" was often breached. The Settlement School programs were based upon a belief that the new knowledge and skills would help families to live better within the changing environment. They did. But the advantages accorded to children who studied at the school also provided them greater opportunities including the choice to leave. Some did. Even so, many others stayed or returned to become the teachers, social workers, lawyers, doctors, business and civic leaders of the region. May Stone did an informal survey in the 1930s and calculated that about eighty-five percent of the Hindman graduates remained in the region. One Hindman student became governor of the state; another, one of the most influential congressmen of his era. Congressman Carl Perkins spent thirty-six years in the House of Representatives during which time he served as chairman of the House Committee on Education and Labor. It would be difficult to find a modern legislator who did more to aid the education of poor children, vocational education and programs for child nutrition and school meals than Perkins. In a real sense, he carried the ideals Pettit and Stone lived and taught at the Hindman Settlement School into the wider sphere of the nation. He used what the Settlement School had inculcated into him to rewrite the law of the land.

It is always easier from hindsight to decide what people should or should not have done or been in the past. The emphasis on moral uplift and overt "do goodism" or "Christian conscience" pervasive in the Progressive Movement has been out of favor with many scholars in contemporary society. It is often dismissed as narrow, misguided, controlling and moralistic. But John C. Campbell described the spirit which moved Stone and Pettit as "social love." He saw it as a form of spirituality–"men and women willing to spend and be spent."[6] This view of the ethos of Progressivism has equal validity with that of its critics.

Perhaps we should let those shaped by the experience of the Hindman Settlement School have the final word on the legacy of May Stone and Katherine Pettit. One student wrote to May Stone, "How can any of us ever tell you all what it has meant to us? It would be like trying to thank one's mother for the gift of life. Hindman has been to us a gateway to the "level land" of knowledge and better living, whether we got "book-learning" or practical experience."[7] Another described the impact of the school as "like a whole world was opening up like a blossom."[8]

To the end, Katherine Pettit and May Stone remained practical idealists. They poured out "social love" to the Kentucky mountaineers. Most of the schools and institutions established in the early part of the century–the ones that sought to imitate Hindman and Pine Mountain–no longer exist. Both Hindman and Pine Mountain endure although in very different forms from their early twentieth-century precursors. Neither Pettit nor Stone would be disappointed with this. In their continuing work with local communities to preserve the natural environment and important aspects of the older culture of the region, and in their continuing efforts to help people to better control their own destiny–whether with programs to fight adult illiteracy or childhood dyslexia–the Hindman Settlement School and Pine Mountain still express the social love of Katherine Pettit and May Stone. The remark of that local citizen long ago during the first, Cedar Grove, summer that, "the good you have done will live with us" remains a reality today.

Endnotes

INTRODUCTION

1. Nov. 13, 1912, Elizabeth Watts to Mrs. Henry Boynton, Hindman Settlement School Archives, uncatalogued Watts letters. The manuscript of the Cedar Grove camp account no longer exists except in typescript form. There is a manuscript copy of the Camp Industrial and Sassafras Summer diaries in the Hindman Settlement School Archive (hereafter HSS). They form items 1-10 in Box 1, Series I, titled, "Narrative Reports and Publications, 1899-1979." A typescript of the Camp Industrial journal was made in 1900 and of the Sassafras diary in 1901. The Sassafras diary published here is based on a more recent transcript prepared by Julia Miller and Sidney Farr in 1977 at Berea College. I have made only minor changes to the 1977 typescript in capitalization, spelling and punctuation to provide consistency for the manuscript. In cases where the typescript presented a question of accuracy, I sought clarification in the manuscript version.

2. Lucy Furman, "The Work of the Fotched-On Women," *Louisville Courier Journal*, Sept. 6, 1936.

3. Ibid.

4. "Books" by Ann Cobb in Jane Halsted Stout, "Miracle on Troublesome Creek," (privately prepared typescript) 106. Stout's mother taught for more than five years at the school.

5. Allen F. Davis, *Spearheads of Reform: The Social Settlements and the Progressive Movement*, 1890-1914 (New York, Oxford University Press, 1967); Robert Crunden, *Ministers of Reform: The Progressives' Achievement in American Civilization* (New York, Basic Books, 1982) 68.

6. Dewey Grantham, *Southern Progressivism, The Reconciliation of Progress and Tradition* (Knoxville, Tenn., University of Tennessee Press, 1983) xv, xviii.

7. Mary Katherine Jasper, "Social Value of Settlement Schools in the Kentucky Mountains," M.A. Thesis, University of Kentucky, 1930, 15; John C. Campbell, *The Southern Highlander and His Homeland* (New York, The Russell Sage Foundation, 1921) 262, 264. Campbell was Secretary of the Highland Division of the

Russell Sage Foundation and a leader in mountain settlement work.

8. James S. Greene, "Progressives in the Kentucky Mountains: The Formative Years of the Pine Mountain Settlement School, 1913-1930," Ph.D. Dissertation, Ohio State University, 1982, 14-16.

9. Melba Porter Hay, "Madeline McDowell Breckingridge; Kentucky Suffragist and Progressive Reformer," Ph.D. Dissertation, University of Kentucky, 1980, 33-34.

10. James Klotter, *The Breckingridges of Kentucky: Two Centuries of Leadership* (Lexington, Ky., University of Kentucky Press, 1986) 189-90.

11. Transcript of a taped interview with Elizabeth Watts, J'May Bertrand, "The Appalachian Settlement Schools: The Rural Response to an Urban Concept," M. A. Thesis, Bryn Mawr College, 1975, 69-70.

12. HSS Archive, I, 1, 15-16. This is a miscellaneous body of materials including the Mitchell letter.

13. Ibid., 16.

14. Anne Firor Scott, *The Southern Lady, 1830-1930, From Pedestal to Politics* (Chicago, University of Chicago Press, 1970) 163. The Federation played an important role in educational reform in Kentucky. It prepared a report in 1906 which highlighted the inadequacies of education in the mountain counties. This led, two years later, to major reform legislation which included taxes to support schools and mandatory high schools. Nancy Forderhouse, "The Clear Call of Thoroughbred Women: The Kentucky Federation of Women's Clubs and the Crusade for Educational Reform, 1903-1909," *The Register of the Kentucky Historical Society* (Frankfort, Ky., 1985) 21.

15. HSS Archive, III, 9, 20-22, 24. These folders contain miscellaneous biographical information on May Stone including a pamphlet prepared for the memorial service held for her at the school in June, 1946.

16. Ibid., III, 8, 97; Greene, 252-53.

17. Jan. 13, 1912, Elizabeth Watts to Mrs. Henry Boynton, HSS Archive, uncatalogued Watts Correspondence.

18. Cratis Williams, the leading authority on the fiction of Appalachia, concluded that Furman's books, "in quietly evoking a sense of the antique quality of the Kentucky mountaineers living in their weathered log houses with moss-covered roofs sprinkled along the narrow valleys in the most remote areas...succeeded better than others in capturing the authenticity of the details of life and character of the mountain folk at the moment when they were poised to step over the threshold into a new age." Cratis Williams, "The Southern Mountaineer in Fact and Fiction," Ph.D. Dissertation, New York University, 1961, 1165.

19. Jan. 12. 1912, Elizabeth Watts to Mrs Henry Boynton, HSS Archive, uncatalogued Watts Correspondence.

20. HSS Archive, III, 8, 97.

21. Stout, 130, and material taken from interviews with the editor and written recollections of the following former students: Alma Pigman (telephone interview 8/8/95); Nancy Stewart Boatright (telephone interview 8/15/95); Gertrude Maggard (letter of July 11, 1995); and Ruby Boleyn Allen, "Room in the Wagon," (Typescript reminiscence sent August, 1995),1-2.

22. 1914 Newsletter, HSS Archive, I, 1, 26.

23. Albert Stewart, "Fesser Clarke: Pioneer Educator in Feud Country," *Appalachian Heritage*, 2 (Winter, 1974) 87-90.

24. Rhonda England, "Voices from the History of Teaching: Katherine Pettit, May Stone and Elizabeth Watts at Hindman Settlement School," Ph.D . Dissertation, University of Kentucky, 1990, 8, 11.

25. July 25, 1984, article by Josiah Combs in the Centennial edition of the (Hindman) *Troublesome Times*.

26. Robert C. Young and David R. Smith, "Professor George Clarke, Buckner Academy," *Knott County Legacy* (Troublesome Creek DAR, C. & R. Printing, 1994), 128.

27. Jane Addams, *Democracy and Social Ethics* (New York, MacMillan, 1902) 180-81.

28. Lawrence Creman, *The Transformation of the School* (New York, Vintage,

1964) 61; Pauline Ritchie Kermiet, HSS Archive, III, 9, 2.

29. England, 84.

30. Lucy Furman, *The Glass Window* (New York, MacMillan, 1927) 218.

31. England, 74.

32. Ibid., 160.

33. 1904 Newsletter, Uncatalogued Watts Correspondence.

34. 1913 Newsletter, HSS Archive, I, 1, 26. Files 21-36 contain newsletters. Sometimes a file contains more than one letter and also letters from more than one year. Much of the information about the operation of the school over its first decade included in the introduction was culled from these newsletters.

35. 1914 Newsletter, Ibid., 28.

36. 1904 Newsletter, Watts Correspondence.

37. 1907 Newsletter, HSS Archive, I, 1, 21.

38. Ibid.

39. 1910 Letter concerning fire, Ibid., 23.

40. 1908 Newsletter written by Lucy Furman titled, "Home Life of the Little Boys," Ibid., 21. Ann Cobb prepared a similar letter titled, "The Home Life Of Our Little Girls." It is hand-dated 1912 in the same file.

41. Greene, 39.

42. Ibid., 5l, 68, 327.

43. *Lexington Courier Journal*, Sept. 4, 1936.

44. "May Stone-The Ladyest," HSS Archive, III, 9, 21.

45. 1912 Newsletter, Ibid., I, 1, 25; Francis Jewell McVey, "The Blossom Woman,"

Mountain Life and Work, X (April, 1934) 1.

46. A typical pamphlet for the Fireside Industries is included in the uncatalogued Watts correspondence. It contains no date; however, the coverlets advertised cost $9, the striped blankets cost $6, and 36" linsey-woolsey cost $1 to 1.25 per yard depending on color. Baskets cost anywhere from 40 cents to $4.

47. Katherine Pettit, "Ballads and Rhymes of the Kentucky Mountains," *Journal of American Folklore*, 20 (1907) 251-76.

48. HSS Archive, I, 1, 15-18.

49. The fight over the teaching position is typed on WCTU Settlement School letterhead and titled, "How They Elected The School Teacher on Montgomery Creek." It is hand-dated "1908" and stamped, "Return to John C. Campbell." HSS Archive, I, 1, 21.

50. Pettit's motor trip is part of an addenda found in the 1977 transcript of the Sassafras diary. HSS Archive, I, 1, 13.

51. Williams, 1122.

CEDAR GROVE

1. A slade (sley) is a comb-like instrument which is set in the batten of the loom. The modern term for sley is reed. This was Katherine and May's first meeting with Mary Stacy whose home would be their headquarters two summers later at Sassafras.

2. Beaten biscuits are a cracker-like bread made by lengthy beating of the dough before baking.

3. In this common method of hymn singing, someone calls out the hymn line by line which is then sung by the congregation.

CAMP INDUSTRIAL

1. A fly is the outer canvas of a tent which has a double top. It serves to provide a cover for otherwise open ground.

2. The Teacher's Institute was held in George Clarke's school, Buckner Academy,

so this must be a reference to one of the rooms in the three-room building.

3. Francis Willard founded the Women's Christian Temperance Union.

4. "The Curfew Must Not Ring Tonight" was a popular narrative poem written in 1867 by Rose Hartwick Thorpe. "The Maniac" was written by Thomas Russell, a minor English poet who lived from 1762 to1788.

5. *Youth's Companion* was originally published in Boston by Willis and Rand beginning in 1834. It was absorbed by *Merry's Museum for Boys and Girls* in 1872 and later by *American Boy* in 1929.

6. This is a reference to ginseng, a valuable medicinal herb growing wild in the mountains. It was often harvested as a cash crop.

7. "announced."

8. This is usually a reference to a tumor or boil.

9. The preachers of the Regular Old Baptists, also known as the Primitive or Hardshell Baptists, were usually uneducated and served without pay. They were known for an emotional, sing-song delivery with a strong rhythmic quality full of pauses. Many "level-landers," Stone and Pettit included, responded negatively to this method of preaching.

10. *The Sweet Songster: A Collection of the Most Popular and Approved Songs, Hymns and Ballads* was first published in 1854. It contains the words to 275 hymns and was widely used in Eastern Kentucky.

11. There seem to be several forms of the triple pledge. One typically administered at WCTU events was a pledge not to use, offer or consume beverage alcohol. The pledge mentioned in this text, however, seem to be a promise not to use alcohol, tobacco or bad language.

12. This was one of the most famous Kentucky mountain feuds centered in Perry County. It is probably the one that Katherine Pettit learned about prior to her first trip to the mountains. It ended in 1895.

13. Uncle Solomon Everidge is the figure who, over time, became the basis of the founding myth at the Hindman Settlement School. He supposedly traveled on foot and shoeless more than twenty miles to urge Stone and Pettit to start a school by

telling them that he had grown up ignorant but wanted better for his "grands" and "greats." In the many renderings of the story he is supposed to have told them, "You are the ones I have looked for all my lifetime." Uncle Solomon's cabin is now on the grounds of the Hindman Settlement School. The story was regularly used for fundraising and a play based on the incident was also performed for these purposes. Pine Mountain had a similar patriarch, Uncle William Creech, who provided much of the land for the school. He was also referred to regularly in fund-raising literature.

14. Sloyd is a system of manual training for wood carving.

SASSAFRAS SUMMER

1. A jolt wagon got its name from the fact that it had no springs to cushion the ride.

2. Light bread is made with yeast causing it to rise as opposed to the typical cornbread of the mountaineers.

3. *Black Rock, A Tale of the Selkirks*, was a very popular novel written in the 1890s which went through many editions before 1900. Written by Ralph Connor, the pseudonym of the Reverend Charles W. Gordon, it is an adventure story set in a lumber camp in northwest Canada.

4. Flux is another name for dysentery.

5. This refers to a teaching certificate.

6. A gnat smoke was the method used to get rid of gnats. A piece of cloth was rolled tightly and then set on fire. It would blaze up and then die down and smoke. The smoke would keep away gnats. I am grateful to Jana Everage of the Hindman Settlement School for supplying me with this description.

7. A "turn" is a sack, hence a turn or sack of corn.

8. The Regular or Primitive Baptists, founded in the mid-eighteenth century, were distinguished from the Free-Will Baptists by a number of theological disagreements including Sunday Schools which the former maintained had no scriptural base.

9. A type of lace.

10. Notching is a procedure much like what is called "pinking" today. It is done to make the fabric more resistant to fraying.

11. This is a loose full dress, usually without a defined waistline. They are often seen in photographs of the time.

12. This probably refers to bleached muslin.

13. A mattock is a digging or grubbing tool. Ann Cobb used the phrase found in this sermon for a poem titled, "An Old Regular Preacher" in *Kinfolks*. It reads:

> And now this body's dwindling down–
> I'm aiming for to die.
> My pilgrimage is almost done,
> My soul will find release,
> And sweep his way triumphant through
> The pearly gates of peace.
>
> Length the brittle thread of life,
> That I may garner in
> Some silly sheep that's lost amidst
> The thorny paths of sin.
> Poor feeble stock, us humans be,
> Unfit for courts above.
> O Lord, dig round the roots of our hearts
> With the mattock of Thy love.

14. "announced."

15. Perry Pictures were an educational tool which consisted of framed black and white photographs of historic sites and buildings such as the Coliseum in Rome. Pettit noted that the teachers preferred any pictures that had color.

16. A letter to Katherine and May from Mary Stacy early in the following year shows that the best laid plans can bring disaster. The boxes arrived and, with much effort, the tree and presents were made ready for Christmas Day. Then something like three hundred people showed up and as she wrote, "what could we do but tie the garden gate and keep them out." She continued that, since the gifts had been for the children in the Sunday Schools, those who were not present had their gifts set aside for them. Many in the crowd had children who had not attended but who expected to receive gifts. They became angry and before long, they rushed the gate

and, as Mrs. Stacy related, "just grabing, wading, stiring and hunting." She and Jasper did the best they could to gather up the gifts that were left and took them into the house. The crowd jeered her and called her "big boss." She concluded the saga by saying, " I am write now going to tell you I never will try to boss another Crismas tree but am willing if you ever come to put one up to help you…but never will I try to boss another. I will tell you now if you ever come you will haft to get in some ones garden and bring a lock and key to lock the gate." She appended a one-line moral to her tale: "You see people believe in presents more than Sunday Schools."

Mary Stacy to Katherine Pettit and May Stone, Jan. 7, 1902. Whatever the two wrote back, it mollified her and a Feb. 1 letter indicated that she had changed her mind and would take on the task again next year. These letters are appended to the Sassafras Journal, HSS Archive, I, 1, 13.

17. Being very untutored in these matters, I asked a weaver if he could give me a translation of how Mary Stacy prepared her loom. He wrote: "I first buy some bale cotton thread, boil it, rinse it, dye it and then make a thick starch of cornmeal to size it. Since it comes in large skeins it must be wound into a ball or on to a spool to make winding the warp easier. Two or four threads are held while winding the warp. After winding the warp it is chained off the warping reel. It is then sleyed (combed) for winding on to the back beam. Then the warp is treaded one thread at a time through the heddles and then back the other way through the sley. It is tied in and the loom is ready for weaving." I wish to thank Robert Young of Hindman for this translation. The warp of a piece of woven goods refers to the threads which run lengthwise in the fabric. These are stretched on the loom and tied to its beams to provide the structural support for the weaving apparatus. The goods are woven by the shuttle adding cross threads (the woof) to this structure.

18. nature.

19. Corn was the principal crop. In September the stalks and all of the blades were cut down, laid on the ground to cure for several days and then bundled and put away for winter food for the cows and horses.

20. This is an open but roofed space between rooms of a two-room cabin. A two-room cabin with a dog trot was very common at the turn of the century.

21. I was not able to identify what temperance gloves were. Neither the published works on the WCTU and the temperance movement nor the WCTU Library in Evanston, Illinois, could clarify this reference.

22. Gross Alexander, *The Son of Man: Studies in his Life and Teachings* (Methodist Episcopal Church, Nashville, Tenn., 1899).

23. The word "charivari" usually refers to a celebration which is noisy or boisterous.

25. A fascinator was a crocheted headcover worn by women.

EPILOGUE

1. Henry D. Shapiro, *Appalachia On Our Mind* (Chapel Hill, University of North Carolina Press, 1978) and Jack Weller, *Yesterday's People: Life in Contemporary Appalachia* (Lexington, Ky., University of Kentucky Press, 1966). For a good discussion of the schools of interpretation in Appalachian studies see, Richard Drake, "Jack and Clio in Appalachia, Comments on Regional Historiography," *Appalachian Notes*, 4 (Winter, 1976) 1-9.

2. Ronald Eller, *Miners, Millhands, and Mountaineers, Industrialization of the Appalachian South, 1880-1930* (Knoxville, Tenn., University of Tennessee Press, 1981) xix, xxi.

3. Harry M. Caudill, *Night Comes to the Cumberlands, A Biography of a Depressed Area* (Boston, Little Brown, 1962), quoted in Drake, 5.

4. David Whisnant, *All That Is Native and Fine, The Politics of Culture in an American Region* (Chapel Hill, University of North Carolina Press, 1983) 11, 78.

5. England, 6.

6. John C. Campbell, "Social Betterment in the Southern Mountains," *Proceedings of the National Conference of Charities and Corrections*, 36 (1909) 133.

7. May Stone, "Education in the Early Days of Kentucky," HSS Archive, III, 9, 28.

8. Jean Ritchie, *Singing Family of the Cumberlands* (New York, Oxford University Press, 1955) 231.

Bibliography

PRIMARY SOURCES:

The Hindman Settlement School Archive was catalogued along with the archives of a number of other mountain educational institutions in the 1970s through a grant provided by the National Endowment for the Humanities. It is divided into seven series. In addition, the extensive collection of photographs held at the school has also been catalogued. The school archive was the primary source of original materials used in the preparation of the introduction and photographic essays in this publication. The papers of Elizabeth Watts who died in 1993 have been deposited at the archive but have not been catalogued. They were also used in preparing the manuscript.

SECONDARY SOURCES

Addams, Jane, *Democracy and Social Ethics* (New York, MacMillan, 1902).

Bellups, Edward W., *The Sweet Songster, A Collection of the Most popular and Approved Songs, Hymns, and Ballads* (Catlettsburg, Ky., C.L. McConnell, 1854).

Bertrand (Rivera), J'May, *The Appalachian Settlement Schools: the Rural Response to an Urban Concept*, M. A. Thesis, Bryn Mawr, 1975.

Bradley, William Aspinwall, "The Women on Troublesome," *Scribner's Magazine*, 62 (1918) 315-328.

Campbell, John C., *The Southern Highlander and His Homeland* (New York, Russell Sage Foundation, 1921).

_____, "Social Betterment in the Southern Mountains," *Proceedings, National Conference of Charities and Corrections*, 36 (May 1909) 130-37.

Caudill, Harry M., *Night Comes to the Cumberlands, A Biography of a Depressed Area* (Boston, Little Brown, 1962).

Combs, Josiah, *The Kentucky Highlands from a Native Mountaineers' Viewpoint* (Lexington, Ky., L. Richardson and Co., 1913).

Creman, Lawrence, *The Transformation of the School* (New York , Vintage, 1964).

Crunden, Robert, *Ministers of Reform: the Progressives' Achievement in American Civilization* (New York, Basic Books, 1982).

Davis, Allan F., *Spearheads of Reform: The Social Settlements and the Progressive Movement, 1890-1914* (New York, Oxford University, 1967).

Drake, Richard, "Jack and Clio in Appalachia," *Appalachian Notes,* 4 (Winter, 1976) 1-9.

Eller, Ronald, *Miners, Millhands and Mountaineers, the Modernization of the Appalachian South, 1880-1930* (Knoxville, University of Tennessee Press, 1981).

England, Ronda, "Voices From the History of Teachings: Katherine Pettit, May Stone and Elizabeth Watts at Hindman Settlement School," Ph.D. Dissertation, University of Kentucky, 1990.

Forderhouse, Nancy, "The Clear Call of Thoroughbred Women: The Kentucky Federation of Women's Clubs and The Crusade for Educational Reform, 1903-1909," *The Register of the Kentucky Historical Society* (Frankfort, Ky., 1985).

Fox, John Jr., "The Southern Mountaineer," *Scribner's Magazine*, 29 (April-May, 1901) 387-99.

Frost, William Goodell, "The Work of the Fotched-On Women," *Louisville Courier Journal*, September 6, 1936.

Furman, Lucy, *The Glass Window* (New York, MacMillan, 1927).

_____, *Mothering on Perilous* (New York, MacMillan, 1913).

_____, *The Quare Women* (Boston, The Atlantic Monthly Press, 1923).

_____, *Sight To the Blind* (New York, MacMillan, 1914).

Grantham, Dewey, *Southern Progressivism, The Reconciliation of Progress and Tradition* (Knoxville, Tenn., University of Tennessee Press, 1983).

Greene, James S., "Progressives in the Kentucky Mountains: The Formative Years of the Pine Mountain Settlement School, 1913-1930," Ph.D. Dissertation, Ohio State University, 1982.

Hatch, Grace, "The Hindman Settlement School," *Kentucky Magazine*, 1 (September, 1917) 385-93.

Hay, Melba Porter, "Madeline McDowell Breckingridge: Kentucky Suffragist and Progressive Reformer," Ph.D. Dissertation, University of Kentucky, 1980.

History and Families Knott County, Kentucky (Turner Publishing Co., Paducah, Ky., 1995).

Jasper, Mary Katherine, "Social Value of Settlement Schools in the Kentucky Mountains," M. A.Thesis, University of Kentucky, 1930.

Jones, Loyal, "Appalachian Religion," in Samuel S. Hill (ed.) *Encyclopedia of Religion in the South* (Macon, Ga., Mercer U. Press, 1984).

Klotter, James, *The Breckingridges of Kentucky: Two Centuries of Leadership* (University of Kentucky Press, 1986).

Lewis, Helen (ed.), *Colonialism in Modern America: The Appalachian Case* (Boone, N.C., Appalachian Consortium Press, 1978).

McCauley, Deborah Vansan, *Appalachian Mountain Religion* (Champaign, Ill., University of Illinois Press, 1995).

McKinny, Gordon, "Industrialization and Violence in Appalachia in the 1890's," in J.M. Williamson (ed.), *An Appalachian Symposium: Essays in Honor of Cratis Williams* (Boone, N.C., Appalachian State University Press, 1977) 131-46.

McVey, Francis Jewell, "The Blossom Woman," *Mountain Life and Work*, X (April, 1934) 1-5.

Miller, John Wayne, "Appalachian Studies Hard and Soft: The Action Folk and the Creative People," *Appalachian Journal*, 9 (Winter-Spring, 1982) 105-14.

Peck, Elizabeth S., "Katherine Pettit" in *Notable American Women* (Cambridge, Harvard University Press, 1971) 56-58.

_____, "Sophonisba Breckingridge" in *Notable American Women*, 233-36.

Pettit, Katherine, "Ballads and Rhymes of the Kentucky Mountains," *Journal of*

American Folklore, 20 (1907) 251-76.

Ritchie, Jean, *Singing Family of the Cumberlands* (New York, Oxford University Press, 1955).

Scott, Anne Firor, *The Southern Lady, 1830-1930, From Pedestal to Politics* (Chicago, University of Chicago Press, 1970).

Shapiro, Henry D., *Appalachia on our Mind* (Chapel Hill, University of North Carolina Press, 1978).

Speizman, Milton, "The Movement of the Settlement House Idea into the South," *Southwestern Social Science Quarterly*, 44 (December, 1963) 237-46.

Stewart, Albert, "Fesser Clarke: Pioneer Educator in Feud County," *Appalachian Heritage*, 2 (Winter, 1974) 87-93.

_____, *A Man of Circumstance & Selected Yellow Mountain Poems, 1946-1996* (Limited Editions Press, Lubbock, Texas, 1996).

_____, *The Untoward Hills*, (Morehead, Ky., Morehead State College Press, 1962).

Still, James, *The Wolfpen Poems* (Berea, Ky., Berea College Press, 1986).

Stout, Jane Halsted, "Miracle on Troublesome Creek," (privately prepared typescript, n.d).

Weller, Jack, *Yesterday's People: Life in Contemporary Appalachia* (Lexington, Ky., University of Kentucky Press, 1966).

Whisnant, David, *All That Is Native and Fine, The Politics of Culture in an American Region* (Chapel Hill, University of North Carolina Press, 1983).

Williams, Cratis, "The Southern Mountaineer in Fact and Fiction," Ph.D. Dissertation, New York University, 1961.

Young, Robert C. and David R. Smith, "Professor George Clarke, Buckner Academy," *Knott County Legacy* (Troublesome Creek DAR, C. C. & R. Printing, 1994) 128-30.

Index

The Jesse Stuart Foundation

Incorporated in 1979 for public, charitable, and educational purposes, the Jesse Stuart Foundation is devoted to preserving the legacy of Jesse Stuart, W-Hollow, and the Appalachian way of life. The Foundation which controls the rights to Stuart's published and unpublished literary works, is currently reprinting many of his best out-of-print books, along with other books which focus on Kentucky and Appalachia.

With control of Jesse Stuart's literary estate–including all papers, manuscripts, and memorabilia–the Foundation promotes a number of cultural and educational programs. It encourages the study of Jesse Stuart's works, and of related material, especially the history, culture, and literature of the Appalachian region.

Our primary purpose is to produce books which supplement the educational system at all levels. We have now produced more than fifty editions and we have hundreds of other regional materials in stock. We want to make these materials accessible to teachers and librarians, as well as general readers. We also promote Stuart's legacy through video tapes, dramas, and presentations for school and civic groups.

Stuart taught and lectured extensively. His teaching experience ranged from the one-room schoolhouses of his youth in Eastern Kentucky to the American University in Cairo, Egypt, and embraced years of service as school superintendent, high-school teacher, and high-school principal. "First, last, always," said Jesse Stuart, "I am a teacher. Good teaching is forever and the teacher is immortal."

In keeping with Stuart's devotion to teaching, the Jesse Stuart Foundation is publishing materials that are appropriate for school use. For example, the Foundation has reprinted eight of Stuart's junior books (for grades 3-7), and a Teacher's Guide to assist with their classroom use. The Foundation has also published several books that would be appropriate for grades 7-12: Stuart's *Hie to the Hunters*, Thomas D. Clark's, *Simon Kenton, Kentucky Scout*, and Billy C. Clark's, *A Long Row to Hoe*. Other recent JSF publications range from books for adult literacy students to high school and college texts.

Jesse Stuart's books are a guideline to the solid values of America's past. With good humor and brilliant storytelling, Stuart praises the Appalachian people whose quiet lives were captured forever in his wonderful novels and stories. In Jesse Stuart's books, readers will find people who value hard work, who love their families, their land, and their country; who believe in education, honesty, thrift, and compassion– people who play by the rules.

James M. Gifford
Executive Director